Soul Connection

Memoir of

A Birthmother's Healing Journey

by

Ann H. Hughes

The longest journey is the journey inwards to the source of being.
—DAG HAMMARSKJOLD

OTTER BAY BOOKS

Baltimore, Maryland
1999

Produced by Gateway Press for
Otter Bay Books, 3507 Newland Road, Baltimore, MD 21218-2513

Cover art "Unmarked Boxes" © 1998 Josephine Tejal Murray
Cover design by Janet Kratfel

Library of Congress Cataloging-in-Publication Data
Hughes, Ann H., 1945-
   Soul connection: memoir of a birthmother's healing journey / Ann
   H. Hughes.
          p.   cm.
      1.   Hughes, Ann H., 1945-   . 2. Birthmothers--United States-
-Biography.   3. Adoption--United States--Psychological aspects.
I. Title.
HV874.82.H84A3   1999
362.82'98--dc21
[B]   99-17435
                                                                CIP

ISBN 0-9614053-2-5

Printed in the United States of America

To Jana—
A healer on a healing journey.
May your journey be blessed —
Your friend
[signature]

To my beloved daughters

and to all who seek their connections

This story is entirely true, but many names and places
have been changed to protect privacy

Contents

Part III
Quest

Part IV
Connections

Acknowledgements

Thanks to . . .

Tom Hall, choral conductor extraordinaire, for demonstrating the power of vision, discipline, skillful communication and creative process—and for teaching me the art of careful listening

Tom Nugent, master writer, for generously and patiently sharing his bag of magic tricks with me

Janet Kratfel, my "right hand" at work, for always supporting me *in everything*—and for her sharp eye and beautiful graphic design work

Barry Chodak for creating a place for me to do meaningful work and for knowing how to challenge me without trying to boss me around

Linda Brady and all my counselors for showing me new doorways

Darlene Bruland, dear, giving friend, for tutoring me in astrology and the mysteries of human behavior

The Baltimore Symphony Orchestra for being a constant source of inspiration on many levels

My clients and friends for supporting my search and asking about my book

The Adoption Reform Community for sustaining me in dark hours and giving me a place to feel normal and a place to make a difference

My mother for her worthy challenges, powerful lessons and devoted love

My husband and soulmate for his constant support and generosity and for so much more . . .

The Higher Powers for their irony and syncronicity, their constant love and for always knowing when the time is "right"

Don't grieve. Anything you lose comes round
in another form. The child weaned from mother's milk
now drinks wine and honey mixed.

God's joy moves from unmarked box to unmarked box,
from cell to cell. As rainwater, down into flowerbed.
As roses, up from ground. . . .

—RUMI, "UNMARKED BOXES"

Men live on the brink of mysteries and harmonies
into which they never enter, and with their
hand on the door-latch, they die outside.

—RALPH WALDO EMERSON

Prologue

Linda seated herself serenely in an upholstered high-backed chair with wooden arms and motioned me to the pillow-strewn couch. A small coffee table stood on the wooden floor between us. It held a few books and a peculiar wheel-shaped chart filled with strange symbols. I took my time sliding into the corner of the couch closest to the door, arranging the pillows around me like armor. In those days, "resistance" was my way of clinging to any bit of personal power I could muster.

No, Sir, she wasn't going to get me with that hocus pocus stuff. I was just going to ask my question and get out. Would I get pregnant again or not? The monthly see-saw of intention, hope, expectation and disappointment was making me a nervous wreck. And my gynecologist couldn't have told me if I'd had the nerve to ask.

I'd been explaining my dilemma to my boss's sister a few weeks earlier when she just blurted out—with people walking by!—"Why don't you go see my astrologer, Linda Brady?"

I shook my head at that. Sounded pretty kinky to me. But I agreed to think about it and took down Linda's number—just in case. When I got home, I mentioned it to my husband Ned. Of all things, he said *he* wanted to see her! That shook me a little.

I decided to wait and see what happened to him.

He came back noticeably calmer, talking about a past life in prison and how he didn't have to choose to be a martyr anymore. I couldn't quite figure it, but something had changed for the better. And she hadn't turned him into a zombie after all. So, I decided to try it, too—one time.

I scheduled my appointment for October 22, 1982, leaving work early to get there by 4:00 p.m. Linda saw clients in a sunny room on the first floor of a rambling house that had been a country home in horse-and-buggy days. Now, it was in need of restoration. Linda and her husband Michael lived on the second floor. The first floor held the kitchen, Linda's office, and several other rooms "under construction."

Linda waited patiently while I fidgeted myself into position. My arms were tightly crossed; my legs twisted shut. Outside, a truck

1

farted up the Route 140 hill in first gear, but inside, a taut silence stretched between us. My gaze leapt past Linda to a window overlooking the back yard. A new crop of colored leaves drifted by, making their autumn transition. A fat, white cat jumped up beside me on the couch, disturbing my musings. When I reached over to stroke it, I risked a glance into Linda's eyes. Kindness and openness stood there waiting, like two still ponds. My stomach twisted, and I retreated to the safety of the cat.

Linda laughed. "That's Crystal," she said, reaching over for the mysterious piece of paper that must be my astrology chart. "What brings you here today, Ann?"

My hands abandoned the cat and squeezed tight around my chest again. I fidgeted with my elbows while I explained "the baby problem."

Ned and I had married last July after a long courtship. I was thirty-seven; he was a few years older. It was a second marriage for both of us. He had a daughter; I had two. (Well, three, in a way—but I didn't talk about that back then.)

Ned had always wanted a son. So, though it put my beloved job in jeopardy to do so, I'd had my IUD removed. But nothing had happened yet. Would it ever? I needed to know. My eyes were tearing up, so I turned them back to the safety of the cat and listened, hardly breathing, for her reply.

"I can't predict the future," she began. "People come to astrologers for that all the time, but we can't do it. There are too many possibilities and man always has free will."

My balloon of resistance must have deflated slightly. I looked up and uncrossed my feet.

"Astrology *can* help you interpret the past, though, and it can also speak to what's influencing you in the present and will influence you in the future," she continued. "All I can do is counsel you about that so you can see the problem more clearly.

"Now, about this baby you're trying to have . . ." She looked down at my chart and compared it with her big red book of symbols and numbers. "I can tell you're re-examining what's important in your life right now. I can also see that there are powerful forces blocking your focused desires."

My brow furrowed. What did she mean? What kind of forces?

She answered by pointing in the red book. "Here's Pluto, which symbolizes your destiny, and Saturn, which symbolizes male energy, work, reputation and career, conjunct with Venus—what you deeply desire—in your Second House of values. Does your husband want the baby? Will it jeopardize your career?"

Clearly, a baby would complicate my career, but this had been my husband's idea, for Pete's sake—(or so I'd thought at the time). Was that the best she could do for me? I gave her half a point and put my attention back on the cat.

She let me give Crystal a few good rubs and then asked gently, "So, why else are you here?"

I bit my lip and slowly raised my head. "I don't know, really," I replied. "Why don't you just tell me something about myself." I was paying for an hour. Might as well get my money's worth.

She picked up my chart again. "You're a very old soul, Ann," she began. A strange tingling rippled down my spine as she continued to speak. "You've lived many lives." She must be talking about reincarnation, like that thing she said to Ned. I'd heard about it—sure—but no one had ever explained it to me before.

"What do you mean?" I cautiously asked.

Her face lit up at my question, and before I knew it, I was drawn into a conversation about the meaning of life.

"We choose to be born here on Earth to build character and wisdom through living," she explained. "We live many different lives—some as men, some as women, as different races, in different places, some rich, some poor. And we all come here with a mission—something to do for someone or the world."

Each segment of the natal chart is called a "house." There are twelve, each symbolizing a different area of life, such as career, health, children, partnerships, etc. We struggle to gain consciousness in each area, in turn, as Saturn transits each one for a 2-3 year period, making a 28-year cycle around the chart. The planets and signs in the natal chart show how we search for consciousness in each area of life.

It sounded like an interesting scheme, but who was to say it was true? I chucked Crystal under the chin again for courage.

"So, what does my chart say about me?"

She studied it in silence for a moment. "Was there a lot of conflict in your early home life?" she asked.

"You could say that," I replied, my eyes cast down, trying not to give anything away.

"Thought so. Mars and Mercury are there in Capricorn, conjunct. My guess is that your mother was an energetic, talkative woman who criticized you a lot. You have a Moon in Virgo."

I shot her an amazed look.

"But with Sagittarius on the cusp, your home was probably well-to-do, with educational advantages. You patterned yourself after your father, didn't you? With Saturn in the Tenth in Cancer, he was pretty easy-going and might have worked with children. Was he a teacher by any chance?"

My mouth was clamped shut, but my head kept nodding in wonder. How could she possibly know this stuff?

"I'll bet you were born with a chip on your shoulder," Linda continued, picking up steam. She winked at me! "South Node in Capricorn children usually feel superior to everyone around. Your Sun is in Aquarius. You don't take too well to people telling you what to do either, do you?"

Saturn in Cancer in the Tenth also showed I had some deep lessons to learn about family values and empathy. I would struggle all my life with that, as well as with forging a good reputation. The Moon in Virgo in the Twelfth also indicated buried emotions and hidden intuition, as well as karma around "motherhood." (Could that explain why I'd had to give a baby away for adoption?) My mind grew dizzy as she went on and on.

I'd been raised in a Protestant church, but no one had ever implied that lives had patterns or that souls had lessons to learn or missions to accomplish. Nor had a stranger ever guessed so much about me in such a short amount of time. I was intrigued—yes—but I was really going to test her now.

Fresh in my mind was something that I couldn't understand at all. My heart had stopped last year. I'd been "dead" for four minutes or so before I was shock-paddled back to life. The doctors never could explain it. Let's see if she could try.

"What happened to me in early September, 1981?" I smugly

asked while Crystal jumped down and sauntered away.

Linda went flipping through the red Ephemeris and her eyes darted back and forth between the line of symbols she was running down with her finger and my birth chart in her other hand. In about thirty seconds, she looked up at me.

"Your illusions about yourself, your body, and who you think you are were severely shaken," she answered. "I imagine your higher beliefs and your very essence were tested as well. Saturn was transiting your natal Neptune in the first house, trine your Sun in the fifth and Uranus in the ninth."

Something zinged through my heart—bulls-eye! I'd understood nothing of the last sentence she spoke, but she'd taken my breath away with what came before.

Yes—"dropping dead" had changed me in just those ways, now that I thought about it. I'd seen first hand that the world could and would go on without me. It had also radically shifted my values. People I hadn't really appreciated before—my mother and Ned—had stayed doggedly by my side. Others I thought would, didn't. The earth itself had brightened by several shades.

Score one for Linda, but could she do it again? I took a deep breath looked straight into her clear hazel eyes:

"Okay, Linda. What happened March 1, 1980?" I'd given her the date of my first human potential training session.

Again, the page flipping and the balancing act with the chart. "This is a time when your entire view of the world and of life shifted. Saturn was transiting your ascendant. A whole new 28-year cycle was beginning. Old illusions were being cleared away so a new cycle of learning could begin."

I untwisted my arms and hissed out the rest of my tension at last. She'd totally nailed my experience twice in a row. I had no idea how. She'd spoken to the deeper meaning of things I couldn't explain before. Now, I wanted to know more.

I got her to go back and tell me again how a soul's next life was chosen and planned on the other side. If astrology worked, that meant *someone* calculated when and where and to whom a soul should be born. How did they do that?

No clear answer from Linda about that. She wasn't privy to the

5

workings of the higher realms and could only imagine what they did. All she knew was that the results they produced were both comically ironic and brilliantly perfect—a master design to get us through those lessons!

"Do you mean to say that the challenges we begin life with—our parents, our talents, our location, circumstances, etc.—are all chosen to set us on our path? Sounds like we're being led to our destiny like slaughterhouse animals!" I objected.

"No, man always has free choice," she affirmed again. "Many paths are open to him. There's no one 'right' way. People are allowed to make mistakes. Over and over if that's what they choose. I think Spirit hits them with cosmic two-by-fours when they do, though. Each time they ignore the lesson, the whack gets a little harder."

I leaned forward slightly. "What do you mean by that?"

"Well, let's say you're supposed to be learning how to stand up for yourself in this lifetime. You start out with an alcoholic father. If that experience doesn't teach you anything, you end up with an abusive spouse."

I could see her point. "Okay, but, if there's a God, why does he allow hurt and destruction?" I asked. I *had* to be able to stump her with one of these questions.

"That's a good one," she conceded. "People are always asking me that."

Our eyes connected with the force of laser beams. "So, do you have an answer?"

"Well, no one can know for sure, but I have a theory that these things have been pre-arranged between souls before they incarnate. All kinds of lessons are needed for advanced learning. Loss is a very significant experience in peoples' lives. It teaches deep lessons. Sometimes people get committed to causes after they've suffered losses. So perhaps these things were arranged so that issues that need correcting here can finally get the attention they deserve."

That calmed me and made a lot of sense, too. Okay— *if* there was a God, maybe he wasn't such a bad guy after all. I'd have to see.

When I walked out of Linda's office that afternoon, my mind was whirling with exciting new questions. Did my life have a purpose? Did my pain? Did the "bad times" really happen to teach me and lead me? Had I lived before? What did it all mean?

But I wasn't about to take her word for anything. No, I'd spend the next six years answering these questions for myself before going back. There was only one thing she gave me that day that I could fully accept: *Hope!* Hope that there was hidden meaning, after all, in my crazy, mixed-up life! Hope that this higher understanding could help me deal more positively with life's future twists and turns.

I even hoped for the possibility that, someday, *something* might shed light on that darkest, blackest hole of all—my unwed pregnancy.

Part I

Beginnings

There is no such thing as an accident. What we call by that name is the effect of some cause which we do not see.

— VOLTAIRE

1 - Switched in Paris

It was a marked moment. A loudspeaker blared the announcement; the train screeched into the station; dust kicked up in tiny tornados beside the tracks. Mother put her strong hands on my shoulders and looked deeply into my eyes. "Be careful," she said with measured tones. And we both knew what she meant.

"I will," I promised, jerking free of her embrace. I clunked up the metal steps, my luggage off-balance, and gave her one final wave. I was a free woman now, bound for Europe, my diaphragm confidently tucked away in my oversized purse.

The train lurched forward leaving Mother behind, still waving, as she would, until I was out of sight. Meanwhile, I stumbled down the aisle with two large suitcases and my purse, until I found an open double seat. I tossed the purse onto the aisle seat, lofted the suitcases onto the overhead rack and slunk into the window seat. A collage of soft summer greenness whizzed by outside as a cacophony of unbending steel groaned underneath me. I fumbled inside my purse for my travel guide and settled in to read up on my European destinations.

Mother has signed me up for a summer job in Europe. My group of American college students was scheduled to meet in Luxembourg City on July 1st, get a three-day bus tour of Luxembourg, Germany, Belgium and Holland, and then go off, separately, to European hosts with summer jobs and housing waiting for us. Mother is sending me a week early so I can also see London and Paris. First I will fly to London and spend four nights with Mother's pen pal Sylvia; then, June 29th, on to Paris for two glorious days of solo sightseeing.

This was the very trip that Mother herself has always dreamed of taking. She was "sacrificing herself," as usual, to give me an early college graduation present. Sure, I was excited about the trip, but, deep in my heart, I knew that Mother should have gone, not me. I didn't deserve it. Yes, I'd always been a good student. But underneath the proper appearances swirled a devious and troubled life I'd always hidden from my "perfect," do-good parents.

"Tickets, please."

I pasted on my automatic smile and gave him what he asked for.

That was the way I did my life: smooth on the surface, but underneath churned a restless, troubled sea.

For instance—was I ever going to figure out what love was?

It wasn't buying someone everything and giving them expensive presents they didn't deserve. And it wasn't controlling, judging and criticizing their every move. My parents *said* they did all that because they loved me. But if that's what love was, I wanted out!

A few years ago, I'd begun looking for love in the company of artistic young men. Mother had made a point of telling me *everything* about sex at an early age, (because her own mother had told her *nothing*). She'd made sex sound like the best thing in the whole world. Of course, she expected me, like her, to remain a virgin until marriage, but curiosity overcame my discretion when I fell in love at eighteen.

Joe, a dark-haired cello player with slender fingers, had won my heart by serenading me with Bach unaccompanied sonatas. We'd surrendered our virginity to each other, but after a year or so of exploring the mysteries of sex and string music together, we slowly drifted apart.

Last fall, I'd found a graduate student poet. He'd wooed me with his record collection—LaPatti playing Chopin. We would stay up until 3 am, listening to music and reading poetry together. But Harold drank a lot, slept on the floor, and never fully took off his pants to make love. He was planning to transfer, so we decided to go our separate ways when the school year ended.

That meant I had just one year left to find a mate. If I didn't find a man in college, I'd probably end up a withered old maid. Here it was—1965, the era of free love. I had never experienced "free love," but I was willing to try a little in Europe if it could help me figure out what love really was.

I arrived in Paris five days later under a New Moon in Cancer. Standing out on my hotel balcony that night, the lights of the city blazed across the landscape. The stars above were blotted out. The glowing orb of the moon was missing from the night sky, too. Like the real me, it was shut away in the void. Yet, the world spun on, and seemed not to notice.

I slept restlessly and was awakened by car horns honking and animated words zinging back and forth at the fringe of my consciousness. But something was wrong: they weren't speaking English.

Oh, yes, I suddenly remembered: *I'm in Paris.*

Wake up! It's June 30. This is your last day of freedom. You have to leave for the job in Luxembourg tomorrow.

Okay. Okay.

I force my eyes open. The sheer, white curtains which cover the partially open French doors to my balcony billow cheerfully in a light breeze.

Try to think in French today, I urge myself. *Leve-toi.*

I poke my feet out from the fluffy, white comforter and plant them firmly on the plush carpet that covers my hotel room floor. I amble over to a nearby desk chair and put on the clothes I spread there the night before. The room contains its own sink, toilet and *bidet.* I am still trying to figure out the latter, a low porcelain fixture with no useful purpose that I can fathom. There is an upholstered *divan* on the far side of the room. The tall ceilings and French Provincial furniture give the room an air of comfortable elegance.

This is a terrific room, I tell myself, closing the French doors and shutting off the street noises. *But I can't stay here all day. This is my one day to see the sights. I promised myself le Louvre, so I've got to go today.*

I check my purse. It's heavy with a camera, a map of Paris, my tour guide, my well-worn French-English dictionary and a few other items. Lots of walking today. Let's see. I can do without these today, I decide, dropping my camera and my diaphragm into my suitcase before closing the door behind me.

"*Bon jour,*" the door man calls to me, as I set off.

I follow my city map to les Champs Elysees, an upscale boulevard with many sidewalk cafes tucked between the buildings and the street. I pick one that overlooks a small park and order a Continental breakfast in my best French.

Here I am in Paris with a whole day to myself, I muse. *Nowhere I need to be; nothing I need to do. Away from Mother—half a world from home. For once, I can be my own boss.*

The void opens before me, and anxiety squeezes my chest. But, thankfully, the waiter twirls by, filling my space with *cafe au lait* and hard rolls. *Now* I have something to do: sip and munch. Busily, I butter my roll, and my chest relaxes. Still, everywhere I look, people are going places, doing things. Am I the only one idle?

Well-dressed office workers scurry past. *"Bon-jour, bon-jour,"* they call to each other on their way to some place important. Across the street in the park, older women sweep the pavement with purpose and determination, using old-style twig brooms.

You'd never see something like that back home, I think. *Pity I don't have my camera. And everyone's speaking French.*

Well, you can speak French. You might even speak enough to get by.

That was it: maybe I could "pass" as a Parisian today? Wouldn't that be fun?

A smug grin creeps over my face. With a flourish of French, I call for my check and pay my bill. Then I'm off for le Louvre.

I arrive early, determined to absorb the entire cultural history of Europe. For hours, I traipse through gallery after gallery. Dutifully, I stand in line to see the Mona Lisa. Face to face with her, though, I am captured. What *is* lurking behind her enigmatic smile? Has she, perhaps, been trapped in a role she has no wish to play? Is her response the simple one I often use—take yourself away and smile? I sigh deeply and pass by.

Now, I've paid my dues to tradition, so I sneak off to see my favorites: the French Impressionists. Here I find freedom of expression, at last. Manet delights me with boring buffoons in black tie picnicking with a sleek, white, naked lady. With him, I spit on tradition; natural beauty's what counts! A Toulouse-Lautrec bar maid amuses me with her round, bold breasts and alluring smile. I breathe in her realness, impress her sensuality into my imagination. I keep walking. But by now, many hours have ticked by, and everything begins to blur. My stomach is empty; my legs ache. It's time to go.

I retrace my steps down the long, wooden staircase, and standing in the great hall at the bottom of the stairs, I spy an exit. I plod toward the light and push open the heavy door that leads to the outside. Blinding sun makes me squint in pain. I draw a long, slow breath, while my eyes slowly adjust to the brightness.

Cobblestone paving wraps itself widely around a large bubbling fountain in the middle of the plaza. Trees and benches are scattered in a grassy area outside the cobblestones. People are spread out everywhere, relaxing in the shade, visiting by the fountain.

I walk over to the stone fountain and pull myself up onto the rim, almost out of range of the billowing water plumes. Tucking my purse's shoulder straps carefully under my leg, I trail my fingers in the cool water, dribbling it on my cheeks as the fountain mists me from the side. My eyes close and the rhythm of the water-plops slowly mixes with the babble of French. Tiredness struggles up my throat and stretches my jaw into a big yawn. I drop my head. In the stillness that follows, I feel someone looking at me.

A trim young man with round, black eyes, stands a respectful distance away, beaming at me. "Hello. You look tired," he says to me in French.

He thinks I'm French! Here's my chance. "Oh yes," I reply, coolly in French. "I've just spent all morning walking around inside le Louvre. I am tired."

"Are you an American?"

Deflated, I drop my head. "Yes. I'm a student," I confess. "Just here for the summer. I guess my French isn't that good, is it?" I look up bashfully, seeking his approval.

"Oh, your French is just fine," he lies, smiling gently. "I'm a student, too. May I sit down here beside you?"

"Sure." I move further over into the dry area. "Do you study here in Paris?"

"Yes, I study medicine at le Sorbonne."

"Oh." I've heard of that school, of course. "Do you go to classes now, in the summer?"

"Yes. Our break will come in August. Where do you study?"

I tell him where I'm from and what I'm up to this summer. My talking is better than my understanding, but I'm doing okay with my French. Just what I was looking for today: a chance to practice my French!

"I was just about to go for lunch," he announces. "Are you hungry? Would you care to join me?"

Should I? Well, we'll be in a public place. Why not? He certainly looks harmless. And if I eat lunch with a real Parisian, I can keep practicing my French.

"What a lovely idea," I reply. "Do you know a place nearby?"

14

"Follow me."

He hops off the fountain ledge and sets off toward the street. As he walks ahead, I notice his heavy limp and how romantically unappealing he is. Maybe I shouldn't . . .

Be kind, Ann, I chastise myself. *He probably has a hard time making friends with girls. He doesn't appeal to you, but that doesn't mean you can't be nice and have lunch with him.*

He tells me his name is Jean-Michel. I call him Jean at first, but he keeps correcting me until I get it right. Before we reach the restaurant, he has a new idea. What if we buy a baguette, some cheese and some wine and have an authentic Parisian lunch at his apartment, instead? Jean-Michel offers to treat.

Well, I can save some money that way, and, by now, I'm quite sure he's harmless. He's so small, he couldn't hurt me if he tried. And he's been so polite. I can't imagine . . . "Okay," I foolishly agree.

We stop in a nearby bakery, and I stand by shyly as Jean-Michel purchases our supplies and banters cheerfully with the rotund storekeeper. Pushing the shop door open ahead of me, he smiles broadly and hands me a long baguette.

We proceed to his nearby tenement house and labor up many dim, grimy flights of steps. I'm panting by the time I reach his apartment. When he opens the door, I walk in and put the baguette on the Formica table in the center of his room. A battered chest of drawers is to the left, near his bed. To the right is a stained sink and a narrow counter which holds a small hot plate.

We enjoy our light lunch together. I'm quite proud of myself for being able to converse in French. My skills are moderate, at best, but Jean-Michel is quite patient and praises me for trying. When I ask his age, he shocks me by saying twenty-eight. He says some other things about himself and his studies that I can't understand very well, but I just nod agreeably and pretend I know what he's saying.

After we finish eating, he gets up from the table and sits tentatively on the edge of the bed. "Come, sit over here," he motions to me. I get up and join him, sitting a careful distance away. I figure the bed must double as his sofa.

"And your parents," I ask. "Do they live in Paris?"

"No, in the provinces. What about your parents."

"In the States. My father teaches music; my mother's a housewife."

"Oh, that's nice. Would you like to sleep with me?"

I know instantly what he's said. Back home, my friends and I have used that phrase as a joke, practicing our French. My breath grows shallow; my eyes widen. "What did you say?" I ask, not believing my ears.

"*Voulez-vous couchez avec moi?*" he repeats.

Yep, that's what I thought he said. Oh boy. Now what?

Fear constricts my throat. My thoughts race and collide.

He's been nice to me, but I certainly don't want sex with him. How in the world am I going to get out of this?

The words come rushing out. "But, no, I can't. I didn't bring my birth control."

Will it work? I hold my breath.

His brow furrows slightly and then he smiles. "No problem," he says. "I'm a medical student. We have shots."

Rising panic gives my voice a sharper edge. "Shots? I've never heard of such a thing." But I already know it's hopeless. The room begins to spin. I try to get up, but he reaches over to restrain me.

"Well, it's experimental. Sure—shots. *Pic-pic.*" He gestures to his arm. Then he grabs hold of me with both hands, using a strength that surprises me.

Boy, was I stupid. I never should have come here with him. He probably thinks I owe him this for buying me lunch. I wonder if he'll force me. He could hurt me if I resist. Why, he could even murder me if he wanted to. No one's around to help. My family doesn't even know where I am. I could end up a statistic!

For a short, dark moment my pride wrestles with my will to survive.

Well, I'm not a virgin. I hate this, but I guess I could just grit my teeth and let him do it. Hopefully, I won't get pregnant. There's no graceful way out. I put myself in this mess. I'd better just take what's coming and get it over with.

I don't say a word; I just pull off my underwear for him. A few quick thrusts are all he requires. I hold myself stiff and unresponsive in protest, but Jean-Michel acts like nothing's wrong. He doesn't even

16

notice me trembling. When he's done, he pulls up his trousers and smiles.

"Would you like to go out and meet some of my friends?" he asks.

I swallow quick, so I can speak again. "Good idea!" *I've made it through this alive. Here's my chance to escape.* I pull on my panties and straightening my clothing in record time. *Boy, was I lucky all he wanted was a little quick sex. It could have been lots worse.*

As we prepare to leave the apartment, I look Jean-Michel over carefully. On the remote chance I do get pregnant, I want to remember exactly what he looks like. I burn his image into my mind. His complexion is dark olive, something I didn't really notice before. Actually, he looks Algerian or Moroccan, now that I look at him closely. His eyes are large and very dark, and his hair, black and kinky. He's a small man, about 5'3", and probably about 120 lbs. His most distinguishing feature is his limp. *Why does he limp?* I wonder. I look more closely. *Does he have some hereditary problem?* A chill pushes up my spine, but I shake it off and follow Jean-Michel out of the apartment building and down into the street.

Outside, the sun shines brightly and the bustle of Paris makes me feel safe again. Anxious to get away but still not wanting to appear impolite, I follow Jean-Michel to a nearby sidewalk cafe. There he hails a group of friends and proudly introduces me.

"This is my new friend, Ann," he grins, as if nothing were wrong. "She's an American student." My skin still crawls, remembering the unwanted intimacy with Jean-Michel. I feel violated and unbalanced, like a top unspun, but I grit my teeth and force a smile.

One of Jean-Michel's friends gets up and brings us each a chair. Wine is on the table, and someone pours a glass for each of us. I gratefully accept the wine, and swallow it quickly to calm my nerves. My glass is refilled immediately. With each swig of burgundy, my senses mellow; gradually, the world takes on a rosy glow.

The people around the table are animated and friendly. Like Jean-Michel, all are students at le Sorbonne. I am immediately drawn to the young man across the table. His name is Claude. Tall, dark, and handsome, he looks Algerian, like Jean-Michel. But he has a broad face and wavy hair, and he's a much larger person. Claude has

17

an easy sense of humor and a warm and gentle manner. He studies history, as best I can understand.

I draw in a deep, slow breath, and, while the conversation rambles on, struggle to put the afternoon in perspective.

Okay, I was violated, I admit to myself. *But sex has always been the one thing that's made me feel special and worthwhile. I can't just give it up! True, Jean-Michel was a frightening exception, but sex itself can't be bad. It's always made me feel loved before. Maybe Claude can make me feel that way again.*

I drink more wine while continuing to talk and laugh with my handsome prince. Gradually, the unpleasant luncheon encounter fades away, and now I can even feel the tiny ember of hope glowing inside me. Slowly, it fans into a raging flame of sexual desire. Claude's eyes gleam and dilate: he feels the same way about me. As soon as it's polite, we say goodbye to Jean-Michel and sneak away together.

When we reach the privacy of Claude's apartment, I can't be worried about birth control. If I'm going to get pregnant today, I probably am already, so why worry, I reason. Claude's sweet, ripe kisses wash away the bitter memory of Jean-Michel's unwanted touch.

Claude's lovemaking is slow and sensuous, the way love *should* be. He takes his time to passionately please my every desire. He strokes me with skillful tenderness, always holding back, until I can wait no longer. I reach for him with my whole being, and in the ultimate explosive moment of union, I feel a connection happen deep inside me. Part of me senses what it is and appreciates that masterful lovemaking like this *should* create the miracle of new life. And if it has, so be it, I tell myself lightly.

Claude suggests douching afterwards, and he goes along to the bathroom to help me figure out the *bidet*.

Later that afternoon, Claude calls up Jean-Michel and asks if he'll give us both a mad-cap tour of Paris in his jalopy. The three of us roar away, giddy laughter consuming us. We buzz through l'Arc de Triomphe, up to Montmartre, around traffic circles, through tunnels, weaving crazily in and out of traffic, horn blaring.

As the tour winds down, I speak up. "Let's go back to my hotel. There are a few things there I really need." I *must* get my diaphragm back before any more amorous encounters!

Jean-Michel heads for the address I recite.

"But why don't you just get your suitcase and spend the rest of your time with me at my apartment?" Claude suggests.

What a glorious idea! Too bad I have to leave tomorrow, but I can still make the most of the time I have left. Claude is such a special, gentle person, and so much fun to be with. My heart beats wildly as I accept his offer. We all have supper together; then Claude and I go off to his apartment to share a night of deep passion together.

Early in the morning, Jean-Michel comes by with his car. Claude and I pile in for the ride to the train station. We go by way of les Halles, the market district, so Jean-Michel can point out yet another tourist spot, the only one open at 7:00 a.m. In the dim light of morning, I peer out the car window at grey-capped men with aprons unloading trucks, hauling bushels of greens, beans, peas, cabbages and carrots through the market door. Boisterous jokes and shouts fill the air. But a quick glimpse of this fecund world is all Jean-Michel allows before he stomps on the accelerator again.

When we get to the station, both men walk me to the platform. I shake hands with Jean-Michel; then I turn to Claude. His big, warm body envelopes me in a long, tingly embrace. While he holds me tight, the memory of his gentle kindness, of our joyous, shared passion percolates through me. How I long to stay in Paris the rest of the summer. But the train whistle blows, and I must put my tugging sadness aside. Claude and I exchange addresses and promise to write. Then I climb into the train.

I linger in the doorway, wrestling with myself. *I don't want to go. Damn my schedule!* But then, the engine shudders; wheels clatter, and I begin to roll, relentlessly, east.

Little did I know that my life had been switched onto a new track in Paris. For better or worse, I'd been connected to—and was already rolling towards—a most unexpected destiny.

2 - The Stunning Blow

The re-routing of my life had, no doubt, been carefully planned in the higher realms. Hypnotherapists, like Drs. Brian Weiss and Michael Newton, during past-life regressions, have had clients describe to them what happened after death. Once liberated from their bodies, people have reported traveling in a spirit body through some kind of tunnel. They are met by loved ones and are gradually drawn towards a brilliant, all-encompassing light of pure, unconditional love. In the light stands Jesus, Buddah or the great spiritual leader of their culture, who embraces them and infuses them with love, acceptance and forgiveness.

Next, spirits go through a Life Review. Surrounded by their personal guides, they re-experience their lives, on a *feeling* level. Because actions beget reactions, they also experience the stone-in-the-pond ripple of consequences caused by their actions. Where they've hurt someone, they sear with that person's hurt feelings and the hurt feelings of all the other people against whom that person acted, in turn. Where they've brought someone great joy, they soar on that person's joy and soar again when that joy touches another, and another.

After they are fully aware of how they've affected others in their life—where they've triumphed and where they've fallen down—they move into a study/learning/preparation phase. Each new spirit now joins a small group of soul friends, some of whom have played roles in their most recent life. They study together in a kind of celestial classroom. Here, under the guidance of one or a team of more highly evolved spirits, they re-examine their lives in careful detail, squeezing the meaning out of each crisis. What blocked them from making better choices? What other openings would have come if they'd made a different choice?

What if Mary hadn't quit her job in anger? *What if*, instead, she had told her boss that, for years, she'd been feeling judged and demeaned? *What if* she'd confessed that this abuse had led her to do "only what she had to?" That sometimes she deliberately left work incomplete because she felt unfairly treated? *What stopped her* from saying all that? *Why* had she walk out in a huff instead?

By studying the past-life "screen," Mary can see where she missed opportunities to learn how to disarm abusers—not by confrontation or running away, but by acknowledging the abuser's feelings, telling the truth about her own feelings, and then seeking solutions that would satisfy all parties. Because she missed that chance, a more abusive situation developed later. The "screen" also shows where her life could have gone if she had learned the lesson there.

After the review and the study, the planning work begins. Mary and her guides start formulating requests to the Life Planners. They send out thoughts about what kind of experiences and alliances might help her get past the old blocks. When a life is chosen later, various friends will sign on to help in supporting roles. The boss will be someone who needs to understand how overcontrolling and judgmental behavior makes others distant and uncooperative. Next time, Mary will have a friend, who owes her a debt, assigned to help her when she gets stuck.

Each soul's possibilities interweave with those of other souls to form a beautiful symphony. Each melody supports and enhances the others—some harmoniously, some dis-harmoniously. The melodies move forward together—except when the needle gets stuck and the same old patterns repeat over and over again. Death can always unstick the needle, if needs be, so that, with a new life and a new plan, the symphony can continue afresh.

The trick to living is keeping the needle unstuck.

My own life was seriously stuck the summer I headed for Europe. From age twelve on, I'd been in an underground power struggle with my parents. They would cajole and shame me, trying to fit me into their mold of perfection. I would covertly rage against their rules in a life-or-death struggle for my own identity, all the while displaying to them my "good girl" act. Underneath, I was a roiling Vesuvius, hissing and steaming under the fire hose of parental authority, unaware that, someday, the top was going to blow.

Sometimes, the new can emerge only when the old is completely destroyed. For a long while, a new energy gathers underground; nothing on the surface appears to change. The new keeps expanding and pressing against the thick crust of the old regime, the pressure building, until one day, to everyone's surprise, the top blasts off. The blast releases all that has been hidden. And when the new matter spills out freely, the old is consumed in its wake.

I first felt my world start to rumble a few weeks into my Luxembourg stay. By that time, my summer job was bogging down in misery. No one else spoke English. I couldn't make friends and didn't fit in. They worked me 13 hours a day, six days a week. And my boss hated me, partly because, feeling totally out of control, I kept dropping his glasses, dishes, bottles of wine—something—every day.

A grimy 100 gallon trout tank was wedged between the sink and a huge wine rack in the hotel kitchen. I stared into it fifty times a day. The fish never looked back. They only swam in endless circles, awaiting the inevitable: the net, the stunning blow, the knife, the skillet. I felt a strange kinship to them without knowing why. And because of them, one day, I discovered a still bigger problem.

It happened three weeks into my stay on my way upstairs to my room. I was on my lunch break. After scrubbing toilets and cleaning rooms until lunch, I would get a break. Then I'd be due downstairs to tend bar or help in the kitchen until they dismissed me at 9 p.m. That day, the steps to the fifth floor seemed endless. With two more flights to go, I paused and leaned over, panting. *Just get to the landing*, I prodded myself. Then, I took a deep breath, lifted my aching right leg, and sprinted up the last few steps. Still breathless, I turned and peered out the little window there, down onto the street.

That's when I saw the trout truck parked below, by the kitchen door. A smiling peasant in work clothes was shouting greetings to passersby as he netted live fish out of a barrel on his truck. Fish that used to sparkle in gurgling streams were now transferred, each in turn, to a large bucket. When the bucket was full, he hauled it inside. *So, that's how they get the trout*, I thought to myself.

When the trout man disappeared into the kitchen, I turned to grab the bannister, and doing so, my arm absently brushed my sore and tender breasts. That's when I put it all together: my missed period, frequent urination, and now, sore breasts. . . .

I'd read up on pregnancy, and I knew very well what all that must mean. But I decided not to worry about it just yet. I'd go to a doctor first to find out for sure.

So, I went on my next day off. The doctor noticed me straining to understand her French, so she spoke slowly. "You are probably pregnant," she told me after the examination. "It's a little too early to know for sure, but I think you are. Come back next month and I can tell you then."

Come back next month? Is she crazy? I'll be back home by then. Oh, Lord, my parents mustn't find out. Maybe I should try to get an abortion here. But how would I arrange it? I can't even speak the language.

No. Just get yourself home as soon as possible. You can deal with it there, I advised myself. *You're only a few weeks pregnant. No need to panic.*

I dressed quickly and left the doctor's office. Outside, the air was bright and crisp. Through swept, cobblestone streets, I scurried back to the hotel, heart pounding. The sun sparkled off the tile roofs of tidy homes. The world looked squeaky-clean, but my life was a muddled mess. How could I just go back to my room? I needed time to think about all of this.

A gentle breeze fondled the leafy treetops across the way, making a dance of dappled shadows on the stone wall edging the park. *I'll sit down and sort this out over there,* I told myself, crossing the street.

I hopped up onto the wall and slid into a sunny spot, where I could feel the stones' warmth beneath me. *Luxembourg summers are cool,* I thought, wrapping my sweater tighter. Or was it that the blood had all drained out of me?

I closed my eyes and took a deep breath. The sun felt so good; its warmth soaked into my body like a lover's embrace. The gentle patter of bird songs and leaf rustling calmed me. Slowly I shifted my attention inside. There, a new wonder glowed.

"Probably pregnant." In spite of myself, I smiled. One afternoon in my whole life I didn't use birth control, and—bang—I was pregnant. What luck! Imagine—a single unguarded moment, and some soul in this vast universe chose me to be its mother—*me*—of all people. How awesome that, in *my* body, a new human being was forming.

I opened my eyes, refreshed. My skin tingled as the mystery and miracle of it washed over me like star dust.

But then my chest tightened. *You need to think about what this will mean for you, for everybody,* I reminded myself. I closed my eyes and concentrated.

"Is pregnancy something to be afraid of?" I asked some unseen force. "What about giving birth?"

"No," came the answer from deep within. "Both are a natural part of life."

My brow unfurrowed momentarily, and then furrowed again. *But, just who is the father?*

I thought back to that infamous afternoon: *I was with Claude when I felt the connection. It must be his child. I'll write and let him know. Maybe he'll want to marry me.*

But I already knew what would happen: he would never answer my letter. I would have to bring up the baby alone.

Me? What do I have to offer a child? I am just an unhappy, mixed-up college student. I could never raise a child on my own.

My mouth turned to acid as a memory surfaced from last spring. I'd gone to visit Amy, my old school chum who'd gotten pregnant the year before and married her boyfriend. She'd dropped out of school when the baby was born. She'd greeted me that day in a faded bathrobe, with disheveled hair and a cigarette dangling between her lips.

"Come in," she mumbled, waving me through the door into her efficiency apartment. It stank of urine, sour milk, and stale smoke. The sink brimmed with dirty dishes. Half-filled baby bottles and overflowing ashtrays littered the counter and table surfaces. Worst of all, her red-faced brat was wailing and continued to wail, overriding everything I was trying to say. Soon my head began to throb. How could she stand it? Something inside me screamed, *Make it stop! Make it stop! Make it stop!* Reeling with confusion, I offered her some weak excuse and stumbled out.

When I opened my eyes and drew my next breath, the sweet, cool air of Luxembourg was soothing my lungs. But my head still throbbed in spite of the peaceful sound of rustling leaves.

That's because now YOU are pregnant, and you have a BIG PROBLEM, I reminded myself. My chest tightened; my breath grew shallow. What in the world was I going to do?

Thoughts started spinning in reckless confusion. *When you get*

24

pregnant, you should get married, but I can't. I'm not even sure who the baby's father is. God! What are my parents going to say?

My heart pounded at *that* thought. In the background, a discordant phrase thudded and repeated like a scratched record: *I can't raise a child alone. . . I can't raise a child alone. . . I can't . . .*

My chest heaved again, this time releasing a sigh of defeat. My eyelids lowered themselves to half-mast. I was just thrashing around, like a fish flopping itself silly on a chopping block. It was hopeless.

"Well, I guess I'll have to get an abortion," I mumbled to the breeze.

The next night I called home and begged Mother to change my return flight. Ten days later, I left for home. I hid out in my room for the rest of August and then hauled myself back to school. By the first week of September, I was back into the classroom routine. Everything appeared the same, even though nothing would ever be the same again.

I remember sitting in my fourth-period English class, two months pregnant, tapping my pen nervously on my notebook. In my mind, I kept flipping the calendar ahead.

How long before I start showing? Another two months, I guess. I'll be lucky to finish fall term without everybody in here figuring out I'm pregnant.

I slouched down in my desk, pretending to take notes, while I frantically plotted my defense strategy. The cute, dark-haired boy in front of me dropped his pencil and glanced up at me. There was something about that boy. . . . I was certainly not in the market for a boyfriend, but I caught him glancing back at me furtively while the rotund professor droned on about the British novel. Then, while I was packing my book bag after the lecture, he stood up and introduced himself.

"Hi. I'm Roger. How do you like it so far?"

We discovered we were both English majors and that we each had the next period free.

"Let's go for a soda," he suggested.

If he only knew . . . he wouldn't be asking me out. But, he doesn't. And come to think of it, I could really use a new friend right now. "Sure. How about the Corner Tavern?"

We each shouldered a book bag and headed for town. The Corner Tavern was just across the street from the main campus. It was a two-story, Tudor-style frame building constructed so that the second-floor corner jutted out over a cut-away corner at street level. The revolving door under the overhang spun us inside. We headed for a majestic, high-backed wooden booth big enough for six people. We slid our book bags onto the ample seat and then slipped in opposite each other. A moment of stillness, surging with possibility, hung between us.

"So, what year are you in?" Roger began safely.

"I'm a senior this year."

"So am I."

"Oh yeah? What kind of stuff do you like to do?"

"I have a Saab. Do you know what that is?"

I shook my head "no."

"It's a little sports car. I run it in rallies."

I stared back blankly.

"That's a kind of a road race. You're given a set of instructions to follow—kind of like a treasure hunt—only you're driving your car down country roads trying to find the right route. It's a lot of fun, but you need a navigator. Maybe you could do it with me sometime." His eyes shone with enthusiasm. "What about you? What do you like to do?"

"Me? I sing!" Last year, I'd finally made it into the prestigious chamber chorus, Singers. Singing was my greatest joy in life. I glanced over at Roger, whose face remained in neutral. "Guess that's about all."

Singers! Then it hit me. *I won't be able to perform with them this year. I'll have to drop out!* My spirit plummeted to the bottom of a deep pit, and reality crushed it like a heavy stone. I bowed my head to keep Roger from seeing the tears that were forming in my eyes. But my face turned red and my bottom lip began to pucker.

"Ah, what's wrong?" he asked.

I glanced up, blurry with tears. His large, dark eyes were full of concern. "Gee, I don't even know you, Roger," I began in a husky voice, "but I have to tell somebody about this." He bent forward, still listening, so I took a quick breath and plunged ahead. "I'm two months pregnant," I blurted out, quickly dropping my head to the table. My arms flew up to cover it while my body began, helplessly, to shake with quiet sobs in the dark space under my arms.

Roger reached over and tentatively touched my arm. Just then, the waitress came. I kept my head down and muzzled my sobs while Roger quickly ordered two large Cokes and sent the waitress away. Then he turned his attention back to me.

"Oh, you poor thing," he said softly, reaching over with both hands to gently rub my neck and caress my arm. His tender touch soothed me. I slowly lifted my head. My eyes were burning; my face was bloated. I grabbed a nearby napkin and loudly blew my nose. Then I dabbed at my teary face and released a long sigh. There! At last it was out.

The waitress returned with our Cokes and we sipped in silence as I gradually recovered myself. Then I began to speak. Roger's brow furrowed, his gaze fixed on me, while I told him the whole long story of my trip to Europe and my mis-adventure with the two French men. "I've been thinking about an abortion, Roger, but I don't have any idea where to go or what to do," I concluded.

He took a sharp breath, breaking the spell, and then reached over, putting his hand on top of mine. "Now, now. Don't worry. I think I know somebody who can help. I can find out about it for you."

My heart jumped. I looked up, eyes shining. "You will? Oh, Roger—will you really?" It was like a fairy tale: my prayers were answered. I was a lady in distress, and Roger was a knight—a champion—coming to my rescue. Maybe he was the one I'd been waiting for. My words rushed out of their own accord. "Oh, thank you so much. You're a god-send."

I gave his hand a little squeeze, but then a wall of doubt stuck fast in the middle of my chest. I dropped my eyes and hastily reprimanded myself: *You fool. This isn't Hollywood. It's far too much to ask.*

True. But maybe . . .

I studied him closely. Then, carefully slipping my hand away, I said, "But I hardly know you, Roger, and I've made such a nuisance of myself, already. Really, you don't need to get yourself involved in this mess."

I folded my hands back into my lap and held my breath, waiting for his reply. I looked away for a moment, but when I turned back, his dark eyes still brimmed with gentle kindness.

"Nonsense. Just relax. I'll take care of it for you." He reached for me again. When I felt his touch on my arm, bliss rippled through me. The corners of my mouth turned upward and my eyes snapped back to life. My hand groped for his. There was a warm connection, a green light on the track. We both sighed. The next thing I knew, angel wings were fluttering in my chest.

3 - Beyond the Veil

Meeting Roger was too instant, too perfect to be explained in ordinary ways. You've seen this in your life, too: the time you got a flat tire on the way to the airport and an empty taxi came along on a highway far from the city—the time a book fell open to the exact passage you needed to read.

Do the Higher Powers use syncronicity to clue us in? Is it like the party game, B.F. Skinner where the person who's "it" must figure out how the audience wants him to pose by their response to his movements? If he's supposed to be the Statue of Liberty and puts his hand in the air, they clap. When he takes it down, they stop clapping. Perhaps syncronicity is the Higher Realm's way of helping us follow some long-forgotten plan.

How *do* souls choose their new lives, anyway? Again, we look to what Dr. Newton reports in his book, *Journey of Souls*. In preparation for a new life, souls are drawn towards a great concentration of light and energy they call the Ring of Destiny. Like some circular, four dimensional movie theater, the Ring shimmers in the round with scenes from Earth. Time and space are manipulated so the viewer can experience selected portions of possible next lives.

As earth life materializes around her, the previewing soul divides her energy and enters the scene. She feels, smells, tastes, hears, sees everything as it happens. For a moment, she becomes that person. Then she retreats before being detected. (Could this explain our sense of *deja vu?*)

Previewing spirits sample a few pre-selected scenes so they can sense how living them would feel. Would this or that life be too easy or too hard? In which life would the soul's objectives most likely be met?

Picture my daughter's soul in the Ring of Destiny. She's developed gifts of intelligence and competence in past lives. But she's gotten on a treadmill of "doing" that has her spinning wheels—so busy doing what *others* want and worrying about what *others* think that she neglects to discover and honor her own being, her own needs. In this new life, she'll hope to begin that inner journey.

She asks her guides: "How can I get beyond this compulsive

'doing?' What circumstances will drive me to discover who *I* am and what *I* value? What will lead me to that place of wholeness within, where stability and peace abide without efforting."

Advanced souls, called Planners, listen to her requests and select several upcoming lives for her to view. When all is ready, she enters the Ring. Empty, shiny surfaces glimmer all around her. She moves to the control panel and throws the switch. The first life to be previewed now comes alive.

She's a baby boy whose mother's a hypercondriac. The baby is left alone in his crib to cry. No one's there for him. He's desperately lonely. He develops a sense of rootlessness, unfulfilled needs, something wrong inside—a subconscious void.

In the next scene, the boy's in school. He's very shy but, because of his intelligence and good work habits, does really well there. He's proud of his good marks. He'll be able to win scholarships and get a good education.

Next, he's twenty-three. He's finishing a master's degree and is late to class. He's speeding downhill on his bicycle. A car pulls out in front of him. Oh, no!

He's lying in a hospital bed. A monitor is beeping. He's in a body cast and will never walk again. His hopes for a busy career are foiled. How could this have happened? Why him? That subconscious void he felt as a child is threatening again.

A special therapist comes into his life and, together, they begin to explore the Inner Dimension. . . .

That scene dissolves; the screen clears.

Here comes another life. This time, a baby girl is being born to a Chinese single mother in a small college town in Belgium. Her mother must work and leaves the girl to be raised by a strict Chinese grandmother.

When she reaches school age, she finds herself the only Oriental student in school. She feels out of place. But she excels in her studies and her teachers, the nuns, treat her kindly. What future awaits her in this foreign society?

Reaching adulthood, she craves more education and yearns to fit in, so she joins the convent and begins an inner journey.

The screen clears again and one more life begins. This time, a baby girl is crying for her mother. But her mother isn't there. This baby will grow up in a closed adoption system. She'll look and feel different from the family she grows up with. She'll long to know who she really is, while remaining loyal to her adoptive family. . . .

After these previews, the soul goes back with her friends and guides to make a final choice. Which life is she more drawn to? Which circumstances better fit her needs? Who will she choose for parents? Who will play other important roles?

This is a busy time with many choices to make. Ten to fifteen key players agree to accompany the soul and play the necessary roles. Now they all go together to another special area for a life-to-come preview cram session. In this place of high energy, signals for recognition are devised and learned. You're taught to recognize your spouse when he pulls your hair in choir rehearsal. You practice knowing your best friend when she tells an incredible story about a therapy problem she solved with astrology. These signals are rehearsed and gone over. They'll be the red flags that will mark turning points in the life to come.

Then, when a soul is finally ready to travel to Earth, her friends and guides accompany her to a spot where bands of light connect celestial energy with earth energy. In this spot, messages can be passed to and received from Earth. Here, fond goodbyes are said.

Spirit friends form two lines close together, like a chute. The traveler is passed down the middle, from one to the next, with a soft touch on the shoulder or hand. Each friend, in turn, whispers a message. The words, moist and warm, gently vibrate on all sides. "Have courage." "Embrace your fear." "Remember your mission." "Speak your truth." "Always forgive." "Love is the key." She soaks in the words, storing them in her inner treasure chest. "Trust the Universe." "We will help you." "You are worthy and wise." "You are loved completely."

The soothing voices and tender touches bathe her in love the whole way down the chute. When she emerges, her guide is there waiting to enfold her quivering essence. They vibrate together for a long moment, spreading a low-pitched tone over the whole area. From the resonance, a golden glow forms and rolls between them.

Afterwards, the traveler lingers. She wanders off by herself to go over everything in her mind one more time. There are deep regrets about leaving but great excitement about the coming mission. When the moment feels right, she rejoins her guide. Stepping to the launching point, they fling themselves onto one of the connecting beams of light. But the guide soon turns back, leaving the spirit to travel earthward alone. She's propelled downward, as if on a giant waterslide. She closes her eyes and surrenders, knowing the beam will take her directly where she needs to go: into the warm, dark softness of her mother's womb. Whoosh! She's there now! She's inside a baby! Now begins the slow, gentle process of joining her soul self to the body of the baby already in residence.

No one knows exactly when "ensoulment" happens. It could vary from case to case. But *my* baby's soul was definitely there on the fateful day I checked to see.

A week after meeting Roger, I still haven't asked him anything about the abortion. I need to talk to him *soon*, but something about it makes me queasy. What if it is botched and I can't have other kids? What if I die? How will my parents feel then? And what about the baby? Is it right to take its life? What if it wants to live?

I certainly have never considered that.

Please, just stop and think a minute before you go any further, my inner voice demands. So, at lunch time, I select an empty bench and plunk myself down to think.

I swing my book bag onto the bench beside me. I'm seated along a tree-lined mall, with a tall, gray stone wall to the south. The wall separates campus from town and muffles the sound of traffic. I sit, idle, absently watching the fat squirrels hoard nuts for the winter. Happy, carefree students stroll past, unaware that fate is pressing down on me.

Pregnant and alone! I carry the child of a stranger I met in Paris—and the full responsibility of what to do about it is mine alone. A tear of self-pity leaks out and dribbles down my cheek.

You're not alone: you have Roger now, I remind myself sternly. *So straighten up and quit feeling sorry for yourself. You have a decision to make here.*

I count my due date over and over again on my fingers. I got pregnant June 30th. July, August, September—I'm starting my third month now. October, November, December, January, February, March. The baby is due in March. If I'm going to have an abortion,

I have to do it *now*, before the third month is over.

I close my eyes, wondering if I can visualize the baby inside me. Hmm. Yes. There it is, a small figure, suspended in dark silence. "Who are you?" I ask. "Why are you here inside me? You won't have a father. I can't be your mother. Should I just abort you now, or do you really want to be born?"

Something grabs my solar plexus. Low vibrations buzz through my spinal cord. **"I have a right to my life. I have a contribution to make to the world. Do not stop me from fulfilling my destiny."** There is no sound, but an awesome command has been given.

I slump back into the bench; my eyes bolt open. I take a shallow breath and slowly twist my neck around, checking behind me, but the squirrels are still busy gathering and the people still nonchalantly amble by. How can one explain what has just happened?

Is this only my imagination? I wonder. A shudder wriggles through my body. *I need some proof here*, I decide, trying to stay logical.

Holding my breath, I close my eyes. "If this is real, tell me again," I demand, addressing the unseen force. Again, I try to visualize the baby curled up inside my womb.

"I wish to live. I have gifts for the world, a purpose to be born for. Do not take my life away from me." The presence is still insistent, but gentler. Gradually, it fades.

"Okay," I hasten to agree. "If that's what you want." I hold my eyes tightly shut as I deliver my promise; then I sigh deeply and open them once more.

It's as if I've been in another reality, but the world is back now. I sit up and let my shoulders relax. I notice a strange feeling of calm. Finally, I have an answer to the question that's been torturing me since July. And I can say goodbye to those many nasty things I won't have to think about any more.

But soon, my eyes fill with tears: this means I'll have to tell my parents.

Dull despair grabs the pit of my stomach. I've forgotten my lines. The scene goes black and pitches me into confusion.

Off-stage, a light flicks on. Thoughts float out from the prompter's box: "Roger will help you. You'll find some way to do it.

You've promised your baby it can live, and your parents will just have to deal with it."

Classes are letting out and the sidewalk fills with pedestrians and bikers. Shouldering my book bag, I get up and join the swarm of students on the mall. I smile broadly, allowing myself to think at last: *I'm pregnant! I'm going to have a baby in March.* It's such a wondrous thought. I laugh. No one can tell. It's still *my* little secret. I know it won't stay that way for long, but it's mine for the moment, anyhow.

Bursting with excitement and joy, I rush to find Roger. We have agreed to meet at this class break, outside the building where we both have our British novel class next period. I spot him as soon as I round the corner. His lanky, boyish figure is leaning on the brick wall near the entrance, his book bag on the ground. His dark eyes flit nervously over the passersby. When he spots me, that broad, gentle smile of his flashes across his face. We move towards each other, and he folds his arms around me.

"Hi, Honey. How's it going?" he asks, as casually as he can manage. Poor Roger. He's promised to support me, whatever I decide to do. But I'm sure he really has no idea what that will entail, in either case.

I set my book bag on the ground beside his. "I'm not going to have an abortion," I announce.

Roger's face relaxes in deep relief. No illegal arrangements or secret trips to make! No cash to come up with! No worries about having to face my parents if I die on the table. He doesn't say anything; he just kisses me and holds me tight.

But still breathless with excitement, I break out of his embrace and babble about seeing the baby *in utero*. "I felt my baby's thoughts. It wants to live, Roger. It said it has some important contribution to make to the world."

Roger stares at me, trying to comprehend. "I know that sounds nuts," I continue, "but that's how I experienced it."

"Oh well, don't worry about it." He gives me another big hug. "I'm just glad you decided against it."

"Roger—I didn't know you felt that way!"

"Well, I didn't want to influence your decision. It *was* your choice." He looks down bashfully.

Students pour past us on the way to fourth-period classes, but Roger and I make no move to join them.

"Let's skip class," I suggest. "I need to talk to you about telling my parents. They're going to be pretty mad, you know. It could be a bad scene."

"Okay. Let's go to the Corner Tavern for a Coke." Roger scoops up his book bag.

I try to lift mine, but it feels like lead weight. Seeing me falter, Roger shoulders my bag as well. "Don't worry," he says. "I'll go with you when you tell them."

My heart melts when I hear his words. I look up to see his beautiful dark eyes fixed on me and brimming with kindness. He winks and, stepping out, links his arm under mine.

I add my hand to our joined arms. "Oh, would you, Roger? I'd be *forever* grateful! That would make such a difference to me—if only I didn't have to face them alone! If you're there, it should help. Mom and Dad will be worried about keeping up appearances in front of you. That should quell their reaction a little bit, anyway. I promise—I'll do the talking. All you have to do is be there and hold my hand."

4 - A Price to Pay

Sunday, October 3—the "big day"—is bright and sunny. I arrange it with Mom and Dad in advance: dinner at home—a chance to meet my new boyfriend. I'm not showing yet, but it will be too late for an abortion, should they suggest one. We'll be there Sunday after church. *God, please fill them with Christian charity today*, I pray as we speed toward my parents and my destiny.

Roger maneuvers his little red sports car over bumps and around curves at motorcross speed with me huddled in the bucket seat beside him. It's just starting to turn chilly. The trees are ablaze in fine fall colors. It reminds me that, soon, my parents' illusions about me will be dropping just like the autumn leaves. I'm glad Roger doesn't look over, because he would see me trembling.

This is no good, I tell myself. *Just try to relax a minute. Close your eyes.*

In the darkness behind my eyes, scenes from the past start playing out. I can see my dad patiently coaxing notes from pig-tailed girls with dry-reeded clarinets. How does he manage not to flinch at their squeaks and squawks? He leans over freckle-faced boys with skinned knees saying, "Take out your gum. Now blow." Air whooshes down brass mouthpieces and burbles out in short blasts. He checks all the spindly fingers stiltwalking on valves—prodding, slipping, pushing. "Now, French horns, trombones, tighten your lips. A little higher." He points upward and croons the note, while drummers, forever happy at artillery practice, tat-tat-tat along. Daddy, in his studio below my bedroom, corrects and praises—groups in the afternoon, private students at night—inadvertently giving me a hundred thousand music lessons.

Now I see his pride and joy, the high school marching band, parading down the street decked out in maroon and gray. They march eight abreast by twelve deep (later fourteen). "Keep those rows straight. Look left, look right, look straight ahead." Ninety-six pairs of white spats stepping in time. Dad, in his glory, sweat pouring off his shiny brow, proudly marches to the drum beat, mile after uncomplaining mile.

He loves his work—quite a bit more than he loves me, I often think. When he's done teaching at 9 p.m. weekdays, he comes upstairs and falls asleep on the big recliner chair, watching TV. Mother hushes us. On Saturday he runs errands, mows the lawn, washes the car, polishes shoes. Sunday morning, it's always Sunday school and church—and sometimes a drive on Sunday afternoon. Occasionally, there's a game of back yard catch or marshmallow toasting around a fire. But, most of the time, Dad's busy elsewhere.

There's no easy love between us, but, I can see Dad's joy, his fulfillment at work—and I want that for myself someday.

According to Dr. Darlene Bruland, an academician, psychotherapist and astrologer, every child adopts the value system of a particular parent. Children born under the astrological signs of Aries, Gemini, Leo, Libra, Sagittarius and Aquarius pattern themselves after their fathers. Taurus, Cancer, Virgo, Scorpio, Capricorn and Pisces children pattern after their mothers. Of course, both parents will influence a child in significant ways, but the child will see one parent as more important and will imitate that parent. Which one, is shown by the child's sun sign.

Often times, one must look below the surface to see what's really going on. The waves may be going in one direction while the current runs in another. In my case, Dad's and my relationship was strained: he was preoccupied with work and had a hard time showing his feelings, so I felt unloved. His unquestioned orthodox beliefs and prejudices grated on me. Yet, what he *valued*—his job and his music—looked far more appealing than my mother's lot—the kitchen, the ironing board, soap operas and yelling at the kids.

Besides, I was blind to mother's love of domesticity. There was no way I could understand the deep personal pleasure she took in making a perfect home for all of us. I discounted the value and self-esteem she found in protecting husband and children, in giving us all a firm sense of security.

What I did see was her preoccupation with my father—how she basked in the glory he reflected instead of generating her own. I watched her always smooth his way. I saw her grow exhausted and short-tempered from holding herself and others to high standards of perfection. She would sacrifice all her time and energy to others and then cry "martyr." Mother was both smart and gifted, but her plate seemed empty to me.

I had no intention of walking down that road! I would rather be out working, doing something I loved—like Dad—and leave self-sacrifice and boring domesticity to someone else.

In our family, Mother always administered the small-time discipline. But if we were really bad, she would get Dad involved. "This hurts me more than it hurts you," he would say before landing blows with the yard stick. "I'm easy on you. Grandpa always used a razor strap on me."

His punishments filled me with hate, but Daddy firmly believed a caring parent must spank a child to teach what's right, or the Devil would take her soul. And when he believed something, you'd better believe it, too, or he'd spank you until you did. That's the way his father, the minister, did to him, and Grandpa's father, the one who lost his money and turned to drink, did before him.

But even Mother knew he got carried away sometimes. It would happen when he put down the yardstick and started beating me with his fists. Usually when we argued about religion or morals. She'd had to haul him off me more than once. . . .

I'm feeling queasy by the time Roger's car pulls up in front of Mom and Dad's "dream house." When I look up, the grand, stone rancher looms before us. Built into a hillside, Mother has designed the house so the family can enter at the top, while band students can use the separate doors in the basement. The extra income Dad earns teaching at home helps pay the mortgage.

Mother comes to the front door, a crisp apron carefully covering her Sunday dress, and invites us in. She has timed the meal perfectly, as always. Roger joins my father in the living room briefly, while I help her serve the food.

At the ringing of the dinner chimes, we come to the table and take our seats. (I'm glad she hasn't made place cards.) A cocktail drink of cranberry juice with orange sherbet rests in the middle of the good china, and a fruited Jello salad sits at the tip of the forks to the left. We join hands for prayers, then smooth out our napkins and sip the juice. Roger, making a good impression, compliments Mother on the place setting. I jump up to whisk away the juice glasses, and the serving begins.

Dad, at the head of the table, carves and passes a chicken-filled plate to Mother at the other end. She piles on mashed potatoes and peas and gives the first plate to Roger, our guest. I'm served next. I'll be expected to empty my plate, so, when everyone is served and Mother has taken her first bite, I begin shoveling down my food, though every bite sticks painfully in my throat.

"Pass the rolls please, Dear," Mother reminds me.

I jerk to attention. The rolls, wrapped warm and cozy in their heated tile box, sit before me. Without a word, I pass them to Mother. Then I pick up the cut glass dish containing homemade jam that I know she'll ask for next.

"So, Roger—Ann's told us you're an English major. What are your plans after graduation?"

Mother plies Roger with questions. After all, she must find out "certain things" so she can assess his desirability as a future son-in-law. Religion, social status, ambition, earning potential, and good manners, of course—these are the things that count. Dad tries to keep some light conversation going so Mom's fixation won't seem too rude. I am feeling enormously embarrassed for poor Roger, who's not Anglo-Saxon or Protestant enough to pass close inspection.

Finally, the meal is over. I quickly propose leaving the dishes until later and lead the procession into the adjoining living room. I know the time for my "big announcement" has arrived at last because a heavy, black cloud of tension has dropped on me, blurring my vision. It can wait no longer.

"Mom, Dad, I have something important I need to discuss with you," I bravely begin.

I have positioned myself in the middle of our tan brocade couch. Roger sits close by my left side. My cold hand gropes for his—it will be my lifeline. Mother sits to my right on the couch, looking at me with excited expectancy. Dad shifts forward in his dark-brown recliner. The tension builds. They're obviously expecting an announcement of some sort. . . .

Oh, no! They think Roger and I . . . I did this all wrong.

My breath is short, and my hands are like ice.

It's too late. Just go! You have to say it now, a voice within me demands.

"Mom, Dad, through no fault of Roger's, I'm pregnant."

Mother is on her feet in an instant. "You're WHAT?" she

shrieks, her eyes wide with horror. "PREGNANT?"

I can almost hear her cherished illusions shatter like glass around us. "The perfect mother," "the perfect family"—smashed to smithereens in an instant. She crosses her arms in front of herself and glares at me in outrage.

"You slut! You ungrateful slut! How dare you do this to us, after all we have sacrificed for you!" she screams, her face contorted. "How could you? You're nothing but a whore! You've disgraced your whole family—me and your father, your grandparents, your brothers—all of us!"

Her body is quaking, her face, red, but then she slowly hardens to stone as a memory from a dark scene in her childhood clicks in. She spins on her heel and turns her back to me. **"I disown you!"** Her words travel upward from a deep pit of rage inside. They reverberate out of her and into my body. "You're not my daughter any more! From this day forward, you are no longer a member of this family!" Then, she collapses in heavy sobs.

My neck tightens, my throat grows raw. In shock, I struggle to grasp her meaning. Then I begin to cry. I'd always thought she would understand. At least I'd always been able to reason with her about things.

Where can I turn now? Dad doesn't love me. He'll flip out and attack me. Mom's been the one who's protected me from his rages in the past, but without that . . . . Disowned? She calls me a whore? In my worst imaginings, I'd never expected that. *Kicked out of the family? Who will pay for college? Where will I go? I'll be stuck in a hovel somewhere with a screaming kid to care for. I'll go crazy and kill us both.*

All I could do was cry. Poor Roger is mute as I bury my head in his chest.

"No!" booms a male voice. It takes me several seconds to realize that the voice is my father's. My heart stands still. "We will not disown her! She is our daughter. A family must stay together. They must stand beside each other." He says it stiffly, like he's quoting scripture. He gets up out of his chair and is standing protectively in front of me by the time I think to look up.

Dad?

The soiled veil of misperception that's hidden Dad's love from me for twenty years is torn away in an instant. He has come through for me just when I really need him. The grace of his act washes away all the petty grudges I've ever held against him. They seem less than meaningless now. If there was a karmic debt between us, he's discharged whatever's owed. His account with me is paid in full for all time.

Somehow, we all recover ourselves eventually. My explanations are made and accepted. Naturally I leave Claude out of my story entirely and hype up the "forced" nature of my encounter with Jean-Michel. He becomes the criminal. I'm an innocent victim. Dad and Mom discuss the possibilities briefly—including my worst fear: Mother raising the baby—but decide, much to my relief, that there is only one thing to do: put the baby up for adoption.

Dad goes out in the foyer to call our family doctor at his home. The rest of us wait tensely, listening as best we can to his side of the conversation. The doctor recommends a home for unwed mothers. That way, no one will ever know, and our family name can be protected. The baby will be cared for by nice adoptive parents, who want children but can't have their own. After the baby is born and surrendered, I will be accepted back in the family "as if" it never happened. This has occurred in other good families, the doctor says. We will all forget about it in time.

It certainly seemed like the perfect solution at the time.

5 - Refuge

My parents drove me to the home for unwed mothers on December 26, 1965. We travelled many miles over icy roads that day. They sat together up front; I cowered by myself in the back. A book lay open on my lap, unread. In the front passenger seat, Mother reapplied her lipstick, attempting to restore her perfect image after our lunch stop. She held her body stiffly in place, like her spray-net-coated hair. When she finished her ritual, she tilted her compact mirror to survey the back seat. I glanced down at my book and shielded my face with a hand to block out her spying. After a tense moment, she heaved a huge sigh and snapped the compact shut. I didn't have to look up to know that her jaw was set and her steely blue eyes were staring straight ahead again.

I squeezed my eyes shut in concentration. *Please, God, get us there quickly. I can't stand this much longer.*

"Forecast for western Pennsylvania. . ."

"Turn that up, Honey."

At her direction, my father reached over and adjusted the volume on the radio.

". . .freezing rain, turning to snow late this afternoon. Highs in the mid 30's; low 28 degrees," the deep voice announced. "Hope you all had a very, merry Christmas yesterday. Now back to music."

"Sure. We had a great Christmas," my mother muttered, slowly turning her head. "And if we wreck this car today, **it will be all your fault**," she blazed at me.

"Now, Mother." My dad reached over and gently placed his hand on her thigh.

"Well, it's true," she said, turning back, her throat constricting. When her body began to quiver, I knew that she was crying again.

Unfortunately, our "plan" hasn't cured my mother's pain. True, our family will stick together and probably manage to avert public disgrace. But Mother's dream of "perfect mother," "perfect child," "perfect family," will never fit back in place. It is gone—completely swept away. My volcanic eruption has obliterated all the old forms she's toiled and sacrificed to create. She grieves her loss. It wails inside her, lashes out at me.

We get attached to our ideas of how things should look. It's really hard to let them go when we deeply cherish something, think we need it to survive. For more than twenty years, Mother has cooked three nutritious meals a day, served dinners on time, set tables properly, ironed the linens, washed and folded underwear, sewed, mended, helped with homework, kept a spotless house, done the dishes, watered flowers, canned vegetables, made pickles, visited in-laws, even educated me about birth control! . . . what more could she have done? And for all that dedication she's been betrayed, disgraced!

If only people would stop believing that "what they do" has, or should have, the power to control how *someone else* behaves. When their partners do the unexpected, the unapproved, people run down blind alleys crying, "What did *I* do wrong?" and "How could he have done that to me?"

The pattern is a relic from childhood. When parents punish a child's bad deeds and reward his good ones, the child concludes he can control how other people react. He sees himself as a magical puppeteer, pulling peoples' strings. If he can be good enough, everything will be okay.

But that game really doesn't work. After all, where is it written that "your being perfect" obligates someone to do what you desire? As long as people have free will, they'll act the way they do, sometimes for hidden reasons. Husbands can be "perfect" and wives can still leave home. No connection, really.

But, if you *say* there's a connection, it's *you* who will be floundering in anger, resentment and confusion.

Why do people do the unexpected? Sometimes it's because of unexamined family patterns. My father was programmed to forgive, my mother to disown, by events buried deep in our family history. Unknown to me, my father's college-age brother had impregnated his girlfriend, and my grandfather, the minister, had stood by them, married them, helped them keep the child. My mother's parents, on the other hand, had once disowned a disobedient college-age son. No one ever spoke of these things, of course, but the shadow they cast was long.

Was Mother so shaken by what had happened to her brother that the association of "not being perfect," traumatic upset and disownment was branded into her subconscious mind?

Could this explain what she'd done on Christmas Eve when I was almost thirteen? I'd gotten into a snit with her that night. I wasn't a baby anymore and I wasn't going to sit through her ritual reading of "Twas the Night Before Christmas." I was too grown up! Mother had flipped out. She terrified us by screaming, crying and locking herself in her room until Christmas afternoon that year. For years, I'd felt responsible for driving her over the edge.

But was it just the old pattern kicking up again? When Mother was perfect, she thought other people should do what she expected. When I didn't, that Christmas Eve, it must have pushed her imperfection-trauma-disownment button. What happens deep in our psyches? Do dark memories leap out like fun house monsters? Do we lash out or recoil in fear?

My pregnancy didn't fit what Mother was expecting either. Disownment had been averted, but a firestorm of invalidation was raging. She and I were jostling for control, trying to protect our egos. No one could get beyond those issues to consider the long term consequences of giving away a child. Mother and I were too entrenched in fighting for our very lives.

By late afternoon, when we arrived at the home, the air was swirling with tiny, stinging flakes of snow. Mother successfully navigated us to the proper address in an old residential neighborhood of the city. The home itself looked new, though. It was a well-kept colonial-style building with an imposing facade.

I smirked. A home for unwed mothers *would* need to keep up appearances.

When we pulled up, Dad got my suitcase from the car and Mother rang the bell. I hung back, preferring to keep a safe distance between me and my parents. Dread knotted my stomach. *Will they be shaming and judgemental here, too?* I wondered.

A moment later, a small, wiry woman with a perky, no-nonsense personality was herding us all out of the bad weather and into the entrance hall. Goldie, the housemother, wore a stylish dress, seamed stockings, and high-heeled shoes, yet I sensed a faint air of unconventionality about her. I hoped so, anyway. Dad set my suitcase down, and we all hung our coats in the nearby closet.

There were introductions all around. Then Goldie asked about my due date and if I'd been to a doctor. As usual, my mother did all the talking.

"Yes," she explained. "We took her to our family doctor just as soon as we found out. He was the one who recommended the home."

I focused intently on my hands, which were tightly clenched in my lap. If only I could make myself invisible. Mother's voice floated somewhere in space, giving correct, responsible answers to all of Goldie's questions, while I sniped at her in my mind.

You always have to look good, I felt like saying. *Why don't you show her "the other you" for once? Why don't you tell her how you wanted to throw me out of the family when I told you I was pregnant?*

The axe-blow memory contracted my stomach.

"One more thing. You'll have to decide on an adoption agency today," Goldie continued. "We have three to choose from: Jewish, Catholic and non-denominational."

My body stiffened. I hadn't thought of this.

Please, no religious agencies, I prayed with all my might. I sat there helpless, while my parents conferred. They were very religious people. They went to church every Sunday. My father sat on the Church Council; Mother was in charge of the Altar Guild. But what worked in my favor was that the "right" religion had not been mentioned.

"We want the child raised as a Protestant," my mother finally reported, "so we'll take the non-denominational agency."

I'd been holding my breath. Suddenly, it released sharply. Goldie glanced over at me, and I quickly shielded my face with my hand.

She stood to end the meeting. "I think that's all I need from you. Ann can receive mail, but no visits from home until this is over. We'll take very good care of her. We provide three nutritionally balanced meals a day, and all our girls have the best medical care. They meet every week with their social worker, too.

"Now, would you like a little tour of the facilities before you go?"

Mother's eyes brightened as she eagerly accepted the invitation for all of us. If there was anything she enjoyed, it was house tours. She was always looking for new house design ideas.

We trotted down the hall behind Goldie, through a large dining room, furnished in well-polished, heavy pine. We were allowed only a peek into the spotlessly clean, stainless steel kitchen at the back, because some of the girls were in there helping with the cooking chores. The home was decorated for Christmas, but with a simplicity that was relaxing. We ended our tour in the formal sitting area, where a small Christmas tree stood in the front window.

"Upstairs are the girls' rooms and a TV lounge, but to protect the confidentiality of the girls, no outsiders are allowed up there."

Mother nodded her head approvingly, and Dad handed Goldie a check for my first month's stay. Coats were gathered, awkward hugs exchanged. Mother looked solemn and sad. "Good luck," she managed. Then they turned and left. As the heavy door swung shut behind them, relief washed over me. I was free of them at last.

Goldie tapped my shoulder lightly. "Come back into the office for a moment, Ann."

All I need is another lecture, I thought bitterly. But I dutifully trudged along behind her, hands clasped in front of me to make a wall.

She closed the door and then turned to look me straight in the eye. "Ann, we only have a few rules and regulations here, but they need to be followed." She explained the sign-out procedure. Two one-hour walks a day were allowed. Chores would have to be done before going out. Dinner was at six sharp. No one went out in the evening; no visitors and no hanky-panky.

I sighed with relief. Was that all? It didn't sound that bad to me. "Okay," I readily agreed.

She touched me on the arm then, and her voice softened. "I live here with the girls, and I'm always available to you—twenty-four hours a day. You can knock on my door anytime. If you ever get blue, you can come cry on my shoulder. That's what I'm here for."

I tried to keep my expression neutral. It was nice of her to offer, but that was just about the last thing in the world she'd ever find me doing. I'd learned long ago to keep my feelings to myself around adults.

"Okay," she chirped, turning around briskly, "Might as well bring your suitcase and come upstairs. I'll show you your room and introduce you to the girls."

We went back out to the hall. I picked up my suitcase and

dragged myself up the steps behind her. Worried thoughts billowed like storm clouds inside me. *What will these girls be like? Will they accept me?*

Goldie led the way down the brightly lit hall to the dorm room I was to share with two other residents. The room was spacious and orderly. There were three single beds, each with a night stand, and one large shared dresser. The bed at the far end of the room would be mine. I put my suitcase down there and peered out the window. The frosty panes showed a deserted street swirling with falling snow. Ice-coated maple trees quaked in the winter wind. I drew back and tried to smile at Goldie.

"Ready to go meet the girls?" she asked.

I took a deep breath and nodded.

I followed her down the hall to the TV room. My stomach was churning now, and my hands were trembling like the tree limbs outside the window. For protection, I pasted my winning smile in place. I needed to fit in here. *Please like me*, I prayed.

"There may only be a few of the girls in here right now, but this is where they usually hang out."

Goldie confidently stepped into a room ringed by comfortable chairs and sofas. An oval coffee table stood in the center and a TV chattered away at one end of the room. Two pregnant girls looked up from their reading, another from her knitting; a fourth was absorbed in the TV. No one gave me a dirty look. In fact, I quickly observed, I'm not *nearly* as pregnant as most of the girls in this room.

"Girls, this is Ann." Goldie waited while the girls introduced themselves, one by one, and then she slipped away.

Typically, the "girls" (as they called us) were my age or younger—mostly eighteen or nineteen—and all were from white middle-class families. Most had been jilted by their lovers or torn away from them by angry parents. They were here to keep a family name unsoiled. As we were all in the same boat, there were no moral judgements, only sympathy and support. Relieved to be "normal" again, I released my tight shoulders and looked around.

I was anxious to hear everyone's story. The youngest person in the room was Marjorie, a diminutive Jewish girl with curly black hair. She was only sixteen years old and, I found out later, had gotten pregnant the very first time she'd made love. She wouldn't be telling her parents that the baby was half black. "How could I have gotten pregnant the very first time?" she kept asking.

The oldest was Susan, twenty-four, who was carrying her married boyfriend's child. (Her "baby" turned out to be twin girls, and she decided to keep them, much to our amazement.)

"What did you say your name was?" I asked the butch-looking girl I ended up sitting next to.

"Name's Rudy," she replied. "The kid's due the end of February. What 'bout you?" Everyone was known by her first name and due date.

"Ann—March 15th," I replied. I clasped my hands together and sat quietly. I'd felt fine before, but as I sat idle, a lump came up in my throat. "Hey, Rudy. What's this place really like?" I whispered. "I just got here, you know."

She crossed her arms and tilted back so she could see me better. "Well, tell you the truth—it's kinda like a reform school," she boomed out. I cringed, wishing she'd pipe down—I really didn't want the whole room to know what was asking—but she continued in a loud voice. "No bars on the windows or anything, but it's still a prison. They have all these rules and regulations, menial jobs—and no visitors! If you want to know what it's like, I'll tell you: it stinks!"

"Quit scaring her. It's not that bad," objected Susan. "Just do your job and follow the rules, and nobody will hassle you."

"At least they don't harp on your 'immoral conduct' and stuff like that," added little Marjorie. "And the food's decent."

"Yeah, they're tryin' to fatten us up for the kill," Rudy grumbled.

"I've been here for two months," volunteered Molly, a nineteen-year-old blond with a story-book face. "There *are* a lot of rules, but other than that, it's pretty okay."

"Watch out for those social workers, though," Rudy interrupted. "They are real bitches." With that, she crossed her arms and turned away toward the TV.

"Well, that can be true," Susan admitted, throwing me a worried look. "But some of them are okay. I hope you'll get a decent one." She put down her knitting. "Hey, not to change the subject, but when did you get here, Ann?"

"Just this afternoon."

"Did your parents bring you?"

"Yeah. They were as glad to get rid of me as I was to get rid of them. They've been so paranoid! When we stopped for lunch today, Mom made Dad go in alone first, to make sure nobody knew us."

"I know what you mean." Molly nodded in agreement. "My parents were like that, too. They made me come here when I was only three and a half months pregnant."

"Good grief. Before you even started to show?" She didn't reply, but I could detect a hard look in her eyes. "I guess you were all here for Christmas Day, then," I said, remembering the tree downstairs.

"Yup," said Molly, shaking the sadness away. "It wasn't so bad, though. We had a real nice dinner last night." She managed a little smile.

"Did you all get maternity clothes for Christmas, like me?" They tittered. How long had it been since I'd heard that sound? The tension in my chest eased up a little more. "And how about 'cover stories?' Did you all have to make one up?"

Little Marjorie spoke up. "I'm supposed to be on an exciting high school exchange program." She sighed. "I'll miss a year of school because of this."

I overlooked the bitterness in her eyes. "That's kind of like mine," I said. "I'm in college, and I'm supposed to be taking off Winter Term—to help autistic children in Chicago. Original, eh?"

"Hey, Rudy. Where are you supposed to be?" Molly asked.

"Dunno. How about working on a chain gang?" she replied sarcastically, never taking her eyes off the TV.

"Ah, come on, Rudy," Susan chastised. Then she turned back to me and picked up her knitting again. "Rudy doesn't like it here, but I was really glad to come. I'm from a small town, where a pregnancy is really hard to hide."

I nodded my agreement. "You should have seen me. All of November, I walked around campus holding a big pile of books in front of me wherever I went. I made myself wear a coat all the time—even in the dorm. I know people were whispering, but at least I didn't get kicked out of school." I met her eyes. "I'm glad that's behind me now. What are you making, Susan?"

"A blanket for my baby." She smiled at me and dug her needles back into the wool. "Do you know how to knit?"

I laughed and shook my head "no."

"Wanna learn? I can teach you?"

The idea trickled through me like pink and aqua rainbows. I was making a connection here; I was going to fit in. My face brightened. *For once, I have some time to myself. I can relax and learn some new skills. This could even be fun.*

The cloak of my discomfort was loosening by the time I stood up and walked over to the window. Outside, the snow flakes were still pirouetting down the dark and lonely street. But now they carried off my fears. Then, a blinding whoosh of white streaked by. My breath sucked in; my eyes narrowed, trying to peer more closely into the unknown. *What forces lie out there in the dark?* I wondered.

A deep vibration seemed to reply, "We are powerful; we will guide you. Cling to us; you'll be all right."

6 - Birthday Present

My mouth sucked in a thin stream of frigid air through the loose weave of my mohair scarf. I held it in my lungs for a moment, then, slowly blew it out, hoping a bit of warmth would cling to the wool. But instead, drops of water formed, turning it soggy and cold.

January had been brutally cold. Five minutes outside and my feet were already getting numb. The cold chiseled straight into my bare forehead, but nothing was going to deter me from my walk this morning. It was my twenty-first birthday and I'd planned a little treat for myself.

I'd saved a new route for today: my first walk to the east. I'd already explored the nice residential neighborhoods to the north, and the park by the water a half-hour west of the home. And I'd been south many times, as well. The business district lay that way, about fifteen minutes away. In fact, my very first outing had been to downtown.

Susan had guided me there the day after I arrived. That first night at dinner, she had quietly suggested that I buy myself a fake wedding ring at the dime store, like the other girls had done. She offered to show me the way and even promised to help me pick out some needles and yarn for my first knitting project.

On the way back, I'd asked to stop at the library so I could pick out some books about childbirth. That was one subject I wanted to study up on, now that I was finally out of school and had the time.

The book, *Childbirth Without Fear* by Dr. Grantly Dick-Read caught my eye immediately. Without fear, there would be no pain, it said. That was definitely for me! I headed for the checkout desk with my prize, making sure the librarian could see my newly-purchased wedding ring. She smiled at me and asked when my baby was due. I chirped back an answer and headed out the door to join Susan, a broad smile of success plastered across my face.

Later that afternoon, I started reading my book. During labor, I learned, the uterine muscles contract to thin and open the cervix, the mouth of the womb. After the cervix is fully dilated, the contractions push the baby out of the uterus and through the vagina. "Don't think of the contractions as 'pain,'" the book said. "Think of it as 'muscles contracting.' Just let your mind and muscles relax so the uterus can do its work." The author explained that women who don't understand the process often tense up from fear and that this tenseness was what created muscle pain. It also slowed the birthing process. If a woman could just relax and let her muscles work, she would experience discomfort from the contractions, but not pain.

The book also suggested that being in good physical shape would help the delivery. It laid out an exercise program that I followed every night from then on. I wasn't going to be able to give this baby much, but at least I could give him or her a healthy start in life.

I started pinning my hopes on a natural delivery because, frankly, the thought of going under anesthesia made my skin crawl. First of all, I wasn't about to let anybody control me! Secondly, I'd heard a hundred horror stories about saddle-blocks, gas, caudals and epidurals. I'd heard about days and nights of splitting headaches, spinal injury, vomiting, stunted awareness. A lot could go wrong. The more I thought about it, the more I preferred to learn to use the book's breathing patterns to control my fear and stick with natural childbirth. If only I could get the doctor to see it my way.

I'd been assigned to Dr. Marsh and went to see him a week later. That first day, I perched on the edge of his examination table, clad in a scanty gown, arms tightly crossed in front of me, nervously jiggling my foot. At last, he twisted the doorknob open and bounced in the room. Dr. Marsh was a small-framed man, about forty, with glasses and a red, plaid bow tie.

"How are you doing today?" he opened cheerfully. "From the home, I see. Well, just relax and we'll take a look at you here. Lie back please, and put your feet up in the stirrups."

So far so good. No lecture. What a break! The noise of shifting myself into position covered up my sigh of relief.

He examined me carefully and quickly, prodding my now-visible pregnancy, measuring from my pubis to the top of my womb. When he was finished, he stepped back. "You can get dressed now. I'll come back, and we'll talk in a few minutes."

I dressed rapidly and sat in a chair by his desk, my downcast eyes fixed on my hands. When he returned, I kept my head bowed and listened, while his head talked on above me.

"Looks good. Normal pregnancy. You're healthy and young.

Should be clear sailing. I agree with your family doctor that your due date is March 15. I'll see you in four weeks, and then every two weeks until your ninth month. After that, it's every week. Are you taking your iron pills?"

When I nodded, he began to rattle on about delivery anesthesia. But I took a deep breath and interrupted him.

"Dr. Marsh, I'd like to talk to you about trying natural childbirth. I've been reading a book about it. I think I can do it. I really don't want you to use any kind of anesthesia on me." I snatched a quick breath and charged on. "Please say you'll let me do natural childbirth. Please promise me you won't put me out against my will."

Still afraid to look up, I held my breath and waited for his response.

There was a long pause. "Well, young lady, I don't do that very often in my practice, but if that's really what you want to do, I guess I have no objection. If it doesn't work out, we can always fall back on one of the more traditional methods."

No arguments? My eyes grew wide. It always took a bitter fight to get anything I really wanted from my parents.

My head was still stiffly turned downward. "Thank you so very much," I mumbled. A hot rush of gratitude began to pulse through my veins. I breathed deeply and my shoulders dropped. At last, I turned my face upwards and looked him in the eyes. When I saw the kindness that glowed there, my eyes filled with tears.

I found my tear ducts were leaking again as I thought about what had happened that day. So, crunching over snowy sidewalks, heading in my new easterly direction, I swiped at my face with a thick mitten. In the distance, a train whistle sprayed a cluster of pitches into the air. I picked up my pace and lifted my chin out of my scarf to look around. Squinting in the bright sunlight, I noticed a row of houses with unpainted porches and old sheets bunched up inside the windows. *I must be on the wrong side of the tracks*, I thought to myself.

"This is the kind of place we'd have to live in if I kept you, Baby Cakes," I tried to explain, patting my stomach. "I don't want that for us, so I've arranged for you to be adopted by a really nice couple. They're well-educated, they're professional people, and they've been

53

married a long time. They really want children but haven't been able to have any of their own. They can give you the advantages you deserve. They'll take care of you a lot better than I could, little one. I hope you'll understand."

The adoption had been easy to arrange. I was meeting with my social worker, Mrs. Day, every week now, and she was giving me free counseling sessions. I was surprised at how young and beautiful she turned out to be—not like some of those other old biddies.

I smiled, remembering our first interview. I was sullen at first, sitting opposite her, staring at my folded hands in silence. She just started talking to me, gently asking why I was there and what she could do for me that day. I swallowed uneasily and took a deep breath. Then I flat-out stated the obvious truth.

"Well, I'm pregnant, and I'm not married." I'd never said it quite that way before, and soon, shame was burning my throat and tears were starting to form behind my eyes.

"It's okay, Ann. Just relax. Can you tell me a little bit about what happened? Just take your time. I know this might be hard for you."

My neck constricted. *Which story should I tell her? The real one or the one I told my parents? I guess it has to be the one I told my parents. They might compare notes at some point.*

My face was rapidly filling with hot tears. My hand jerked up to cover it. "It was the only time in my whole life I didn't use birth control," I squeaked out. "I didn't want to have sex. He forced me to do it."

Mrs. Day handed me a box of tissues. "It's okay," she said, trying to calm me down. "Where did this happen?"

I could no longer control my sobs. Mrs. Day walked out of the room to get me a glass of water. Eventually, I quieted myself down long enough to tell her the story of my miserable summer in Luxembourg. When I finished, my eyes were red and my fist was full of soggy tissue.

"You've been through a really rough time, haven't you?" Mrs. Day finally interjected. "How did your folks take it when you told them you were pregnant?"

I let her know what had happened in a few short, bitter

sentences. Then I wiped my eyes and blew my nose. I was still clinging tightly to the used tissue. She hadn't judged me so far. Maybe I could get her to help me.

"Mrs. Day, I've been counting the years until I could leave home since I was twelve years old. I've even thought about suicide a few times," I confessed. "I know there has to be something wrong with me. I've needed counseling since high school, but my mom thinks it would cost too much, and, besides, she would be absolutely mortified if anyone in our town ever found out anything was wrong with us. No matter how bad things are, our family always has to look good, you see. I asked for help a long time ago, but she said 'No.'"

"What if I could change their minds for you?"

I picked up my head and looked straight at her for the first time. "You mean, you think you could?" Sparkles of hope zinged through my body. "Would *you* talk to them? Every time I try to talk to them about anything, we end up in a big fight. Maybe if you could talk to them . . ." I held my breath, waiting for her reply.

"I'll be glad to do that," she said, handing me another tissue.

"Oh, if you would, I'd be really grateful," I said, blowing my nose again. "I know I've been bad, and I want to change, but I need some help."

"I'll be your counselor for now, Ann. And I promise to talk to your parents by the next time we meet," she said, rising to her feet.

She was going to be my ally. My heart leaped.

"After that, we can talk about making plans for the baby," she added.

"Oh, I'm going to give it up for adoption," I offered, eager to please. For better or worse, that had already been decided.

I was coming to a slushy main street crossing now. I took off my glove and fumbled for a tissue. My nose was running again. Then, I glanced at my watch. I was time to turn around or I'd be late getting back. I stomped the snow off my boots and pivoted. Then, I gave my tummy a little pat.

I hope you're a girl, I told the baby, who was rumbling around inside me. *You're my little kicker. I like it when you play footsie with me. You hiccup all the time like me, too. Are you nervous, little hiccup baby? Are you afraid to be born?* I wondered.

55

Did this child somehow understand that he or she would be torn away from me? That it would to be forever separated from the familiar sound of my heartbeat and my breathing? I was its world, right now, but after the squeeze and pull of birth, after it was cut free of me, it would lose me.

"Do you know that already? Is that why you hiccup? Are you afraid? When you chose me, you chose 'no mother,' because I will not be there for you. No—you will be alone. All, all alone."

Regret rippled through me. The sky darkened.

What a mess you've made now, Ann, I told myself. Snow crunched menacingly beneath my rapid footsteps. *Bad enough that you've harmed yourself. But what about Mom and Dad—and what about that innocent baby child you carry?*

I gave the ground a hollow stare, and stopped walking. The sound of my footsteps ceased, too. In the distance, traffic rolled, chains clanked through slush. The train whistle blew again, and a dog barked.

"Chirp-chirp."

I looked up: there was a rustle of wings, and a bird flew to a bare branch in front of me. My eye slowly drifted upward to a dark cloud billowing in the bright, blue sky. The sun behind burned it silver at the rim.

A thought popped into my mind: "Every cloud has a silver lining."

Now, where did that come from? I wondered, looking around. But the world—white, silent and still in shadow—gave no reply.

Oh, I know. It's just one of those stupid cliches. It's something Dad always says.

But what if it's true? Look and see, my higher self insisted. The cloud hovered, iridescent. It, too, seemed to demand an answer. A chill moved down my spine.

Okay. I'll just pretend a moment. Getting pregnant is definitely the cloud. What's the silver lining?

Now a breeze fluttered. My mind was blank as a gray sky. Then a thought formed: "Your parents are hurting; your baby won't have a mother. What did you learn from that?"

I felt like a stupid school kid who didn't know the answer, but, finally, I knew: *When someone does something self-destructive, others suffer, too.* It was true! I hadn't thought of that before.

My heart quickened. I'd discovered something. A really valuable lesson. Wow!

A channel opened; more thoughts poured in: *And then there's Dad. I feel entirely different about him now. I used to hate him. But now I've learned that people aren't just the way they appear on the surface. There's a deeper level, too—one that really counts. I never knew that before.*

I started walking again. By now, I felt like I was floating . . . and the sun had come back out. *This is fun. What else can I think of?* I asked myself.

I know. My talk with Mrs. Day. I'm finally going to get some help. I'm going to learn how to deal with my parents, how to be happy. I'm not going to be angry all the rest of my life.

Glancing up, I noticed the cloud in the sky had dispersed. And so had the cloud in my heart. The rays of the sun penetrated my coat, wrapping me in warmth. *What a great birthday present that little cloud gave me,* I mused. Gratitude flushed through me, bathing me in its gentle glow all the way back to the home.

7 - The Promise

The door of the TV room cracks open.

"I thought I heard somebody in here."

I'm startled to see a head of black and silver hair over pink curlers appear in the doorway. It's Goldie, in her bathrobe.

"Are you getting some contractions?"

I nod and we wait together for another. When it arrives on schedule, Goldie springs into action.

"You go get dressed and meet me downstairs with your suitcase. I'm calling a cab, and we're going to the hospital."

"So you think this is the real thing?" I timidly ask.

"Yes, indeedy."

My heart jumps. This is the moment I've been waiting for all these long months. I snatch up my things and tip-toe back to my room. My suitcase has been packed for weeks, so it's just a question of dressing. *This is the last time I'll be wearing maternity clothes*, I gloat, throwing them on. I grab my coat and suitcase, sneak back past the sleeping bodies, and hasten downstairs to meet Goldie.

We see the lights of the taxi streaking through the silent night around 1:40 a.m. Goldie bursts out the door and into the driveway with my suitcase as he pulls up. I step behind her into the clear, dark night. The barest hint of spring hangs in the air.

Goldie catches my eye and cautions me not to speak, so the only noise is the purr of the car motor. She opens the back door of the cab for me. When I ease myself in, she gently pushes the door shut and hastens to get in the other side.

"General Hospital," she commands. "And hurry. There's a baby on the way."

As the taxi speeds in reverse out of the driveway, I feel like I'm being swept backwards down a large, swift river. The current of events swirls around me, pushing me where it will. I flounder and struggle merely to keep air in my lungs. When another contraction hits, I close my eyes and take long, slow breaths. The feeling passes, but my hands are cold. I can't stop their small tremble, even when I clasp them together on my lap.

When Goldie spots the lights of the hospital emergency room, she nudges me and tightens her grip on my suitcase.

"You wait here," she tells the driver. "I'll be back in a few minutes."

My heart sinks as I realize for certain that she doesn't plan to stay. Goldie leaps out of the cab, and high heels clicking, runs for my door and helps me out.

"I'm going to help you get registered, and then I need to get back to the home," she explains, ignoring the look of panic in my eyes. She walks me in and sits me down facing the receptionist. My suitcase hits the floor with a little metallic plunk.

"This is Ann. She's from the home."

As the receptionist flickers acknowledgement, Goldie turns to go. She looks at me briefly. "They'll take good care of you. You'll be fine. Good luck now. See you in a few days." As I hear her clicking off behind me, my heart free-falls into a deep pit of loneliness and despair.

I'm in the earliest stage of labor, when the cervix softens and thins. This can last for hours or days, so they give me a tranquilizer to sleep. Unfortunately, I'm allergic to it and toss in agony until it wears off the next morning. I remain in pre-labor limbo throughout the day until 9:00 p.m. when my water finally breaks. Now my cervix starts dilating for real. It's 2:15 a.m. when they finally strap me on a gurney and bump it through the delivery room doors.

I squint under the bright lights as my draped, mounded body is wheeled in. White oxford shoes squish on linoleum, steel pans clank. Like a mirage, white-masked figures in blue robes take form and look up at me. I'm sure they've all been told: "She's an unwed mother." My fake wedding ring will be useless here.

Then the hardening of my abdominal muscles begins again—incredible pressure. My body is possessed by an unrelenting force. I try to surrender, but its raw intensity rips at my will.

Just relax and let the muscles do their thing, I tell myself for the ten thousandth time. *Breathe steadily. Relax.*

Sure, I testily reply. *That might have worked before, but these new contractions are positively vengeful!* I've reached my limit. *I can't do "slow and steady" any more. God, this is way beyond uncomfortable.*

Will it ever end? Why do I have to go through this all alone? If only I had one friend to comfort me. . . .

You don't deserve to have anybody, I remind myself. *Outcasts from society are supposed to be isolated. This is your punishment.*

But I need somebody. I'm afraid.

Do NOT lose it now! Not in front of these strangers. You're going to show them you can give birth as well as any married woman. To hell with whatever's written all over your chart in big red letters. Show them you're strong. Don't panic. This can't last much longer. You've read the books. It's almost over. You can do this. Just think, when you get to be a real mother, you'll have already had a trial run. Just pretend it doesn't hurt.

One of the blue-robed figures unexpectedly touches my leg. "Let's shift you onto the delivery table now. Please put your legs up in the stirrups."

They want to truss me up like a turkey. God, this is medieval, I think, silently doing as I am told.

"Now your arms. We need to strap them to the table."

Finally, I *must* speak. "Please don't do that," I beg. "I'll be good. *Please* don't. I *promise* I won't touch anything. Please."

They yield as another contraction grips me, distracts me. *Breathe slowly. Hold tight to the ball. Oh no, it's not working. Should I be panting now? Damn, I can't remember. I'm so confused. I'm in a giant vice. Please let this be over soon.*

Dr. Marsh enters, robed in blue. His kind eyes look down at me over the sterile white mask. I try to smile.

"You're doing just fine, Ann," he says, placing his hand on my taut, draped abdomen. "I think you'll be delivering soon. Let me take a look." He positions the goose-necked lamp behind him and peers between my spread and strapped limbs.

I can't hold back. Another contraction comes. But this one is different. Could it be time to push?

"Would you like some anesthetic?"

What? Now? When this is almost over? Don't be ridiculous! "No thanks. I'm fine."

My energy surges. This is it at last—the moment I've been waiting for—the beginning of the end. *I've been pregnant for a long time, but very soon I won't be pregnant any more. Soon. Yes!*

Another contraction. No mistake. This one *screams*, "Push!" I bear down with all my soul. *Out, child—come then. I give you life, but I am not your real mother. You will belong to someone else: a nice married couple. A real family is waiting for you.* Sadness and shame silently ooze out of me like birth fluids. *It has all been arranged.*

"That's good. I see the head."

Another strong contraction grabs my gut. *Inhale. Bear down—push!* ("It's like a watermelon moving through your bowels," I remember Rudy saying three weeks ago. She was right; that's exactly how it feels.) I close my eyes, hold my breath, and force the watermelon down and out, out . . . *out!*

Oh, relief! Deep satisfaction floods my body. *It's over.* I draw a deep breath. *Is that all? Did I do it?*

I open my eyes and look down. Doctor Marsh is suctioning the mucus from my newborn's mouth. *It's slippery and wet. Look at all that dark hair.* He slaps it gently and it gives the cry of life.

The baby's alive. (Oddly, dread grips me now. This is real, after all!) *Will they tell me if it's a boy or a girl?* I wonder.

"You did a good job, Ann. It's a girl," he says, handing my infant to the orderly, who disappears into a distant corner of the room.

Since when does an unwed mother get praise for giving birth? I ask myself. *But she's a girl! That makes her like me. I'm glad. What are they doing with her back there?*

The nurse at my left suddenly begins kneading my sore abdomen. *(Bitch! How dare you? That hurts more than the god-damn delivery.)* I raise my hand to stop her, but then, remembering the threat of straps, I retreat.

"That hurts," I say in a small voice.

"We have to deliver the placenta. I need another contraction," she replies with cold, medical formality, continuing to punch and pull my muscles.

I keep my eyes on the back of the delivery room, where they're holding my baby. Now, they're putting drops in her eyes. They clean her, weigh her and wrap her clean, pink body in a little flannel blanket.

I assume they all have strict instructions not to show her to me. I expect them to whisk her straight off to the nursery; however, since they've all been nice so far, I motion to the nurse.

"May I see her?" I ask shyly.

"Sure. She's *your* baby," she replies with kindness.

MY baby? How strange that sounds. Well, I guess she is—technically, anyhow. Would that make me a real mother? I wonder.

The nurse tucks the baby under my arm after they transfer me to the gurney I'll ride to the recovery room. We lie together in silence under the bright delivery room lights. I hesitate, then reach over towards her. A thought jabs back at me: *Don't touch her, you sinner! You might defile her.*

My hand retreats. *Okay—but I can look, can't I? It won't do any harm just to look.*

Now her beaming face compels me to stare at her fully. Her eyes open and close. Her perfect features, crowned by a full head of thin, dark hair, are cradled in flannel. I'm transfixed by her beauty and her smell, all fresh and new.

It's amazing, I muse. *She's a real human being, and she's so beautiful!* Pride streams through me. I love her entirely.

Stop. Remember: she doesn't belong to you, an inner voice warns.

Deep sorrow floods out the sweet trickles of joy. The world silently drowns.

Well, I console myself with a sigh, *we'll have this tiny bit of time together, anyhow.*

Soon, the gurney rattles forward, and we are beyond the delivery room doors. Endless green walls begin sliding by. Her little body feels toasty and warm lying there beside me. I simmer with pride; then, strangely, I sense a strong power radiating from her body. But how is it possible for a tiny baby to be so full of the life force?

Then it happens. My ears start ringing, and all at once, an enraged mob is clamoring at me, slashing me with furious allegations. My body tenses. Now, a tidal wave of feeling tries to drown me—I gasp for air. Accusations pound and howl through my whole being. Deafening me, a voice thunders, it seems, from somewhere deep inside her: **"It's not right to give away your own flesh and blood."**

Perhaps it's just my guilty conscience speaking, but I'm so jolted that I tear my eyes away to look around. But no accuser lurks in the empty hallway, so I turn back to my baby—just as the awesome force rips at me again. **"She'll never know her real name, her family connections. She'll think you gave her away because you didn't love her."**

Brutal awareness presses in from all sides. It compresses my chest; I fight for breath. A vision floats before me: my dark-haired beauty adrift in the world without her heritage. I feel her powerlessness, her aching need to know.

"Poor baby! I never intended to hurt you like this. I never knew I'd love you; I never knew you belonged with me. Everything's so different, now you're born." Tears rise, warm and fluid. "I made a huge mistake!

"But how could I ever keep you now? I've promised everyone I'd give you up for adoption. Mrs. Day's been so nice. What would she say? And what about the people waiting to adopt you? What would everybody think of me if I broke my promise? Besides, I've got to get back to school," I plead, knowing in my heart that if I could only find the courage, it could all be changed.

"But my parents. . ." Air catches, tears at my throat. "They'll disown me. Where would we turn?"

The gurney rumbles on. Slowly, heavily, a solid wall of hopelessness slides across my life, and a possibility closes off forever. Tears of regret trickle hotly down my cheek.

"How could I have been so stupid? Everyone said adoption was the *right* thing to do. But in all this time, I never once saw what it would actually mean *to you. No!* All I could think about was getting myself back in everyone's good graces. I kept telling myself I could never raise a baby anyway—that my child would be better off with anybody but me.

"Well, I was an idiot, and maybe I do deserve to lose you. But there's more to it than that. . . ."

All at once, a realization slaps me hard in the face: the closed adoption system will erase her birth family ties forever.

"That's not fair! You'll never be told about me or the family you were born to! They'll hide all that from you—imagine—to protect my reputation—our family's reputation."

All at once, I can see the mindless tragedy, the unspeakable waste and horror of it: a child's identity—sacrificed for pretense! So the birth family can pretend no child ever existed. So the adoptive family can pretend the child they're raising was born to them. I squirm; my face flushes. I clench my fists and impotently rage against the faceless authorities:

"Well, I want to take it all back! I don't *want* to hide from her. Just because I can't raise her doesn't mean I don't care about her! I *long* to know who she is and how she'll be like me. Why *can't* I know that? Why *can't* she know who I am? It's not fair—it's not right! And I won't agree to it—not forever, anyway!"

The gurney slows and turns a corner. *They'll be taking her soon. Quick! What can I do?* My mind flits and darts in search of an answer.

"Make her a promise for the future," a husky voice whispers.

My eyes widen; an idea forms. *Yes! That's it! I'll make it up to her later.* I study my baby's priceless face. "I make you this solemn promise, my daughter. When you're grown, I'll come back and find you. First, I'll need to somehow find myself, but we *will* meet again. Then I'll give you back the heritage that's rightly yours. I won't be bound by their lies and secrecy. I promise you, I'll tell you everything about me, your blood family, and about why you were given away. You will come to know me, and I, you. We will be friends someday."

I squint for a second, trying to peer into the future, but it looks impossibly murky. "I don't know how I'll find you, but I promise, I will," I say at last.

At the juncture of the hospital hallways, the gurney grinds to a stop. Looking into her innocent face, I bless her. "Goodbye for now, Little One. Be a good girl. With all my heart, I wish you a happy life. You'll have to be a big girl and take good care of yourself for now, but I'll be back someday. I love you. . . . Fare well until we meet again . . ." *Yes, I will speak her name* . . . "my dearest Jennifer Lynn."

The nurse takes her then. She carries my clean, new baby away, down the long, empty corridor. I listen to her footsteps fade and watch her blue gown recede until she turns the corner. My baby is gone. The spot under my arm where she nestled grows cold. The gurney jerks forward and continues down the hall toward the recovery room. I dry my tears and straighten my arm.

I am all alone in my body again.

Part II

In the Maelstrom

*Out of every crisis
comes the chance
to be reborn.*
— NEDA O'NEILL

8 - "As If" It Never Happened

Two days later, Goldie comes to fetch me from the hospital. I climb into a cab with her and head back to the home. The place is filled with the warm, homey smell of simmering chicken soup, but it's entirely different—"a twilight zone" where I no longer belong.

When I look at people I used to consider friends, a chill spreads up my spine. *All these girls think they're doing the right thing. No one knows about the sacred connection of birth. No one suspects that when they leave their baby behind, a part of them will die.*

They gather around me, like green recruits eager to hear the veteran talk about the war. I avoid eye contact. "It wasn't so bad," I say softly. "Just try to relax. Don't fight the contractions. You'll get through it okay." I excuse myself then and go upstairs to pack.

The next day, Mother comes for me. She's waiting in the hallway when I walk down the stairs with my suitcase in hand. I stop and stand before her stiffly, my downcast eyes brimming with silent tears. She reaches over and gives me a little hug, then lifts the suitcase out of my hand. "Is everything okay?" she asks.

My head bobs shallowly. I open my lips, but only dry air escapes. "Yea. Fine, Mom," I finally croak out. "I had a baby girl."

She never asks more. . . .

Three days after that, April 4, I'm back in school. Surely now, my life will come together, I assume. But, just like at the home, no one knows me anymore. Last week my womb was joyfully bursting with kicks and pokes and hiccups. Now it's a gaping hole.

Was it all for nothing then?

The events that traumatize us the most are the ones where things that matter a great deal to us turn out the opposite of what we expect. And if you've been a member of a group that shares a common belief, which you now know to be false, it's even more difficult. How does one individual share his truth with the hundred who still believe? What makes him right? What makes the hundred wrong? Will you judge yourself to be "not normal," isolate yourself, huddle in shame with your dark secret, afraid to speak?

Men in combat have experienced this kind of trauma. They go into war starry-eyed, to be patriotic, to prove themselves as men.

They encounter lying, cheating, chaos and horror; they violate their own standards of right and wrong because they must do as they are told. Minds and lives can be torn apart trying to reconcile it all later.

With a birthmother the battle is over the fruit of her body and her very soul. Before her baby's born, the mother is swamped with fear, low self-esteem, shame, guilt, confusion. The people she looks to for help tell her: "If you love your baby, you'll put his life and welfare before your own. What kind of a life can you provide for your child?" "If you keep the baby, no decent man will marry you." "There are hundreds of wonderful, loving couples unable to have children of their own who can provide your baby with the best things life has to offer. Surely you don't want to be selfish and deny him a wonderful, happy life. He'll grow up hating and resenting you for your selfishness. If you love him, you'll let him go." Her pregnancy has embarrassed and disgraced the unwed mother, has possibly estranged her from her family. She doesn't have any money, is emotionally unsupported—and from this place of negative resources, knowing she's about to be sucked into the maelstrom, she decides to save her baby. Basically, she agrees to surrender because she loves her baby and everyone tells her it will be the best thing for him.

This appearance holds until the child is born. An emotional and physical peak experience, the birth wakes the mother up to what's really true. She and the baby are connected. They belong together. They need each other. To separate them at a time when they've both been prepared by nature to work together as a team is cruel and painful beyond words for both. The mother knows this, of course, and her tortured choice is to honor her heart and break her agreement—or honor her agreement and break her heart.

If she gives up the baby, more guilt pours in and mixes with the deep, fierce love she feels for her child and a new double dose of rage: she hates herself for agreeing to the surrender; she hates the system for betraying her, for leading her on, for not telling her the true consequences of what they were asking her to do at a time when there was no way she herself could know.

It's a toxic mix of feelings, and the women we call birthmothers go into emotional shock, suffering a shame-filled, primal grief. The secrecy she's sworn to only makes it worse. No friends know, so no one can sympathize or help. Birthmothers enter a "zone," a limbo-land, where they wander aimlessly for a while. Eventually, most start functioning again. But a black hole divides each birthmother's life, a deep pit of pain and incompletion that will need her attention—some other time.

Even though I started therapy right away and was on anti-depressants, I remember walking across campus late in April, mumbling out loud, making important calculations. "Tomorrow, my baby will be one month old. Ten months ago today, I was just arriving in Paris and none of this had happened yet. But by ten months ago tomorrow, I'll be pregnant, my life will be changed forever." I repeat the facts like a mantra. The evidence is gone; I am the only witness. If I don't recount it, I, too, might vanish. I drag my memories with me everywhere. Yet, at the same time, I hide them under loose-fitting emotions, like I hid my pregnancy under loose-fitting clothes. But guilt and sorrow has stained my life like blood that can't be washed or wished away.

A cool breeze ruffles my hair, gives my face a gentle pat that late-April day. I lift my eyes then, and a row of fluffy, pink cherry blossoms tumbles up the sidewalk to greet me. All around, springtime sings out, sweet and lush.

A recent rain has washed everything clean. The buildings across the lawn glint in spring sunshine. In front of them, two flags snap and flap, casting sharp, flitting shadows. Along the campus sidewalk, a line of trees stands at attention. New yellow-green leaves are just beginning to push out of their winter-sleepy branches. I tilt my head back then, and above me, a thin dressing of light clouds fringes the bright blue sky.

I spy a low, stone wall, and the old crabapple tree behind it seems to beckon. Some of its blossoms billow white and full, while other younger flowers are still in pink, close-fisted buds. Above, on limbs, birds chatter like excited children. I perch on the low wall under the blooming canopy. Nearby, cautious robins hop, cocking their heads to the ground. Hop, cock, watch, always alert—hop, hop, cock, watch, dig for worms, fly away. How simple their lives seem. Those robins—they remind me of the trying-not-to-be-foolish girls at the home. . . .

Just then a friendly voice jolts me from my revery, pulls me back to robins and crabapple blossoms. "Ann, hi. How are you? You seem so down. What's the matter?" I paste on a smile and look up, squinting into the sun. It's Adrian, a skinny, blond tenor who sang with me in Singers last year. He sat behind me at rehearsal and pulled on my long pigtail. We had a casual friendship back then, before my life derailed.

"How come you didn't try out for Singers this year?" he innocently inquires. "Where have you been anyhow? I don't think I saw you at all winter term."

At his questions, my face clouds over again. I sit unresponsive and numb for a moment. When my reply comes, it's flat and lifeless. "Do you really want to know?" My chest aches again from the crushing weight of my secret sadness.

"Something's *really* wrong, isn't it?" He puts his hand on my knee for a moment, and then lifts himself up on the wall beside me. "Why don't you tell me about it?" he gently coaxes.

"Oh, Adrian." My eyes fill with tears and I jerk my head away in shame. At last, I squeeze out my reply. "This is really hard for me to talk about."

He waits patiently for me to compose myself. After a while, I open my eyes and stare off into space. *If he shuns me, it really won't matter,* I tell myself. So, I cross my cold hands over my chest, drop my head, and bury my eyes in my lap; then, heaving a great sigh, I begin to speak. "Adrian, I had a baby last month. That's why I wasn't here last term—I was in one of those homes for unwed mothers." My eyes start to sting with uncried tears and my face crinkles up again. "That's why I'm not in Singers this year. Got pregnant in Europe last summer," I choke out.

The words hang heavy between us.

"Oh, you poor thing. No wonder you're so down."

I lift my eyes. Through a watery film I can see Adrian's face tremble with sympathy. The tightness in my chest lifts a little then, and a whoosh of air escapes through my open lips. I drop my arms to my side. Adrian reaches over and places his hand on top of mine. I allow mine to lay limply under his for a moment, then slowly take it away.

He waits for me to speak again.

In that moment of calm, a long-ignored anger begins to surge and tumble in my chest. My face tenses, my eyes blaze; and soon, stinging words are spurting out through my clenched teeth. "I've really screwed up my life," I storm in a guttural tone I hardly recognize as mine. "Here I am, graduating from college in two months, and I have no idea what I want to do with my life. All I'm qualified to do is teach school. And I'm only doing that because my family expects me to." My chest heaves. "I was hoping to be married to the man of my dreams by now. Ha Ha. I'll probably end up an old maid. I don't think things are going to work out with the guy I was seeing before I went away." A heavy sigh deflates my tirade.

"Are you still dating him?"

"Yea . . . but. . . . Roger was really there for me when I was pregnant. I'll always love him for that. But I guess I needed him so much then that I never noticed until now that we really don't have anything in common. . . . I *thought* I loved him." I shake my head in confusion. "I don't understand anything any more."

Adrian stares at me blankly.

My gaze wanders up to the crabapple blossoms. They are still sparkling in the sunshine. "Well, thanks for listening." I sigh again. "I do feel better. Oh, Adrian, please don't mention this to anyone. You, Roger, and one girl in my dorm are the only ones who know."

"I won't. I'm honored you told me." Adrian gives me a quick, tender look and then glances down at his watch. "Um . . . I've got a class at 2:00; I've got to run now." He hops off the wall. "Keep your chin up. I'll be seeing you around." He flashes me a smile and trots off, scattering puffy piles of fallen blossoms.

To think, that's how it all began between us. . . .

I graduated in June, stayed in therapy, took a summer job as a nanny, and began teaching junior high English in the fall. With the job and my own apartment, I was hoping I would "finally make it." Instead, my work made it feel like life imprisonment without parole. Every day, long, green institutional hallways stretched before me, lined with lockers, swarming with gangling, pimple-faced kids. I would plod by, unseen, while combination locks twirled and metal doors snapped open, then banged shut.

Girls would huddle in bunches, their giggles leaking out from behind hand-covered mouths. "Do you think he noticed me? Tee-hee." Furtive glances would spring up out of the circle like arrows, then all eyes would turn back to the safe closed circle.

The bell would grind a loud warning. Everyone would groan. Some would poke along; others would race for their next class. Could they get there in time to set a tack on the teacher's chair? Hide the chalk and erasers? Scribble messages to friends? Later, there would be time for spit ball tournaments, switching seats, and that all-time-favorite game, "Get the Teacher"—me. I would trudge to my next class, feeling my dream of happily-ever-after slowly fuse into a tortured lump of pain.

Four weeks into the school year, early one Saturday morning, Mother called my apartment. Her tone was guarded. "The papers from the adoption agency came in yesterday."

The room started to spin before I could answer.

"What do they say?" I finally eked out, feigning nonchalance. Meanwhile, my heart was racing. *Can they put me in jail?* I wondered.

No. All you have to do is sign the surrender papers. After that, everything will be okay again, answered my mind.

"We have to get them notarized and then appear at the courthouse before a judge for a brief hearing," Mother said.

A judge? The courthouse? A hearing? I tried to force a reply past the lump in my throat, but my doubts and fears jammed the opening. My cat unbalanced me by rubbing against my leg. I put one hand on the table to anchor myself.

"We should be able to do both things in half a day," Mother continued. "When do you think you can come home?"

I cleared my throat. "Uh, let's see." I took a deep breath and seized control. "Just a minute. I need to look at my calendar." My heart was pounding wildly, but I pretended I couldn't feel it. "I think I have next Friday off." Like a robot, I extended my left hand towards my date book. I breathed deeply, swallowing down my fear. "Yeah, I do. I'll meet you at home, around 9?"

"Okay," she said. "See you then."

Stumbling forward, I replaced the receiver in its cradle and considered my next move. My brain whirled with new words: legal papers, notarize, courthouse, judge, sentence, jail. It was all too much. And it was still too early. I rotated my body and plodded stiffly back to bed.

I passed the cinder block book shelves, the card table where I ate and the hand-me-down couch, back to the safe cocoon of my double bed. It was cold between the sheets, but I drew my knees up in a ball and soon new warmth snuggled me. Brain numb, I stared off into space, eyes open.

The room was silent, except for far-off traffic noises and the ticking of my wind-up alarm. Then I saw them: the particles of dust drifting down through a shaft of morning light.

Where do all those tiny specks of dust come from? I mused. *Why are they here? Am I as small as they in the scheme of things?* I watched the dust drift. *So where does it go?* I shifted my focus. It was gone, replaced with the usual view: off-white walls; a straight-backed, wooden chair hung with jeans; Picasso's blue guitarist, sad and drawn, strumming on the wall behind.

Maybe the light shifted, I told myself. *When it shifts, I see a whole new scene.*

I tried to feel the numbness again . . . the drifting, the unfocused gaze. The dust reappeared. Then I blinked and looked straight ahead. It cleared. Two worlds. Like magic.

Can I make my mood change like that, too, by shifting point of view? I wondered. (It was something Dr. K. and I had discussed in therapy lately.)

I gave a quick twist to my kaleidoscope of thoughts and started thinking about the many welcome changes that had come into my life this summer. My face softened into a smile. *Ah, yes. I do feel better now. Maybe Dr. K. was right.*

9 - First Light

Dr. K.'s office was located in an old established neighborhood in a city an hour's drive from home. Mother and I first made the trip in late April, when a bough of pink dogwood was blooming next to the brass name plaque. We entered without knocking, through two sets of wooden double doors. A slightly musty smell lingered in the carpet that covered the narrow hallway.

To our right was a waiting room that had once been a proud parlor. Mother stepped inside and seated herself near the doorway, close to the reception desk. She pulled out her *Reader's Digest* and pretended to read. I strode in behind her and headed across the room to examine the row of medical textbooks lined up on the fireplace mantle. I brushed by the small reception desk, which held a closed appointment book and a stack of unopened mail. I couldn't help but notice a neat pile of business cards and a leather-covered pencil holder arranged near the brass desk lamp.

Mother looked up from her magazine, annoyed, but didn't say anything to me.

I shot her back a sharp look. The room was ringed with wooden chairs. At the far end of the room was an imposing set of carved-wood sliding doors. I walked in that direction and slumped down in a chair where I could watch the clock above the reception desk: 2:55.

The room was dead still. I ran my left thumb over the rough edge of my ring finger. Then I put it in my mouth. The wet smoothness of my tongue flicked over the jagged end of my finger. Then I pried off a loose piece of skin with my teeth. Somewhere down the long, dark hallway, I heard a door open, and two sets of feet padded towards us. The next thing I knew, a tall man with a neatly-clipped white beard stood in the doorway holding wire-rimmed glasses. Behind him, a shadowy figure exited through the double doors.

Mother immediately rose and introduced us. I looked up, but didn't stand. Dr. K. said something to my mother, then nodded and gently asked me to follow him.

When I got up, I could feel my heart racing. And all the while my feet shuffled after him, my thoughts leapfrogged over each other like acrobats: *Sure glad she's not coming, too. What a relief! Anyway, I'd never talk to him in front of her. He looks kind of old. What's he going to do to me back there? Will he hypnotize me? Try to reprogram me? Does he think I'm crazy?*

Keeping my eyes down and my arms crossed, I followed Dr. K. to his office at the end of the long, dark hall. His massive wooden desk stood in front of a big bay window. The window was heavily draped with plush, deep-green velvet. He smiled politely and invited me to take the seat in front of the desk. Then he stepped around to sit facing me and put on his glasses. From his desk drawer, he took out a new manila folder and a ballpoint pen. When he opened the file, I could see it contained fresh sheets of lined paper for note taking. He lifted his pen and adjusted his sleeve—then looked me square in the face.

"So *vhy* don't you begin by telling me *vhy* you're here today," he said in polite tones, revealing a light Russian accent. All the while, he peered at me over the gold rim of his reading glasses.

His question made me shift in my chair. I'd almost forgotten that this whole thing was *my* idea. I was so used to my parents forcing me to do things that "why I'd come" had completely slipped my mind. I cleared my throat, swallowed, and tried to think.

When I remembered, I flushed with hot embarrassment. I pulled my arms closer to my chest and looked away. "Well," I said reluctantly, "I had a child out of wedlock a short time ago." My ears filled with a ringing sound. I let it pass before I spoke again.

I glanced up then. He was still looking at me, so I took a deep breath and pushed on. "But, there's really been something wrong with my life for a long time now, Dr. K. I've been unhappy since I can remember, and I can't get along with my parents."

"Tell me about that, please." His pen began to scribble on the lined paper.

Well, this is what I'm here for, I reminded myself. *Might as well let it rip.* So I sat up and filled my chest with air.

"My parents try to tell me what to do all the time, and yet, their value system *stinks*! They're superficial 'do-gooders.' What's important to them is looking perfect on the outside. Meanwhile, my mother always acts like a big martyr. She'll do stuff for you—and then you're supposed to be grateful for the rest of your life and do everything she says."

Now that the dam was cracked, the rest came gushing out. "Worse than that, they're hypocrites! They go say prayers in church on Sunday morning, yet they'll rip you to pieces on Sunday afternoon." My eyes narrowed to slits. "Whatever I do, I don't want to end up two-faced like them!"

"Hmmm, I see," he said, scribbling furiously in his secret file.

And so it began, week after week: the long, silent drive over and back with mother, pills for depression, and in the privacy of the doctor's office, one bitter memory spilling out on top of the next, from a seemingly endless source. Dr. K. prodded me with questions about my life and attitudes; then he became the *tabula rasa* or "blank slate." While I spilled out my darkest thoughts, he took notes, nodding solemnly, gaping like a loose-jawed trout. Sometimes I felt a little better, and most of the time I went home wondering if it wasn't all a waste of everyone's time and my parents' money.

A few months into my therapy, however I scored a breakthrough. Dr. K. asked me to lie back on his brown leather couch that day. I slipped my shoes off and put my feet up, while being careful to arrange my skirt modestly. The smooth leather behind me felt cool, so I reached for the Granny-square afghan, which was always neatly folded at the end of the couch, and wrapped myself in its wool warmth.

As soon as I was settled, he began probing into my early childhood. "I'd like you to think back now, please. Can you tell me about *when* this problem with your parents began?"

"I don't know, but I remember that by the time I turned thirteen, I was counting the years until liberation day."

"*Vhat* made you so angry back then?"

"It was my mother, mostly. She'd watch my every move. No jumping rope, no running. She always treated me like a baby."

"*Vhy vas* that?"

"Oh—big deal—because I was sick, once, when I was four."

"Can you tell me about that, please?"

"Oh, there was supposed to have been some damage to my heart. So she never let me be a normal kid!"

"And you resented that, I see."

"Yes, I hated it."

"*Vill* you just close your eyes now and tell me about *vhen* you got sick. Just let yourself drift backwards in time. . . ."

I could see him out of the corner of my eye with that trout-jawed look again, crossing his legs and getting ready to write. *This is stupid,* I told myself, *but I guess I'll have to play along.* So I closed my eyes.

"Good. Now take a deep breath . . . and another . . . that's good . . .and tell me . . . how did your illness begin?"

"It started with an earache."

"Okay. Where were you at the time?"

In the dark space behind my eyelids, the scene slowly formed. "I'm at home in the living room." I could see myself lying on our old yellow couch.

"Good. Is anyone there with you?"

I could pick up more details now: the gray feather pattern woven in the yellow material covering the couch—the swirl patterns in the plaster ceiling—ladders—bright lights. "Yes. My parents are there painting the living room. I'm lying on the couch thrashing my head from one side to the other. I can't get comfortable. My ears hurt horribly."

"Yes. And *vhat* happens next?"

"Mommy gets down off the ladder and puts some hot, oily drops in my ears. But I'm burning up with fever and the pain won't go away. So, she calls the doctor, I guess. Anyway, I remember later that night he comes out and gives me a shot. After that, night blurs into day and blurs back into night again—I can't remember anything but sleeping. When the doctor comes in to give me another shot, I open my eyes, but then I go right back to sleep again. . . ."

"Sounds like you were pretty sick."

"Yeah, I was. But then I got better. I'll never forget that day!" A smile spread over my face.

"I wake up one morning and the sun's pouring in my bedroom window." How magically the world had sparkled—like glitter had been thrown everywhere, willy-nilly. The sunshine vibrated through my body, filled me with such tingling energy. "I remember standing on my bed, and jumping for joy, just because I feel so good!" I was singing away at the top of my lungs, bed springs creaking away, covers bouncing off the bed, reaching for the sky with every bounce. "But, pretty soon, Mommy comes in screaming, 'What are you doing? You're going to hurt yourself. Get back in bed.'"

"'But Mommy, I'm all better now,' I tell her.

"'No, you aren't. Get back in bed. Go back to sleep. Do as I say. You're sick. You almost died.'

"She forced me back into bed and tucked the covers in around me tight. When she left the room, she cracked the door open so she could hear me."

"How did that make you feel?" interjected the good doctor.

My jaw tightened. "I was upset. I thought I was all better, but she was saying 'no.' I had always tried to be good before that, but the longer I lay there, the more bored and upset I got. How could I just lay there all day like a lump when I felt so brand-new? Why should I always take her word for everything? Maybe I should start listening to what *I* knew, instead.

"I remember getting up and dangling my feet over the edge of my bed. I kept wondering if I'd fall down dead, but I didn't, so I kept playing. But I was really quiet, so she wouldn't know."

I heard the doctor shift in his chair. His pants rustled, as if he were crossing or uncrossing his legs. "So she thought you were following her orders, but you did what you thought was right for you," he observed.

"Yes. Part of me still wanted to be a 'good little girl,' but I had to do what I thought was right for me." I opened my eyes and twisted my head around to look at Dr. K., hoping that would satisfy him. When he finished taking notes, he furrowed his brow and shot me a pointed look.

"Does what you did then sound familiar in any way?"

I tried to brush off his question. "Why? What do you mean?"

"*Vhen* your parents tell you to do something, *vhat* do you do?" There was an unfamiliar edge of excitement to his voice.

My stomach began to churn; my skin bristled. "What I think is right for me," I retorted.

"And *vhy* don't you do *vhat* they say?" he probed, gazing at me steadily.

I looked away. *He's starting to sound like them now. I knew he'd turn on me eventually!* My heart pumped harder; my breathing grew shallow. "Because"—How could he *be* so stupid? What have I been telling him now for months on end?—"I'm *not* going to let them turn me into a hypocritical robot. I'm not going to live my life like that!" My words came in short, hard bursts.

Dr. K., in contrast, still spoke calmly. "So you do the opposite of what they want you to do—right? If they say, don't drink, you drink. If they say be chaste, you have sex?"

"Right!" I declared, feeling a little less sure now. But I needed to defend my position. "I *won't* let them tell me what to do. I'm *not* going to turn into a hypocrite like them."

Then Dr. K. took out a key and inserted it in the keyhole of my mind. "But aren't you, nevertheless, very much under their control?" he asked slowly—quietly—looking me steadily in the eye. "If they say 'do,' then you must 'not do.' If they say 'don't do,' then you must 'do.' Aren't you really allowing yourself to be controlled by them—only, in an opposite way. If they say 'don't drink,' are you not *compelled* to drink?"

The key was in the keyhole—if I wanted to unlock the door, all I had to do was turn it. My head buzzed in confusion. While I followed his logic, another part of me clung desperately to my old rule. I put my hands to my head to keep the new idea out, but it was too late: it was already slowly seeping in.

"True freedom from your parents," he continued softly, *vill* come only *vhen*, for instance, you can be free to choose not to drink even if your parents say don't drink."

He paused while I puzzled over that.

"In order to grow up, you *vill* need to stop thinking of yourself as an extension of your parents. You can separate from them now and create your own value system."

My body softened, listening to the gentle ripple of his words. I dropped my arms to my side and looked him full in the face.

"You may even decide to keep some of your parents' values if they suit you." He paused and leaned forward. His eyes twinkled. "But *you* must be the one to decide *vhat's* important to you. And then—whatever you decide—*you* must take responsibility for the consequences. You must stop blaming your parents for everything and be responsible for your own life now."

The truth filled my eyes with tears. I knew he was right. For all these years, I'd foolishly tied myself to my parents' wishes without even realizing it.

I looked away and felt my muscles go limp with sadness. My past life was a sooty, black pit of confusion with no escape. For so long, I had groped around it blindly. But now, thanks to Dr. K., I could *see* the pit—for, shimmering at the top was a light. It was distant, but it shone with radiance, like the first light of dawn. And the way out lay right beside me—a long, steep stairway, strewn with dark debris. It stretched ever-upward, awaiting my footfall.

The way up would not be easy. But I knew the light above would grow stronger with every step I took.

10 - Man's Law

A ghostly wall of fog hung outside my apartment window on Friday morning, October 7th. Everywhere, the pretty, shifting mist covered yellowed leaves, discarded things, as dead inside as me. My hearing was today.

Just routine, I told myself. *Sign some papers, then go on with your life.*

Something sharp jabbed deep inside, but I sighed and ignored it, as I'd trained myself to do. I pivoted away from the window. I was due at Mother's soon. Better get going.

I shrugged myself into my coat and opened the door to an all-gray world. Smoky webs of fog hung in the grass. My car whirred to life. I clicked on the lights, and started groping my way out of town. The fog turned to drizzle and made silver ribbons of moisture in the worn channels of the road. Along the way, legions of spent cornstalks stood at attention, channelling me towards the mountains and beyond, to Mother's. At the higher elevations, the dogwoods were blood red, though all fall's colors seem dulled by the heavy grayness of the day. Ten minutes later, the forest ended and I turned off the highway at the bottom of a steep hill. Slowing down, I followed a dirt road past three miles of farmland until I spotted my parents' private lane.

In June, Mother and Dad had sold their big house in town and moved into a brand-new one on their 40-acre wood lot. I drove up to the entrance around back, where I knew Mother would be. By the time I got out of the car, she was already standing at the door, her hair freshly coated with spray net. She wore her beige wool suit with the fox-fur collar.

"Come on in. I'll be ready in a second. I'll drive."

I stepped inside, staying close to the wall. The thick envelope lay on the kitchen table. I slid over and picked it up. Delicately, I extracted the document. I squinted over a page of tightly typed sentences, but the verbiage was "legalese." *What difference does it make what it says?* I asked myself. *I have to sign it, anyway.* So I flipped through the papers with my thumb, folded them up and stuffed them all back in the envelope.

Mother leaned into the hall mirror, applying her lipstick. When she finished, she pulled on her trench coat. Then, she selected a beige purse from the hall closet and swooped up the papers on her way to the back stairs.

"I'm ready. Let's go."

I followed her down to the basement garage and slipped into the passenger seat of her Chrysler sedan. She walked over to the wall beside the garage door and pushed the button, then got in beside me, while the door clattered open. The car motor whirred to life.

"Where were you last night, anyway? I tried to call . . ." she began.

"Went out to eat with somebody." I grimaced and looked at my lap.

"Oh . . . Somebody new?"

"Just a friend . . . a boy I met in Singers." I angled my body away from her and pretended to look out the window. It was still too private and fragile to talk about the miracle that had brought Adrian into my life.

In the summer, after my breakthrough with Dr. K., I'd resolved to try to make my life work. The thing I wanted most, of course, was to be married— but I knew it wouldn't be to Roger. We'd gone our separate ways at the end of the school year.

I lay across the bed I was using in the playroom of my parents' new house and looked back over my life. *Might I already know a suitable someone?* I asked myself.

That's when I'd thought of Adrian. He'd been my friend for years. We were both interested in music and the arts. He already knew about my "shame" and hadn't rejected me for it. I began to hatch a plan: he'd be back at school to finish his degree in the fall. Maybe I could interest him in getting together. I only lived 40 miles away. I had a car and so did he. . . .

So I wrote him a letter—first, on lined paper. Then, I crossed out the parts that didn't work and did it over again. I wanted to show interest—without sounding needy . . . just something brief and casual . . . an invitation to renew our friendship when he got back into town. When it was just right, I copied it over on my best stationary and sent it off in a flurry of bravado.

I patted myself on the back: Adrian was someone my parents would actually approve of. He was white, Protestant and upwardly mobile. (There was something else I didn't know about him that would cause a very serious problem later, but it would be nine long years before we'd deal with that.)

When school went back into session, I waited by the phone. One evening, a few weeks ago, he'd called and invited me out to a fancy restaurant. By candlelight, his heavy eyebrows stood out on a ridge over his piercing hazel eyes. They made me overlook his skinny, triangular face and big French nose. I just watched his eyes sparkle while he talked on and on about musical performances he'd been in, beautiful gardens he'd studied, exotic places he'd visited. His mustache, blond with snatches of red, bobbed up and down. He made me laugh—and dream—again. And he was always a complete gentleman. He told me he respected me and didn't want to do anything to make me feel cheap. We should wait for sex. By then, I knew I was falling in love. . . .

Mother pulled into town and headed straight for a flat-topped, yellow brick building, post-World-War-II vintage. It contained the office of the notary she'd selected—someone who won't know our name. Dirty green walls with plaster cracks led us down a hallway until we found the words "Mary K. Marudas, Notary" frosted into a glass panel on one of the doors. Mother walked in, stepped up to the formica counter, and hit the call bell twice. I trailed behind, eyes on the ground.

At the sound of the double ping, a dark green curtain was drawn aside by a middle-aged woman with stringy black hair. She stepped forward into the light. A waxy sheen glowed on her pale forehead, dark hairs protruded from a mole on her chin.

"Yes, how can I help you?" she crackled in a heavy, smoker's voice.

Mother flipped the document to the signature page before she lay it down. "Here. Please notarize my daughter's signature," she said. She shoved the $2.00 fee over the counter as the notary handed me a ballpoint pen. Without looking up, I scribbled a few broken strokes.

"But what kind of papers are these?" she asked, trying to turn to the front of the document.

Mother slapped her hand down on top of the papers. "It's none

82

of your business," she snapped back. "This is a family matter. All you need to do is witness her signature."

My eyes widened but I didn't look up. I could feel the heat of shame creeping up my face. The notary fingered her pen. I held my breath while Mother stared her down with quiet ferocity. Finally, the notary dropped her eyes and signed the document. Then she clamped the paper between the metal jaws of her seal and slowly squeezed it closed. Our faces were all flushed by then.

"Thank you," Mother said, snatching the papers back. She pivoted toward the door, coat swishing. I pulled the door shut behind us, and soon quick steps echoed down the empty hallway.

We drove to the courthouse and parked nearby in a little lot. I followed Mother down polished hallways, past a warren of offices until we were standing by the hearing room door. Mother rapped. A moment later, the door swung open. A judge with thick jowls and piercing blue eyes, wearing the customary black, showed us in and then stepped up behind his oak desk. Mother clicked open her beige purse, extracted our papers and lay them in front of him. He picked them up and began to read, while we took seats on a bench below his platform.

There was a long silence. Mother sat solemnly. I slumped in my chair, my stomach churning. I glanced around the big, sterile, white-walled room, but the blank walls stared back, uncaring.

Finally, the judge straightened the papers and looked up at me. "Are you Ann?" he boomed out.

I nodded my head slightly.

"Do you understand. . ." he said, slowly and deliberately . . . "that you are hereby relinquishing *all* rights to your child?" He looked straight into my eyes. "If I grant this order, all ties will be severed between you. You will surrender the right to have any future contact with this child. You will not even have the right to know if she lives or dies."

He stopped talking then, but his words continued to pound inside me. My breath grew short; my brow crinkled. My feelings hardened into tips of steel. When I could no longer hold his gaze, I jerked my head away.

No right to know if she's dead or alive? Never contact her again?

That's totally unreasonable! I made a solemn promise that I'd find her someday. I can't agree to this. . . .

But then my old beliefs kicked in: *I wouldn't know how to be a mother. My life would be ruined if I tried to raise her alone. I've already promised. The papers are signed.* My mind darted down one dead-end tunnel after the next, looking for a way out. My eyelids fluttered shut; all I could see was blackest black.

The silence grew weighty. *Please, God, don't strike me dead,* I prayed. Then, drawing a shallow breath, I stared off into space and uttered the words they required me to say: "Yes, I understand."

"Do you agree never to contact your child again?" he asked pointedly.

I speared him with a look of hate. His question burned like a knife point twisting in my throat. My rage flared, but I quickly doused it and forced out my "yes" through clenched teeth.

"All right," he declared, striking his gavel firmly on the desk top. "I'll grant this petition."

We were finished. I bolted to my feet and swept out of the courtroom, leaving my mother behind to do whatever else needed to be done. I moved briskly down the hall, as if swift walking could clear the confusion that buzzed in my brain. But soon, there were words forming on my lips.

"The Law's supposed to be about *justice*, is it? Huh! How is it *just* to separate a mother and child absolutely and forever? The Law is an Ass! I won't agree. Eighteen years should be enough. Why should my baby and I be punished with 'not knowing' for the entire rest of our lives? To Hell with the Law!"

I muttered it all, wanting them to hear . . . but no one even looked up. They were probably used to the utterings of impotent rage.

And, after all, I'd signed the papers. I'd answered "yes." I was the agent of my own destruction. But I discounted how I'd been manipulated and dominated by the beliefs of others. I couldn't see that. Not when their beliefs dove-tailed so neatly with the ones I carried in me, unexpressed, unexamined and unchallenged.

We all operate out of these "transparent beliefs"—things we think we know. They act like a magnet, collecting "evidence" as we walk through life. Since we're constantly bombarded with conflicting evidence, we're always selecting what to notice, what to ignore. This is how we create our personal reality: by choosing what to notice. And this is where the power of creation lies, if we only realized it. But we're seldom conscious of our choices. Instead, we habitually collect more experiences that support the things in which we already believe. As our evidence piles up, we know we're really right!

At the hearing, I only added to the evidence I'd been collecting for many years—that I'd make an unfit mother. If I were fit, wouldn't I have fought to keep my child? I realized a closed records adoption would hurt her, yet I'd agreed to all their rules. Why couldn't I see that I'd made myself powerless, that I was sabotaging myself with my own beliefs?

First, I "believed" motherhood would drive me crazy. It had driven my mother crazy a couple of times, hadn't it? And what about the way I myself had felt during my visit with Amy? Did I ever question my fear? Did anyone else? No one even thought to, because *they, too,* believed that adoption was the "right" thing to do. My parents, my family doctor, my social worker—they all agreed. Not only that, but giving up my child and keeping silent about it forever would be the one thing that could save me and my parents from public disgrace.

The second belief that sealed my fate was that I took everyone's word that my unwed pregnancy was a deep disgrace. I'd never thought to question that! Yet, some native societies, I now know, *require* a girl to have a baby before she's considered eligible for marriage. Isn't childbirth the highest achievement of nature? A girl's passage into womanhood? What made modern man throw all that aside for something else? Why did no conventionally-raised WASP ever question that in the '60's? Did the entire society have a transparent belief?

My fear of inadequacy had dovetailed with their indoctrination about disgrace. It was all working together now. And like Peter with Christ, I had denied my daughter three times: before birth, at birth, and now before the judge.

Trapped by my invisible beliefs, I stiffened and stared up at the gray sky. I couldn't say if there were a sun up there beneath the layers of clouds. I drew my coat around me. Then I took up my rusty armor—indifference—and strained to buckle it back in place. But it wouldn't quite fit any more. Puzzled, I rotated my body and limped back to the car to wait for Mother.

11 - Nine Long Years

The moment of surrender seared *persona non grata* into my heart with the hot iron of shame. Flesh blistering, I wandered off into a wilderness of guilt and secrecy—a lost mother of a lost daughter for all eternity.

Negative forces pulled me down into a black void, swirled me into a maelstrom. Gathering speed, they sucked me down, covered my face—forced their way into my ears, my mouth, my nose. I snorted and spit to keep them out, but they dripped down inside my throat—my nostrils. They tickled; then choked me. Air. I need air. My throat constricted. My breathing was blocked; my last strength drained away. As the dizzying void closed over me, I could only surrender and let them have their way with me.

The blackness whooshed around me then, tunneling me down into the void. Then it gave me a violent shove and popped me to the surface. Half-drowned, I found myself bobbing in the bubbly surf. I gasped, and with my last thread of strength, rolled my head to the side. I fought to open half an eye. Near me, all I could see were churning waves, but in the distance, a little light flickered.

A lighthouse? Could it be?

Dim hope spread through me like the lantern's glow. My promise to Jennifer Lynn! To find her, I would need to make myself strong and survive this ocean of despair. My head began to clear. Like a thirsty babe, I sucked in sweet, nourishing hope. Yes, it would be a long swim through the flood tide of my life, but there in the distance was the shoreline—eighteen years away. . . .

In July, my parents gave Adrian and me a big church wedding. I carried white orchids and wore a beaded white gown . . . and no one guessed I'd had a baby only fifteen months before.

If only I can be a perfect wife, I told myself, *life will be okay again.* So I eagerly learned to cook gourmet meals, keep a perfect house, weed the garden . . . and always do his bidding. Adrian was my king. His beam of approval made me feel worthwhile again, and soon, contentment settled into my life like a welcome guest I hoped would stay forever.

He waited two years before asking me to bear his child. He had

87

told me he wanted children long ago. I remembered back to when we would turn out the lights and snuggle on the couch in my old apartment. Even back then, before we'd become intimate, we would discuss our dreams, and Adrian would tell me how he *loved* children. He wanted lots of them. How about four?

Well . . . I demurred. Maybe . . . some day.

In my heart, I wasn't sure. Would I abuse them? Would my brain turn to mush if I became a household drudge? But, always, what was most important was *pleasing Adrian*. I couldn't disappoint him . . . especially about this. So I quit a new job I liked a lot and gave him two little girls.

He rubbed my back and squeezed my hand through my labors and the miraculous moments of birth. We watched together in awe as our daughters slipped into the world, uniting us as never before.

Before, when pregnant, I'd learned to stay detached. So it took me by surprise when I fell in love with these new babes. But when their nibbling released my milk—when I felt it streaming into their little baby mouths—they became the center of my world. Soon, gourmet meals became a thing of the past. I tried to do it all, but there was no way I could.

Adrian said he understood, but he began spending more time away from home. And he started getting moodier. He needed some time to himself, he said. Would I mind if he went out to have a few drinks with his male friends? Of course I didn't argue, though I'd often wake up and pace the floor in the middle of the night, waiting for his headlights to bounce down our country lane.

Then, six months after our second daughter was born in 1973, the crucible of Life began melting down the world I knew, piece by piece. It began quite unexpectedly when Dad got cancer. I rushed to his side when I found out. I remember our visit . . . how he wobbled down the hospital hallway wearing his old purple, wool robe . . . how it hung off his thinning, slumped shoulders. My heart ached to see a proud man so mortal. He looked up with a thin smile, then dropped his head. Embarrassment misted the air.

The usual greetings rang hollow, and tears burned my eyes. "Dad, I never thanked you for standing by me . . . you know . . . when I got pregnant. Thank you. I'll never forget. . . ."

When he looked up at me, a soul-gate opened between us. He

enfolded me in his arms, and we held each other long and tight, our hearts beating together in that space beyond time, beyond words.

A second blow of fate struck a year after that. It was December, 1974. Adrian's new business was floundering and the company I worked for was going bankrupt. Buy the food and pay the bills without a paycheck? Worry slammed me into a concrete wall of pain nearly every day. Migraines pounded through my head, sickened me, deafened my thoughts, until late April brought the long-dreaded pink slip. Now there were ten slim unemployment checks between the four of us and financial ruin.

Adrian helped me with my resume. "Think back over all the work you've ever done. What types of things do you do well?" he asked. "And what do you like to do?"

It was easy to list my skills, but what had I ever done that I really liked? That was harder.

But then I remembered: preparing material for publication. When everyone else had been laid off at my last job, I'd put the sales magazine together. I smiled to think how, on those days, there were no headaches and the hours flew by. And there was so much more I wanted to know about layout, about printing. That was it: I'd look for a job in printing or publishing.

I'd been job-hunting for three futile weeks when Mother called. "Daddy's dying. He doesn't want to go to the hospital. I'm trying to keep him here at home, but I can't do it alone anymore. Please, can you come?" Adrian offered to keep our older daughter, so, I packed up our two-year-old and headed for home.

The rhododendrons were blooming along the driveway that wound up to the big house in the woods, but, inside, the mood was somber. "He still won't admit he's dying," Mom reported in hushed tones. But we could hear his labored breathing from the hallway. He lay there, barely conscious, the look of death plain on his face. His skin was sallow. His perpetual look of ruddy vitality and youth was gone forever. Cancer had aged him forty years in two . . . ten years, at least, since I'd seen him ten weeks back. I was almost surprised to see his eyes flutter partly open when Mom and I walked into the room.

"Ann's here, Darling," Mom said softly, stroking his forehead as she always did to comfort him.

Dad looked over and tried to speak. Mother choked up and fled the room. I took Dad's hand and sat on the edge of the bed. I tried to beam some life into his warm, dry palms. I could sense he had something important to say to me.

"I'm afraid what will happen to Mother . . ." he managed to rasp out.

Oh, my God, I thought to myself, *he DOES know he's dying after all, but he's feeling responsible for his mother. He's afraid to let himself go, because she might not be able to handle it.*

"Oh, Dad," I said confidently, thinking of his mother—ninety-one years old, in perfect health, and a marvelously accepting human being. "She's a strong woman. She'll be fine. It's okay for you to die."

He squeezed my hand and his faded blue eyes filled with gratitude and relief as deep as the ocean. Then he turned away and started to prepare himself for death.

I knew I'd helped my dad. At first, I'd glowed with pride. But a chill shuttered through me later, when my mind played back our conversation. I'd said the right thing, alright, but only by dumb luck. It wasn't *his* mother that worried him. No, it was *my* mother! And what would I have said to that? She told everyone she'd die of grief without him.

Two weeks later, I huddled under the funeral tent at the cemetery, staring at the shiny gray casket filled with the empty shell Dad had left behind. After the benediction, one of Dad's students blew taps. While the mournful trumpet call echoed through the valley, my eyes surveyed the large crowd assembled there. Men and boys stood solemnly, heads bowed, hats at their sides. Silent women wobbled in high heels on the uneven grass. The sun sparkled off the trumpeter's raised brass bell the same way it had sparkled off my dad's cornet so many times before. Mother saw it, too, and her reddened eyes filled once more. Somewhere above us, Daddy's spirit hovered, free again.

He had made his transition. Now it was time for me to make one, too. I needed a new job. What might Life be trying to teach me about transitions? Perhaps the key was to do what Dad had done: let go of fear; embrace the unknown.

What if Life were to bring me something better? It had already brought me one blessing: the chance to be at Dad's side when he really needed me. What could be more positive than that? Then, a few weeks later, it happened. I was offered my "perfect job" publishing family history books. In a city an hour away.

An hour away, I gasped. *I have two little kids. How will I do it? Get up at 6, get home at 7? And, sure, it's publishing, but why family histories?* My stomach contracted, knowing every day I'd be thinking of my lost daughter and how I'd cut off her roots.

I floundered in a raging sea of indecision. But unemployment checks were running out and there were no other jobs. *A BIRTHMOTHER . . . publishing family history books?* The life preserver was floating nearby, yet, I looked away distracted. Then a giant wave began arching over me. "Look out," throbbed the voice in my chest. So I grabbed for the ring.

In less than a year, Alex Haley's *Roots* had given the American people a new dimension of connectedness along with a new word: genealogy. On the day I couldn't jam another sample book onto my shelf, Haley's spark lit a torch for me. *What if I can help create a "critical mass" of this information?* I wondered. *What if, some day, every American, adopted or otherwise, can find his family roots because of published genealogies?*

When I spoke my vision, a wound deep inside began to heal. And, from that day on, every time I put a new book on my shelf, I dropped a pearl into a secret treasure chest for my lost daughter, Jennifer Lynn. My book shelf would become her shining legacy.

But events were racing forward now, and the third and cruelest hammer-blow of fate was about to fall. It was a bitter cold January morning in 1976. I rose at 6 am. Adrian had stumbled in a few hours earlier. I padded to the bathroom, sat down on the toilet, felt something crawling on me, reached down to scratch my crotch, and then I yelped. Body lice!

Sex partners passed them back and forth, and it wasn't *me* who'd been unfaithful. **That son of a bitch!**

The shock ignited something inside me, but I carefully kept my smoldering thoughts to myself. I dressed in haste and left the house without waking the children or him. All the while, I could feel a fire of rage growing hotter under a thickening layer of ash.

I waited until lunch time to call.

No sweet talk. "This morning I found some body lice on me. You know—'crabs,'" I opened. My chest was tight. I could barely breath. My feelings had frozen into a solid block of ice.

The little suck of air I heard told me everything. Oh yes, I knew his tongue would spin a pretty lie. Out it came, light-hearted and slippery. "Oh, I must have got them in the bathroom at the bar. You know how bars are."

My mouth fixed itself in a frown; my eyes narrowed to slits. "Adrian." My words were weighted. "I *know* how you get crabs."

"I told you what must have happened," he bantered. "Hey, you're making too much of this now. I've got to run."

I repeated it one more time. Slower. Louder. *"Adrian! I know how you get crabs!"* It came out with the force of two boulders clonking together, and I let it resonate . . . before I smashed down the receiver.

It was the next day before he made his confession. He did it on the phone. I was glad he couldn't see me when my heart fell through the ground.

"I've been keeping a little secret from you," he began. His eye must have been twitching. I could feel him falter. His voice slowed and deepened. "Darling, I don't know how to say this . . ."

"Go ahead," I gently urged. I heard his breath suck in as I held mine tight.

"I'm gay," he whispered at last. My mind's eye could see the tears of shame and regret glistening on his long, blond eyelashes. He cleared his voice to speak again. "Please know I love you," he murmured.

But I had gone away. Slipped beneath the icy surface of a pool of grief as deep as an arctic sea.

He had cheated from the beginning, he explained over time. Only never with a woman. (So maybe it wasn't really cheating.) No serious relationships; merely casual sex. I was the only *woman* he'd ever loved, but he had other needs—powerful needs—I couldn't fill.

How could this have happened? I asked myself. *Two children. All those years together. How could I have been so blind?*

Yet, there had been a million clues. His nausea on our honeymoon. Mechanical, infrequent sex. The late nights out drinking "by himself." His "moods."

(Why had I always blamed them on myself? Why had we never talked about our feelings in all those years?)

The illusion of our perfect marriage burned away in a red-hot blaze, and what was left, after all? Had it merely been gossamer talk of music, art and landscape wonders—the fun of singing and travel? Had our common interests tricked me into imagining an intimacy that was never there at all? What remained when the small talk was gone? Our children, surely—but what else? All I could see was ashes drifting away in the wind.

A few weeks later, as previously planned, we moved to a rented house near my new job. There was talk of an "open marriage," but things went on as before, and Adrian and I were still in limbo when our ninth wedding anniversary rolled around July 1, 1976. Walking to work that day, summer heat simmered on the pavement beneath my shoes. I hardly noticed, however. My thoughts were elsewhere. I'd invested nine years in a relationship that was no good for me anymore. Yes, it had been a god-send once, and it had given me two priceless daughters and many life lessons, but now what? Adrian and I had to talk.

After the girls were in bed that night, we spread a blanket and some pillows on the living room floor and lay down next to each other. Gazing up at the ceiling, we talked, for the first time, soul to soul. Yes, he loved me. No, he couldn't change the way he was. Well, I said, I loved him, too, but I couldn't live like this. We'd have to go our separate ways.

We talked about our time together, the joys and the sorrows. And, all the while, the soothing waters of forgiveness lapped at our wounds until talking was done. By the time we finished, the fires of anger and shame had sizzled off into misty vapor. Then, for the last time, we stirred the ashes of our marriage and dissolved them into love.

By the end of the month, we'd split our worldly goods. Adrian took a three-week trip, then started a new single life in an apartment around the corner, where he could stay in touch with our girls.

When he was gone, a person called "me" stood quaking naked in the wind. Dark clouds inked out the stars. I was alone. All, all alone. I wasn't a perfect wife anymore. I teetered back and forth in agitation, hands over chest, head bowed in shame. I shuddered to feel a shadow-hand stroke my soft skin, brush the hair from my wet face.

"Come," it said, "there's nothing left here. We need to journey on. Somewhere within hides a lost soul. Without it, you are nothing. Follow me."

12 - Release from Shame

The dark, wooden floorboards creaked under the tramping of twenty pairs of legs.

"Stop. Face forward," the trainer barked. "Now drop your hands to the side. Look straight ahead."

Then his manner softened and his words flowed like liquid chocolate. "Now just 'be' with someone out there," he said. "And, people in the audience—notice every detail about the appearance of the people in front of you and then recreate what you see them feeling."

A deafening silence filled up every molecule of space in the room.

Had I followed my midnight guide straight into the mouth of Hell? It had been five years since my breakup with Adrian. I had a new man now—Ned—and we were both deeply involved in human potential work, sifting through layers of pretense, sorting through unacknowledged feelings in the search for our inner selves. The work was teaching me, personally, a lot about something I'd always tried to deny: my feelings.

Now, when my chest tightened and my head buzzed, I knew I was *angry*. And instead of lashing out at people with, "How dare you say so-and-so after all I've done for you," I was learning to say, "When you did so-and-so, I felt angry and powerless because I was afraid you didn't trust me." That switch was making a lot of difference in all my close relationships.

Human potential work was also teaching me how to release my old anger and sadness using a technique called "re-creation." We would practice it in pairs. The "sender" would imagine some unexpressed anger or grief with his father, boss or lover, and then he'd scream or cry it out to the "receiver" sitting opposite. The receiver would just let it all in . . . *really listen* to the anger, try to understand how the sender must be feeling . . . let tears of sympathy well up in his eyes. If he offered no resistance, no judgement, no evaluation—if he would merely feel the emotion and "let it be"—then, a magical thing would happen. The sender could be ravingly angry or hurt like there was no tomorrow, and then, every time, his hurt or anger would pass like a storm, leaving fresh air tingling in its wake.

In May of 1981, I'd scheduled myself for a one-week course called the Intensive Training. They promised it would transform my life. And in one way, at least, it did.

The "Swim Suit Process" was held on the third day. I was in the second group of people paraded out to face the audience. Twenty of us were lined up back stage, then marched out in single file, barefoot, in bathing suits. Heat from the spotlights seared us; the small wooden stage felt like a torture box.

I'd been watching the man in front of me walk across the stage when we came out. Unappealing, really. He had a funny wad of black hairs sticking out of the waist band of his green boxer shorts. His splayed feet had plopped across the floor. Gracelessly. He looked like a heron, his body perched on hairy, match-stick legs.

And now something else occurred to me. Whoever was behind me was seeing me like that, too.

I knew that I walked with my pelvis tipped forward, like an empty vessel needing to be filled. Could they see my neediness? Would they notice that my eyes were too close together? That my hair was dull and mousey brown? They were all probably gawking at my flat chest and the dimples on my upper thighs.

Oh my God, I forgot to shave my crotch!

I could feel sweat seeping into the cracks of my face by then. Silence buffeted me like an invisible wind. Nearly eighty people faced me in the small campground auditorium, built out of wood and screening. People I didn't know, middle-class men and women, 20 to 60 years old, sat tightly packed in the three front rows. They stared at our lineup without speaking. I stood stiffly, mesmerized by the vast silence in the room. Then a strange chill made my arms bristle. I turned my head and looked down to my left. My arm was coated with prickly goose bumps; thin hairs stood erect between them like naked poles.

"Eyes straight ahead," the Trainer's powerful voice exploded. My head jerked forward again.

My stomach roiled. *What am I doing here?* I asked myself. *Why did I agree to this anyway? This is "humiliation," not "human potential training."*

Just be patient, another part of myself argued rationally. *Of course, you're feeling fear, anger and shame. That's the purpose of this: for you to uncover your "shadow self." Only when you've dealt with "the shadow" consciously, can you use it to create opportunity and growth in your life, instead of sabotage and pain. You paid a bundle for this Training. Better stick around and get something out of it.*

The Intensive Training was a week-long commitment to being the best you could be and to loving other people, no matter what. We'd been motioned off the secondary road by a grinning woman holding a sign. They were there to serve us, and the help started even while the gravel still crunched under our tires. "Park it here." "Get your luggage." "Put it on the baggage cart." "Please proceed to the main building for processing. Quickly."

I'd jogged up the path to the big camp building, hardly noticing the newly-leaved valley that enclosed the camp complex, hardly feeling the chilly breeze that tickled the trees. All I saw was the dust kicking up under my sneakers. In the main building, a squad of volunteers sat behind numbered tables, busily processing the new arrivals. Registration and name tags first, then room assignments, schedules, a Polaroid photo snapped in front of a white screen. "Next, please."

Now I'd made it through half the week, but I was still wondering what it was all supposed to mean. The late hours, the arduous exercise, the ridiculous "processes," endless classroom lectures. So far, I'd seen people sweat, cry, throw up, have fits of rage and freeze with fear. "Don't quit," they warned us: "You'll be jumping off a roller coaster, mid-ride." One person had packed up and left the very first day, but everyone else had stayed. Now, we would all stay no matter how tough things got. Why? First and foremost, because we liked the results we'd seen in our friends who had done it before us. Secondly, because we knew that, however we acted, whatever happened, we'd be loved and cared for here.

When I ran up the mountain path every morning, I stumbled and my lungs burned, but a hundred people cheered me on. Yesterday . . . when I quivered on that tiny platform in the middle of a tree, looking *way down* at a lake sparkling *miles* below, only a thin cord of wire between me and eternity . . . they reassured me. They told me to live by my word—and jump. Or was I going to let Fear

97

make decisions for me the rest of my life? My mind went white with fright, but I'd clamped my eyes tightly shut and allowed the bottom to drop out of my life. My stomach had seized in terror when the wind began rushing by me like a tornado. Then I'd heard the little whizzing sound of a metal ring slipping over a wire line, and, when I opened my eyes, I saw myself flying over the lake toward the soft, sure shore. A crowd of cheering angels was waiting there to catch me. No, I wasn't going to die.

Whee, this is fun, I realized, just as the ground pulled up fast below me. Strong hands steadied me, removed the safety line. I hopped out. Then, I wanted to go again—without squandering my turn in fear. But my turn was over. Still, there was something I could keep forever: the knowledge that, once, I was afraid, but I'd kept my word. I had experienced my fear and lived to tell the tale. . . .

My mouth crinkled into a smile, and feeling my muscles move jerked my awareness right back into that auditorium. I shook my head. *Where am I?* Then I remembered: wearing a swim suit, standing in front of a roomful people. The silence pounded. The hot lights glared. And all those people stared at us, stonily, from below. *Now, what did he say? Look out into the audience and "be" with somebody?*

My ears buzzed. Someone was looking at me. The young man with the dark, floppy hair. I'd noticed him yesterday. One of those classroom exercises . . . forget why. He was staring straight at my crotch. *He'll see the kinky, brown pubic hair I forgot to shave off.* I could feel it bushing out the sides of my blue bikini bottom. I blushed.

But his gaze captured me. It was moving up my body and it stepped into mine. A tug of energy pulled between us. My brow furrowed and froze; my eyelids burned and dropped to half mast. Our eyes locked, and a magical door opened.

He *saw* me. He saw inside my life to where the shame lived. He knew I'd given myself to men to get the approval I could never give myself. He knew I'd slept with men I didn't like, that I'd disregarded both my dignity—and safety—to please them.

Our souls blended, and the pain he saw in me welled up in both our eyes. Time stood still while silence rang around us, and when it began moving once more, my pain slowly released. As if a thick elastic band had been cut loose from my arm, healing pulsed through my body. My eyes widened while tiny prickles chased down my arms and out my fingertips. My shoulders dropped, I breathed freely again, and then I looked away.

Every shameful sex act—things I'd never told a living soul—mystically, magically—this young man knew about me and accepted. I could feel the poison draining out of my body, and, as it did, a new space opened up. I lay down my heavy sack of shame and a lighter, freer me stepped into the new room that now loomed inside me. He'd followed me into that black pit of shame and just "let it be." Now, I could just let it be, too. My soulmate had set me free.

My eyes flooded with gratitude. I looked down to thank him, but his eyes were locked with someone else's by now. Even so, my cracked lips whispered, "Thanks."

How could he have known all that about me? We'd never even spoken. Where *had* I seen him before?

Then I remembered yesterday's distressing classroom session on sex. When they asked who'd ever been a prostitute, he'd been one of the ones—as we held our breaths—to stand.

13 - The Place Within

"So, Ann, do you remember back when we did the Intensive Training in May?" Lucy asked me over the hum of the air conditioning and front-seat chatter. It was July, 1981. Three new friends and I were headed to Washington to be trained to assist in yet another Intensive Training scheduled for the beginning of September. "Do you remember that classroom on 'sex' when they asked people to stand up if they'd had homosexual relations and stuff like that?"

(How could I forget? Especially that mortifying moment when I'd had to stand. My knees had buckled under the weight of the hundred bricks that seemed piled on my lap!)

"Did I see you stand when they called for people who'd had children out-of-wedlock?"

I gave a slight nod, while a bomb exploded inside my gut.

"I thought so." She cocked her head and looked at me quizzically. "I was surprised you'd never mentioned it before."

Lucy and I had been carpooling together to human potential trainings and seminars for over a year. We had discussed our dominating mothers, Lucy's love life and career, my first marriage, my relationships with my kids and the man in my life, Ned, but never . . . that. . . .

"Do you mind me asking about it? How was that for you?" Her dark eyes punched a hole in my soul.

"Well-er-ah," I stumbled, nervously clearing my throat. I knew she'd never be judgemental, but my mouth felt like it was stuffed with wads of cotton.

She backed off gently. "I see this might be hard for you to talk about."

"Oh, no, it's okay," I lied, while swallowing hard and squirming in my seat. "I'll be happy to tell you about it."

Listen, Ann, you haven't talked to anyone about this for ages. You say it's something you want to get resolved. It will be good for you to get a little practice in a safe space, I lectured myself, even while tall stone walls closed in on me.

I stretched my lungs with a slow, deep breath and groped for Lucy's hand. Then, I told her the whole story in five quick sentences.

"Did you have a little girl or a little boy?" she asked when I finished.

"A little girl," I managed hoarsely. Tears welled up and I turned away.

"It's okay. I understand," Lucy said softly. "I probably would have done the same thing myself."

Then, like a cyclone ripping down a canyon, an old anger welled up inside me. I jerked my hand away and snarled out to her the "terms" of the surrender.

"That's not right, Lucy! Why can't we know each other some day when she's grown? Why should I live forever never knowing if she's okay? And don't you think she'll wonder where she came from?" My head shook back and forth. "I wronged her when I gave her away. I know that. . . but I think I should have the chance to make it up to her some day. Damn it, why can't I give her back what's rightfully hers?"

My outburst of passion surprised even me, but the storm passed with a sigh. I dropped my arms uselessly into my lap and waited while sorrow flooded back in to drown the fire of anger. "I can't forget about her, Lucy. Every time she has a birthday, I get depressed for a week."

Strong thoughts echoed through our minds in the long pause that followed. "How old would she be now?" Lucy finally asked.

"Her birthday was March 30th . . . she was fifteen this year," my tight throat croaked. *(Oh God—fifteen!)* Then I made a connection that shot through my heart like a firecracker. My eyes widened. "Lucy, I've only got three more years to wait."

"To wait? To wait for what?" she asked.

"Till she's eighteen. Then, I can go find her!"

Now the words came spilling out. "Lucy, when she's eighteen, I can put my name in the reunion registry, and then, if she registers too, they'll match us up and I'll find her!"

"What are you talking about?" Her eyes expanded.

"Two years ago, I was looking through one of the *Genealogical Helper* magazines we get at work, and there was an ad for adoptees. It said, 'Adoption Search? Register in the International Soundex Registry.'

"I wrote right away to their address in Carson City, Nevada, and a week or so later, I got a form back. I filled it out, but I can't send it in until she turns eighteen. Then, when she files, too, they'll match us up. I can't wait!"

Soon after getting the form, I'd looked up the address of my adoption agency in the library's city phone directory collection. A week or so later, I sent them a letter, and they even replied.

"Yes, you were our client," they wrote. "We will keep your letter and new address on file." I was thrilled to think I'd already begun my search in a very small way.

"Did you name your baby?"

"Yes—Jennifer Lynn." The mention of her name washed a wave of memories over me. "She was a really beautiful baby, but she didn't look like me. She had dark hair and olive skin." I stopped talking and stared out the window. The landscape whizzed by outside, turning the clock in my mind back fifteen years.

I could almost hear my slippers scraping down those polished hospital floors on the way to the nursery. With each step forward, my stomach was twisting in knots. There were the babies, all lined up in a row behind the thick glass window. I searched all the bassinets, but my baby wasn't there. What had they done with her? I finally summoned the courage to rap lightly on the nursery room door. I showed them my hospital bracelet and pointed to the bassinets. "May I see her, please?"

The nurse rolled a bassinet forward from the back of the nursery. My baby was asleep. No, she didn't look a bit like me, but maybe that was for the best. I searched her beautiful face. Who was her father? Was it little limping Jean-Michel or my big dreamboat Claude? Lying there in innocent contentment, my baby held the answer. I held my gaze unfocused and tried to concentrate . . .

When Claude's broad smiling face slowly formed before my eyes, relief washed through me.

Pretty soon, my mind was whirling with a plan of action. *I must write to Claude and let him know he has a daughter. I'll do that right away. Too bad I only told the agency about Jean-Michel. Too late to change my story now, but I'll have to record the truth somewhere. Where?*

I knew a moment later: the birth certificate. When it came time to do that, I would tell the truth.

The next day, I went back to the nursery again, but this time, the baby was twisted up in sobs. Poor little thing. She needed someone to care for her. I knew it could never be me: I wouldn't be able to cope. That was the real reason I had to give her up. This sharp truth jabbed at me like a knife blade, shredding my last thin hope of keeping her. I turned and fled to my room in tears. The following day, I left the hospital without seeing her again.

The car jolted over a bump, snapping my mind back to the present. I looked up at Lucy once again. Her soft, dark eyes were waiting for me to come back. "When she was born, I promised to find her someday," I murmured. Then I sealed my lips and slowly turned my head away.

Lucy gently touched me on the shoulder. "So, when will that be?" she asked.

I jolted. "What do you mean, 'When will that be?'" Then I snapped at her. "How the hell should I know?"

Lucy withdrew her hand but not her support. "You know . . ." Her voice drifted off towards infinity.

"Huh?" It was a possibility I'd never considered.

As I slowly mulled over her suggestion, a channel opened in my mind. Lucy must have seen my face soften.

"Close your eyes. Look deep inside yourself," came her slow, steady instruction. "Somewhere inside you is the answer you seek. You know when you'll meet your daughter. Look and see."

My mind drifted inward through a dark, mysterious cavern. There, in front of me stood the answer. "1990," my mouth said, though my mind did not believe.

"Good," said Lucy. "Now, when in 1990?"

My eyes flew open. "God, Lucy. How am I supposed to know that?" I protested, rubbing my hands over my head.

"You know," she calmly affirmed.

I shut my eyes and looked again. I peered deep, deep down in the dark cavern this time, way beyond where light lived. I'd forgotten about this space, but it was the same place I'd gone to when I'd seen my baby in the womb. It was the place of knowing, deep in my subconscious . . . the place within . . . the place within us all, where we connect to the Source, to all events and all people, past, present and future. It was the place into which we speak our word, knowing it must then manifest in the material world. There, glowing in the dark was the word "July."

Suddenly, my eyes flew open again. "Lucy! I know!" I gasped. "July, 1990! I'll meet my daughter in July, 1990!" Shivers of wonder pulsed through me and tears brimmed up. "God, I'll be forty-five by then, and she'll be twenty-four." *Nine more years—a long time to wait, but not forever. So, it will happen!* I squeezed myself in glee.

I raised my hand to my mouth and gently let my top teeth scrape over the rough top surface of my chewed off thumbnail. If only I could heal myself by then.

14 - Changing Perspective

I was drifting . . . drifting . . . through a long, silent, black tunnel. Then I heard a steady beep, beep . . . like a hospital monitor. I lifted my head. Wait! Tape plastered my face. I struggled to free myself; my eyes burst open. Two people jumped to my side, grabbed my hands, leaned over me.

My mother and my boyfriend Ned. What were they doing here?

Worry had etched deep lines in their faces. Mother reached over and stroked my forehead, the way she used to rub my dad's. I hated her touching me that way, but I couldn't reach up to grab her hand. The beep-beep accelerated. I shook my head. Ned pressed his warm palm into my cold one. "It's okay." His steady voice comforted me. "You're in the hospital. Just relax, now. You're going to be okay." He and my mother exchanged knowing glances.

I struggled to speak, but my mouth chafed against the tape. "What?" I croaked, eyes bugging out. "What happened?" My mind raced with terror, imagining motorcycle crashes, building collapses.

Now Mother spoke. Her fine, white skin rutted with concern, she clutched the metal railing of my hospital bed. "Your heart stopped," she explained. "You were assisting at the Intensive Training." (Oh, yes, I could remember that.) "You collapsed while dancing."

While dancing? My ears began to ring. *What do they mean, "My heart stopped?" Am I going to die?* My chest constricted; breath came in shallow spurts. I closed my eyes to block out the horror, and drifted back to safe unconsciousness. But each time I woke up, I picked up another bit of the story, and then another. Slowly, like assembling a 1000-piece puzzle, I started patching together the two missing days of my life.

I could remember packing my suitcases before leaving for the closing party that night. It was called the Completion Workshop. It was for all the participants and all the assistants, and it would celebrate the end to our very special week together. I was bone tired from many days of push-yourself-farther-than-you've-ever-gone-before and very little sleep. Still, I'd sprinted down the path to the main building and stood in line with the others, ready to cheer the participants when they ran in. We screamed like banshees, hooted, shouted and whistled—until our lungs and voices were bursting. We raised our arms, waved our hands, stomped our feet, jumped up and down. The valley echoed back our bedlam as the participants poured through the doors. Let the celebration begin!

I can only imagine what must have happened after the party got into full swing. The blaring music, sweaty stomping, a blaze of red, orange, yellow, green shirts and shorts bouncing up and down to the rhythm; and then, somewhere in its midst, I crumple on the floor.

My partner sees me close my eyes and fall. He reaches out to steady me; the weight is leaden. The girl beside us gives a shriek; heads turn. I'm down by then. Someone shouts to stop the music. Excited jabbering surges through the crowd. "What happened?" "Someone collapsed." "I think she needs a doctor," someone says. People take up the cry. "Is there a doctor? We need a doctor!" "I'm over here!" shouts a male voice. The crowd parts. The doctor rushes to my side, feels my neck for a pulse.

There is none.

"Stand back," he must have said above the pounding of his heart. No doubt he loosened my belt, unbuttoned my shirt. My soul must have hovered above and watched while he breathed into my mouth and pounded on my chest. (A warm, white light was slowly drawing me away.)

"I'm not getting any response here. What time is it?" Someone scrambles for a clock.

"The defibrillator. Get the defibrillator! Quick!"

The assistant in charge of medical supplies takes off at a full run, back down the hall. There's a spooky silence in the room. A weight presses on the chest of each person there as the doctor's hands press on mine—pumping, pumping. They stand agog, mouths partway open, eyes partway closed, wincing away tears. One of us lies suspended between life and death. One of us could be any of them.

"Here it is," huffs the assistant, a minute and a half later. He slides the black box on the floor. "I just fixed the handle on this thing this morning," he comments. Chills run up and down his spine.

"Okay. Plug it in. Let's go! Hustle! How long's it been?"

"Three minutes," someone calls out.

"We're running out of time, folks." The doctor's eyes dart up to the paddles. He stops kneading my chest and opens my blouse wider. Then he takes the paddles and spreads them on my chest. "Stand back! Do it!" he charges.

My body jolts up, thumps down. He sets aside the paddles and lays his ear on my chest. Disappointment turns his mouth down.

"Time?" he asks. His voice sounds strained.

"Three minutes, 45 seconds."

He looks at my lifeless form and sighs. "Let's try again." He lays the paddles on me. His eyes squeeze shut as if in prayer. "Okay, Annie. Come on back," he whispers. Then he hollers, "Do it!"

At that moment, I must have chosen to turn away from that soothing, blissful white light. "No! I can't die yet. My children! I can't leave them! And there's a promise that I made . . ."

The rest I heard from Mother and Ned. Paramedics carried me out, taking the prayers of a hundred and fifty people with them. I was bounced up the access road and zoomed, comatose, to the hospital. The coma lasted twenty hours, and things were still touch and go. The doctor said there was a funny double passage structure in my heart. They speculated it had short-circuited under stress. No one knew exactly what to do with me next.

When I closed my eyes, tears oozed out and trickled down my cheeks. I'd been trying so hard to improve myself. A year and a half of human potential work and still I was screwing up my life. An unwed pregnancy. A failed marriage. Now this. What in the world was I doing wrong? Would I ever stop sabotaging myself? Would I ever figure out how to be normal?

* * * * *

I'd been pitched off my lifeboat and was tossing around again in turbulent seas. But I had my knowledge of the mechanics of the mind as a life preserver this time. Still, that wasn't big enough to explain everything. If I'd only known that larger ideas were standing like ocean liners in the fog just out of sight! As Linda the astrologer would teach me next year, one often needs to look beyond this life, beyond this plane, to see that there is sometimes a higher purpose for things, after all.

The astronomers tell us that our Universe is in constant motion.

The Earth is rotating at a speed of 600 miles/hour or more and, at the same time, revolving around the Sun at a speed in excess of 60,000 miles/hour. However, from our perspective here on earth, it appears that the stars and planets are spinning around us every day.

It was from the Earth perspective that ancient astrologers mapped the sky. Astrology means "study of the stars," and originally included what is today called astronomy. The first astrologers mapped the stars and kept track of what was happening here on earth. They believed in the principle "as above, so below." For instance, the constellation of Aries was on the horizon in spring. Aries, therefore, came to stand for new beginnings, fresh energy and assertiveness. It was said to be ruled by the planet Mars, the god of war, masculinity and action, because Aries and Mars had similar traits. Thus, these observations evolved into the symbols we still use in astrology today.

Astrologers calculate where the Sun, Moon and planets appear on the ecliptic, the plane of the Earth's orbit around the Sun. A map of these calculations, figured from the time and place of birth, is a person's natal chart. The ecliptic plane is a 360 degree circle, divided into twelve pie-shaped wedges of 30 degrees. Each 30 degrees is said to be ruled by the constellation that appears in that area of the sky. There are twelve: Aries, Taurus, Gemini, Cancer, Leo, Virgo, Libra, Scorpio, Saggitarius, Capricorn, Aquarius, and Pisces. The natal chart is divided into twelve houses, which symbolize various areas of life—birth, values, communication, inner self and early home life, children, health, relationship, shared values, religion and learning, career, hopes, and the unconscious, i.e., the matrix out of which we are born. These houses correspond to the constellations—Aries/birth, Taurus/values, Gemini/communication—and these correspondences are called archetypes. Each house contains one or more of these archtypes and is slightly more or slightly less than 30 degrees, depending on the angle of the ecliptic plane at the moment of birth. The First House shows what constellation and planets were on the eastern horizon at the moment of birth, and the Seventh House shows what was on the western horizon. Because matter is said to take on the character of the time and space in which it exists, astrologers say the natal chart gives symbolic information about a person's strengths and weaknesses. It also shows what their path of learning will be in this lifetime.

To gain deeper insight about what's going on currently in someone's life, a map of the present ecliptic plane is superimposed on the natal chart. This overlay of transiting planets, tells how the present archtypes are working—as crisis, calm, blockage or opportunity.

In addition to the twenty-eight year Saturn cycle of life lessons that I learned about from Linda in 1982, the transits of the three outer planets—Uranus, Neptune and Pluto—are also significant. These outer planets spend a long time in any given house of the natal chart. Thus, their effect on an area of life, though profound and sometimes dramatic, is far slower. Uranus stays in a sign for approximately seven years; Neptune, about fourteen; and, because Pluto's orbit is elliptical, it can stay in a sign anywhere from thirteen to thirty years. Transits tend to be felt most intensely just as they enter a house of the natal chart, just upon leaving, and when directly aspecting a natal planet.

Of the twelve natal chart Houses, houses one through six—the bottom half of the chart—represent the realm of self-development and self-expression. When my heart stopped, Neptune, the planet that symbolizes empathy, intuition and the unconscious mind, was just leaving my Third House of learning, thinking and communication. Neptune's greatest power is to dissolve the ego so people can see through their illusions and learn about deeper realities. I began this transit back in 1966, when I entered the home for unwed mothers. Since then, my experiences had been slowly dissolving my old, inflexible thinking so I could reexamine what I thought was true. Now, Neptune was about to enter my Fourth House. My new task would be to use my changed thinking to produce a corresponding change in my inner self. I would have the next sixteen years to work on it.

When my heart stopped, Uranus, the planet of awakening and quick change, was also in my Third House. It had entered that area of my chart when my boyfriend Ned and I had begun human potential work. Uranus in the Third House in the sign of Scorpio, as it was at that time, stands for quick, insightful change in mental attitudes. With this transit, I was being offered potent opportunities to look at my life in new ways. As old habits of thinking and communicating fell away, I would be turning to new interests, such as astrology. Learning from these new interests could later lead to a fundamental reorientation of the inner self—which is the purpose of Uranus transiting the Fourth House.

As for the outermost planet, Pluto: it was in my Second House of values and self-worth when my heart stopped. Pluto symbolizes bringing to the surface all hidden thoughts and feelings that must be eliminated to make room for the new. It was just shifting into my Second House when Ned and I began our human potential work. That work was operating to create a complete metamorphasis in my personal values, for sure!

A week after my collapse, I was transferred to a hospital in Philadelphia where the doctors did a lot of tests. First, they threaded wires into my heart looking for blockages, but there weren't any. The next day they probed it again, testing my heart's electrical circuits. They tried to recreate my problem with electrical stimulation. But after all their tests, they were still unable explain what happened. They gave me a pill and sent me home, hoping for the best.

I went away without an explanation, but after visiting Linda, I created my own metaphysical one. What if my soul had been floundering during that Completion Workshop. What if I'd been flirting with someone, for instance? Often when one is breaking up old habits, they still float around loose, like plaque. They can unexpectedly jam up your life again if you're not vigilant. Did I let down my guard that night? Did I need to be pulled up short? This shock made me pay close attention. When one commits to a new course, the changes must be made for real, and not just played at. Old plaque must be completely flushed away—or the spirit realm brings out a cosmic two-by-four!

In a month or so, I recovered enough strength to return to work. Mother stayed with me a few weeks to help with the house and the kids. Ned's and my relationship shifted, too. He was now far more than just the-man-I'd-been-with-for-four-years. We'd had an exclusive relationship, but neither of us had been sure if we would stay or go. So, when I found out that Ned had dropped everything and driven seven hours in the middle of the night to be at the hospital with me, and that he had stayed by my side, even though the doctors said I might be brain damaged, our relationship shifted for me. I could finally see that Ned had a deep commitment. By spring, he had moved in with me. Over Fourth of July weekend, he asked me to marry him. "When?" I asked. "How about tomorrow?" he said. We settled on Friday. I bought a Laura Ashley dress and took a half day off work. With two witnesses, we got married at the courthouse. The ceremony was short, but it was solemn and it was the real thing. The go-or-stay conversation was over for good.

The next day, Ned started talking about "little Neddie." I got my IUD removed and we got on the baby-or-no-baby merry-go-round. After a few months of that, I'd gone to see Linda. I had scoffed at her question about whether Ned wanted the baby. It had seemed he was the one pushing it! But then Ned did the week-long Intensive Training, and by the time he returned, he knew he didn't want another baby after all. So, we suspended our efforts and found a house together, instead.

The next five years were challenging and full of change: making our relationship work better, figuring out step-parenting issues, raising my girls, building careers, and travel. And what I'd learned about "having" a mind instead of "being" my mind was gradually helping me take control of my thoughts. I started to canoe the raging river of life sometimes remembering to point my boat into the current and let it push me downstream. Still, like an unwise paddler, I would forget and fight the current, getting my canoe swamped from time to time. I was learning from my mistakes though, and with each new awareness, my canoe ride through life began to feel more and more like an exhilarating white water ride.

15 - Profound Relationships

Life sloshed along, and in the summer of 1988, I decided to review the two weekend basic human potential training I'd done eight years before, one last time, specifically to see if I might learn something there to help me find my daughter. It had been four long, silent years since I'd sent my information to the reunion registries. I'd had a chance to meet with two other birthmothers over lunch, once. They were nice respectable people—one a lawyer, one an airline stewardess—hardly the three-headed monsters I'd somehow imagined. But they didn't seem ready to search yet, so I went back to my solitary vigil. For a year, I'd run a "reunion wanted" ad in *People Finder's* magazine. But my only reply was a vast, deep silence. What else could I do now? My dream of meeting my daughter in July of 1990 was starting to fade.

Nearly two hundred truth-seekers met in a large hotel ballroom that third Sunday in June. It didn't matter that it was hot and sunny outside. We would be freezing under florescent lights all weekend. We sat in seven neat rows of straight-backed chairs, twenty-eight across. The room was carpeted in red and hung with fake crystal chandeliers. We were surrounded on three sides by glass mirror walls. Our trainer strode back and forth across a low wooden platform at the front of the room, droning on and on. It was Father's Day, and he was in the midst of a long, boring lecture about fathers and family relationships, when one young man stood and made a claim that sounded perfectly logical to me.

"I don't *have* a relationship with *my* father," he asserted. "My father abandoned me at birth. I don't even know who he is!"

The trainer suddenly stood still. He turned to face us and pointed directly at the young man. "Oh yes, you do!" his voice boomed. The veins on his neck stood out in bold relief. "Oh *yes*, you *do!*" he repeated with intensity. "You have a *profound* relationship with your father." He paused and dropped his hand to his side. By now, everyone's mind chatter had stopped cold. "Even though you've never seen him—even though you've never talked to him—you most certainly *do* have a relationship with him!" He said it slowly, letting every word twist into our guts.

I held my breath, waiting for him to speak again. At last he did. Now, his words rolled out on a soft, safe carpet of tenderness. "Look at the effect that father of yours has had on your life. Pretty profound, wouldn't you say?"

I turned my head to look at the young man standing. Shaking with emotion, he nodded his bowed head and sank to his seat.

The trainer launched back into his lecture, but time had frozen for me. "Oh yes, you do!" was still ringing in my ears. If that was true for this young man, what about *my* relationship with the child *I* had abandoned at birth? All these years I'd been telling myself we had *no* relationship. Suddenly, it looked like the most important relationship of my entire life!

My eyes stared off into space while a picture formed in my mind. My little, dark-haired beauty had been my guiding light, indeed. Later, the trainer asked us each to write a letter to someone we'd never acknowledged about how important they'd been in our life. I wrote to Jennifer, of course. Because of her, so many good things had happened: I'd reconciled with my father; I'd gotten the counseling I needed then, and there was so much more. She'd given meaning and purpose to my work publishing family histories for thirteen years now, and she'd motivated me to keep working on myself—to keep trying to understand myself better, heal myself. I had to do this because, more than anything, when we did meet, I wanted her to be proud of her mother.

When I finished my letter, I closed my eyes and expanded my chest all the way out. I knew, now, that I loved her with all my heart. And I also knew that nothing could break our souls' connection.

I couldn't wait to meet her, if only to try to give her back something half as valuable as what she'd already given me. I vowed to stop waiting for her to find me. I'd start an active search for her myself. And more. I'd make another promise: to tell her how much she meant to me by her 24th birthday, March 30, 1990.

But starting my search was easier said than done. All my long-suppressed fears attacked me like boogie-men. Would finding her disturb her life or harm her in any way? Would she hate me? What would her parents say? There were so many frightening unknowns and no answers to be had. After five months of immobility, I went back to see Linda, the astrologer. She'd given me an answer before when none existed in conventional reality. Maybe—just maybe—she could help me again.

It was November, 1988. She had relocated since my first visit six years before. Her office and home were now downtown in an elegant 1860's townhouse. She looked different, too. She came down the narrow hallway smartly dressed and 100 pounds lighter. I could hardly recognize her body, but her steady voice and penetrating gaze were exactly the same.

She greeted me with a hug and invited me back to her office. A large bay window behind her desk overlooked a small walled city garden. I took a seat on the comfortable couch with big loose pillows. Opposite me was an ornate fireplace, flanked by bookcases filled with metaphysical books and a glass coffee table. Linda pushed the door closed and settled herself nearby, in an old-fashioned upholstered high-backed chair that I recognized from my prior visit.

She studied my face and asked, "So, how have you been, Ann? It's been a long time. What brings you here today?"

I got to the point immediately. "I have a new problem I want to discuss with you, Linda. It concerns a child I surrendered for adoption back in 1966." I watched her face carefully. Her eyes closed briefly, registering my unspoken pain, but she didn't flinch in disapproval. She had passed my test.

"I'm thinking about beginning to search for her." I paused and looked down.

"How would you *do* that?" She uncrossed her legs and leaned forward.

I told her briefly about the steps I'd taken with the registries and about my lack of results. "I'm not sure what else to do, but I have to do something." My shoulders slumped, and I sat looking at my lap for a long while. I had never admitted it before, but I may have hit an impenetrable wall.

"This is something you feel very deeply about, isn't it, Ann?"

A wave of sadness rolled over me. "I'm really incomplete about this, Linda. Everybody thinks I'm lucky—and I am. I have a wonderful second marriage, two great kids, and a job I love—but—I don't know—the better my life is, the worse I feel about this mess."

"It doesn't match the rest of the picture, eh?"

114

"Something." I shook my head. "I realized a few months ago that I can't just wait around forever for her to find me. She might be in trouble, or something. She's my *daughter*. I love her. I have to know if she's okay."

"So what can *I* do for you?"

"Well, I'm scared—mostly about whether the timing is right for me to do my search now—or whether I should wait. I have to get this *right*. I can't mess it up, because I'll only get one chance.

"Also, I'd feel more comfortable about searching if I could know something about what her reaction to me might be—what kind of a person is she—stuff like that. I have a zillion questions, but you're the only person I could think of that might be able to give me some answers."

Linda bowed her head in concentration, absorbing the enormity of my problem. Meanwhile, I reached down beside me, touching the smooth brown leather of my briefcase, feeling for the piece of paper I'd slid into the outside pocket earlier. "I have her birth chart," I announced. I had sent for it through the mail last year.

With pride, I held it out toward Linda. It wavered between us—a map of her soul's path. Linda looked the chart over carefully, then ran her finger across it from top to bottom. "Uranus opposing Saturn is the cosmic seal for adoption, you know," she said, looking up at me.

"You mean her soul wanted her adoption?" My eyes expanded in astonishment.

"Yes, it did," came Linda's calm reply.

"My God, I always thought I'd committed a terrible sin when I gave her up! You mean that's the way things were *supposed* to be?" I asked with breathless surprise.

"It's what her soul wanted for her, Ann," Linda said, looking up at me. "It was her plan for this lifetime. You see, there's an important lesson that being adopted will allow her to learn. See this North Node in Taurus? She needs to find her center, deep contentment, find out who she really is. That's her soul mission in this lifetime. What better way to learn to value identity and stability than to be born without?"

"Oh," I choked out. This changed everything I'd ever thought.

All that guilt I'd laid on myself . . . all those rules I'd made up about the way things should have been . . . all those years of torture and self-blame . . . had it all been needless?

I lowered my head to stop the spinning feeling. A face flashed before me—another guilty soul in pain—a young woman, Kathy, whom I'd met during the human potential workshop last June.

"Linda—what about women who have abortions?" I asked. "Do their babies choose to be aborted?"

Before I could hear Linda's answer, Kathy's smooth face came back before me. I could see her at our workshop, in the hallway next to me, speaking softly, not wanting to be overheard.

"I got pregnant out of wedlock, too, three years ago," she murmured, ". . . only I aborted my child." At that, Kathy burst into tears. I reached over to hold her and mourn her loss with her. "I wish I'd been as brave as you," she finally managed to choke out in a small voice.

"What do you mean?" I pulled back, bewildered, to study her contorted face.

"I mean I wish I'd had the courage to have my baby, like you did." She sighed deeply. "I was too scared. I wish I'd been brave. I've regretted the abortion more than you can know." She stopped speaking—shook her head.

"Of course you were scared," I reassured her. "I was scared, too, far too scared to keep my child. All these years, I've been ashamed of getting pregnant, ashamed of hurting my baby by giving her away."

"I know." Kathy looked up at me and we both swelled with deep sadness. "I was a student . . . I couldn't face telling my parents." The space around us buzzed with the buried memories we shared. "But at least, you have something to show for your choice," she added, breaking away, crying again.

I touched her on the shoulder. "Now, now. I know you did what you thought was best at the time."

"I know." She sighed. Then her head snapped up. "But you have something to look forward to. You have a live child out there somewhere. You have a chance to reconnect, be whole again." She paused, then bitterly squeezed it out: "I have nothing but a dead baby."

"But you can claim wholeness for yourself, too," I reminded her, putting my hand on her shoulder. "You have a relationship with the child you aborted, the same way I have a relationship with the child I abandoned. Your child has taught you valuable lessons the same way my child has taught me." There was no difference there. "Why don't you write your child a letter, like I did to mine. Tell him how important he's been in your life and what a wonderful contribution he's made to you. Pour out your regret and your love for him, the same as I did."

Kathy's eyes reddened again and looked deeply into mine. "Maybe I'll do that someday," she said softly, "but I'm not ready yet."

"But why not do it now?" I asked gently.

But she turned and walked away, awash in fresh tears. "You'll be okay," I called after her. I stood there, watching her blend into the throng of people, the raw edges of her grief still showing in the way she slowly meandered down the hall. . . .

My head jerked when Linda's voice interrupted my revery. "Souls choose to be aborted, to die young, to be born retarded, and deformed," she said.

The door creaked open. Linda's shaggy little Shih Tzu, Ti, nudged his way into the room. He scrambled up on the chair beside her and nuzzled down while the tangled wreckage of human life twisted in anguish before me. Linda got up and closed the door.

"But why, Linda? How can that be right?"

"Some souls need lessons like that," she continued, retaking her seat, stroking the dog. "It's their karma." She leaned forward and looked into my eyes then. "If a person has taken his own life, wouldn't it make sense for his soul to be aborted in his next incarnation so he can learn the value of life? Everything happens so souls can learn what they need to know."

"Ah, yes. We talked about that last time."

I nodded, remembering well what she'd said before about how our souls choose the circumstances of birth. "We think we know everything when we talk about genes and DNA, eh?" I smirked, looking away. "Okay, I'm going to stop beating myself up for giving my baby away right now." I closed my eyes, and in the dark space behind my eyelids, I absolved myself. A weight floated away.

"Thanks. That was certainly worth far more than your fee today, Linda!" I reported, opening my eyes and smiling at her. Then my gaze dropped onto Linda's snoozing dog.

I had to ask her one more question. "Before we run out of time, Linda, tell me something else about my daughter. What kind of a person is she?"

"According to this chart, she could be somewhat mysterious and exotic-looking—secretive even. She may have had a hard time of it growing up. It looks like she's very bright and talented in the work place."

"Do you think she'll be open to knowing me, Linda?" I had to ask, even though I was afraid to hear the answer.

"Yes," she replied without hesitation. "She has a Moon in Cancer. That will make her very sensitive to her mother."

"What do you think would have happened if I *had* kept her as a baby, Linda?" I couldn't resist asking.

"Let's see." She compared Jennifer's chart with the one on file for me. "I would say it would have been tough for the two of you to have been together when she was a baby. See this," she said, pointing to my eighth house. "Her Sun's in Aries, and Aries ruling here indicates you may have been an abusive mother for her early in life. It looks clear now, though."

"Linda," I confessed, "that's the very reason I didn't keep her! I was afraid I'd abuse her."

"That could be past life stuff," she commented, without censure. "You could have been abused yourself as a child in a past life and come back now as an abuser. That's over for you now, though."

She paused to let me absorb what she'd said. Then she looked down at her watch and lifted herself out of the chair. The dog jumped down and stood, panting, at her side. "Your fifth house, the house of children, is in Capricorn," she said. "That could mean your search will be difficult and that exact timing will be important." She handed me back my charts. "How do you plan to go about finding her?" she asked again.

I rose, clutching my briefcase, and stuffed the charts back in. "I have no idea," I replied blankly.

Linda invited me to join a beginning astrology class she would be starting in January. I accepted eagerly. I had a funny feeling that, to find my daughter, I was going to need all the resources I could lay my hands on: material, spiritual, and otherwise!

16 - A Figure in the Mist

The Meyerhoff Symphony Hall has always reminded me of a chambered nautilus. The outside is smooth and round, while the inside writhes with stairways, outer hallways and inner hallways, each leading to a different section of the hall, each sealed off with a heavy oak door. I scampered up two flights of stairs one Thursday evening in early March and headed down the hallway to the door marked "Box B." Pulling the heavy door open, I stepped into a tiny space, just big enough for three chairs.

When I looked out, I could see people streaming down the aisles below, while others poured into the two silver-railed balconies that protruded from the back of the hall. Suspended along the sides of the hall, a double layer of sculpted white boxes plunged downward like ship prows, ready to encounter rolling waves of sound. For a while, I watched the red seats steadily disappear, and then I closed my eyes. The murmur of pre-concert chatter sounded like the patter of gentle rain.

My thoughts turned inward. Jennifer's 23rd birthday was only three weeks away. One year left to keep my promise, and what did I have to show for it? An empty notebook. Well, not quite empty, but it might as well be.

Shortly after my visit to Linda last November, I'd read a book about adoption search. It suggested setting up a "search notebook." I could do that! No one would know what it was for. My heart beating swiftly, I went to the drug store picked out a bright blue, three-ring binder and three pocket dividers. A green one for "correspondence with the agency," a blue one for "correspondence for records," and a yellow one for "documents" . . . so shiny and new . . . so empty. When I looked at them my stomach sank. *I must have something I can put in this notebook after all these years.*

My head was buzzing, so I stilled my breath and waited for an answer. *Yes, I do! Downstairs. My letters.*

That sent me dashing for the cellar doorway. I flipped on the light switch and clattered down the open wooden stairs, brushing past Christmas decorations, wicker Easter baskets with pink plastic straw, orange plastic jack-o-lanterns—past green sleeping bags, rolled and stowed—to the gray cardboard files. I tugged open a drawer. There, in the brown plastic folder . . . pull it out, thumb through the marriage certificates, wills, car and house deeds . . . and neatly folded at the bottom were my letters to the agency, and, too, the ones I'd penned to Jennifer Lynn, including the one from the training last summer. I took them out, closed my eyes and blessed the day I'd kept them.

First, I unfolded my letters to the agency, those carefully qualified requests. (I knew my thinking then: maybe if they know how grateful I am, they'll like me and be nice to me.) I winced.

Then I fondled the other letters, penned with a cramped hand, addressed to "My Dearest Daughter" or "Dearest Jennifer." I sighed with satisfaction to think I'd kept them all these years. The only thing I hadn't kept was Claude's full name and address. Damn!

My knees were cementing into cramps. I put my letters to Jennifer back and grabbed the others. Shoving the file drawer closed, I stood and dashed up the steps. Upstairs, I arranged them by date and proudly tucked them in the pocket labeled "Correspondence with Agency." *Well, at least now I have something!* I gloated.

What else could I do?

"Birthparents may request non-identifying information about the adoptive parents from the adoption agency," I read in my search book later that afternoon. There were eighteen questions I could ask without breaching confidentiality. "What was the adoptive father's hair color?" for instance. "Did they own their own home? Did they have other children at the time of the adoption?" I composed a letter, polite but assertive. It came to three typed, double-spaced pages. After each question, I left a space for their reply. I sealed it with a prayer and sent it off in the next morning's mail.

But I received no answer.

So, four weeks later, I sent a follow-up letter. But another month passed without an answer.

Then, I began calling—and calling. But the social worker I needed to speak with was never available. And she never returned my calls.

They stonewalled me for three whole months. Was it a conspiracy? Ignore the birthmother, wear her down; the poor, defeated, guilt-ridden thing will give up eventually. Even now when I thought about it, my chest heaved in anger. Two weeks ago, I'd fired off an indignant letter to the director of the agency. Finally, last week, I'd received a brief reply: "We decline to answer any of your questions or give you any further information about the adoption." It made me feel like screaming. All that time wasted—just to reach a dead end!

I blinked my eyes open and sighed in frustration.

So, where does that leave me? If I'm supposed to contact her by her twenty-fourth birthday (next March) *and meet her four months later* (July, 1990) . . . *that gives me exactly twelve months and three weeks. And I have yet to unearth a single clue.* I rubbed my face and shook my head.

What now? Go to some Pennsylvania courthouse and check long lists of adoptions? My eyes shot wildly across the concert hall. *I don't have time for that. There has to be an easier way.* I looked down at my fidgeting hands and tried to stop my thoughts from spinning. Finally, after a long, slow breath, I let my vision blur and drew deep within myself. *What in the world can I do to get this started?* I asked the Universe.

The house lights were dimming; the orchestra's tuning ritual began. And, suddenly, an idea flashed in my mind: "They're playing Mahler's First Symphony tonight. Mahler always speaks of deeper mysteries. Maybe I can find something there to help me with my search."

Get real, I chastised myself.

But then my higher self argued back, *I know it sounds ridiculous, but it's a small, easy thing that can be done right now. What harm can come of trying?*

The conductor entered and bowed as polite applause rippled through the auditorium. In that moment when the air was cleansed of talk and shuffling, I closed my eyes and prayed. "Let me hear something tonight that will help me find my daughter." When I released my intention and opened my eyes, the conductor's arms were hovering over the orchestra. He was conjuring up dense fog and mystery.

Out of a mist of violin tremolos, musical figures flit—quick—hardly glimpsed. A spot of fog clears and a ghostly figure beckons. My imagination is guided, surprised, into a delightful sunlit meadow. The cellos lead me there—to where animals gambol in a spring-time, flower-filled field.

But then the wall of mystery shimmers in front of me again, and a ghostly figure quakes behind a veil of tremolo. What can it mean?

Horns call; flutes and a solo cello answer. Then I'm back in the meadow. But it's late afternoon now, and dark clouds are filling the horizon until they're blasted away by an earsplitting burst of trumpets and horns. When the meadow reappears, it's painted with heavier brush strokes, more intense colors. And finally, hard, throbbing, life-filled summer stampedes the movement to an end where the dust of life still hangs in the air.

Now the mood changes, the music goes raucously off balance. In my mind's eye, a youthful, drunken buffoon staggers onto the stage. Tipsy, he weaves and circles, until a waltz shoves him behind the curtains. Next, onto the stage sweep perfumed ladies in beaded gowns, escorted by leering gents with black, slicked-down hair. The couples glide flawlessly across the polished wood floor. The room's mirrored walls reflect the light that sparkles out of crystal chandeliers.

Back comes the stumbling buffoon theme. He still reels, but he's old, now, and wears a spotted clown suit, tall hat and funny shoes. Again, he does his off-balance dance and twirls us to a dizzy end.

Low instruments begin the Third Movement with a "Frere Jacques" theme. The round tune plods in a circle, one phrase behind the other, eyes down, like a donkey grinding corn, around and around. High woodwinds impose, on top, a lighter countertheme. All is steeped in mystery by the constant, soft beating of a kettle drum. A second theme emerges, lyrically, sadly spun in minor by the oboe and violins. Now I hear the "Frere Jacques" theme return—faster, higher this time. Then, the trumpets bring in a Slavic countertheme. A zany march idea tries to intrude, too, but is pushed aside by the plodding "Frere Jacques" theme again and the steady beating of the timpani . . . fading.

Suddenly—Cataclysm! Gongs, trumpets, violin glissandi, horn fanfares, and the heavens open. A triumphant march begins now, led by brass and reinforced by strings—punctuated with cymbals. It struts along boldly, and then suddenly sinks into mystery—out of which, twisting its way in and out of the mist, a mirage forms: I see a figure. It quivers . . . motions for someone to grasp its hand. The violins reach out and take hold. Instantly, they seem infused with deep-throated Wisdom. The music they saw into my heart is round and warm.

The figure fades back into mystery. Trumpets and cataclysm return—surging urges of sound. Confusion. Anguish. Not knowing. Pain. . . .

When the march returns again, it's a confident parade of universal truth and love. It slips in, high and quiet at first, then steps forward with strings, winds and brass all joining in an orgasmic statement of God, Life, Love, Light—All Triumph! They blaze unmistakably in our clear view.

But the veil of uncertainty drops yet again, and the march theme becomes shrouded in flute mystery. Snaking through the fog, a convoluted figure slithers near, and, like a distant memory, I hear the sunlit meadow theme recalled. Everything hovers on hold. Through the veil, something shows itself again, like a ghost . . . before drawing back into the shadows.

From this fragmented nothingness, the ultimate march of truth and love returns. Its way is sure now . . . light-footed and joyful. Triumph is at hand. Trumpet fanfares overtake the march and broaden it. Clear, steady, open-eyed tones ring out. Then, with cymbal bursts and timpani rolls underscoring all, I see truth and love standing in full sun. I watch in awe as they are borne heavenward and, with brass fanfare shaking the hall, begin merging into the Light.

I stood and clapped my hands together. My body was shaking. *There was a message: "Have faith; gain triumph." What did that mean? That what we want is always there, but we can't see it because of our confusion? That faith is the blade that can slash the veil that separates us from our beloved?*

I stared blankly into space while the hall emptied.

So, did that mean my daughter was out there somewhere and I simply had to let Faith guide me through my confusion? Was it saying the way might be illusive, but I'd find her sooner or later if I believed? I shook my head and stared blankly at the floor for a moment before hoisting my coat to my shoulders.

Suddenly, two ideas connected in my mind.

Just last week, in Linda's class, we'd discussed Jung's idea of the "collective unconscious," the One Mind into which we think and through which we "know." It's the medium of dreams and, too, it's used to pass subconscious messages (like when someone calls you on the phone and you already know who's there).

What if I project my thoughts into the collective unconscious? I began asking myself. *If my daughter's thinking about me, she might receive my message!*

As the plan slowly took shape in my mind, I shivered with glee.

Her birthday's soon. I know she'll be thinking about me then. I don't need the adoption agency! I'll find her myself by using the collective unconscious! I'll bombard her with mental messages to "come find me." My search will be over in no time!

So, I began sending mental messages that very night. I sent them several times each day—in the morning when I first woke up, during the day, and before falling asleep. "I'm thinking of you. I love you. Come find me," I broadcast that message over and over again.

And incredible as it may seem, exactly fifteen days later, I received a phone call that changed my life forever.

Part III

The Quest

You gain strength, courage and confidence by every experience in which you really stop to look fear in the eye. You must do the thing you cannot do.

— ELEANOR ROOSEVELT

17 - Call to Action

Our receptionist's voice floated through the intercom. "Ann, it's a collect call from your daughter, Jennifer."

From my daughter, Jennifer, did she say?

My eyes drifted away from the computer screen to a blank space on the wall above my filing cabinets. My mind groped while the buzz of background noise blended with the dim images of nearby objects: piles of manuscripts; a parchment map of the Chesapeake Bay, printed with dark brown ink; the green glossiness of philodendron leaves. On a piece of plaster molding near the corner of my office, a white vine climbed up my light yellow wall.

". . . from my DAUGHTER? JENNIFER?"

My eyes shot to the phone, and I seized the receiver. "Oh, YES, Alice, YES!" I gasped. "I'll accept!"

My heart was racing by the time the smooth, cold plastic of the phone bumped against my ear and chin "Hello?" I said. "Hello? This is Ann Hughes. . . ." I held my breath, and the world stood still.

At last, a faint voice drifted through the receiver. It was a mere wisp. "Hello? I think I might be your daughter, Jennifer."

A throaty, primal sound escaped my lips. "Oh—Oh!" I cried out, and a huge knot, buried in my heart, released. My head spun; my lungs contracted. "I've been waiting so long for this moment," I choked out with half a voice. "Jennifer, I've been *calling* to you these last two weeks. It will be your birthday next week. Did you *hear* me calling you?" I started shivering; tears were trickling down my face. "I've thought of you every year at your birthday. Did you ever think of me?" I fumbled for a tissue and hastily dabbed my eyes.

"Yes. Oh, yes!" She opened like a flower. "I think of you all the time. Thank you so much for giving me life. I've had a good life, and I've always wanted to thank you for not aborting me."

My breathing halted. My face turned white. *All those years, I thought she'd curse me. Instead, she's forgiving me? She's blessing me?* I reeled; I choked on tears. And then, a heavy weight lifted from me. I could almost see it floating away.

It was a little while before the room stopped spinning. "Thank you for telling me that," I managed to say at last.

"I've thought about you at every birthday, too," she continued happily. "Every year I find a special present for you. I keep all the presents in a box in my room. When I was younger, I'd find a feather or a special stone. Now, I add poems, prayers, a lock of hair."

I smiled. "That's so beautiful. You're so sweet to have done that!" With each new thought she shared, my chest was expanding. I could feel it starting to glow with a warm, inner light. "God has surely blessed me. Oh Jennifer!"

Now I cleansed myself by drawing a deep breath. My whole body was tingling with joy. "Jennifer, I've waited so very long to hear your voice. Oh, I'm *very, very* happy you called me! Almost twenty-three years. Such a long time to wait." I breathed again, rinsing away still more tension; then, shifted forward in my chair, arched my back and slowly rotated my shoulders. "I want to know all about you. But first . . . give me your name, address, and phone number in case we get cut off!"

I slid my note pad in front of me and picked up my pen. There was a sickening pause on the other end of the line. "I . . . I can't give you my address," she stuttered at last.

"Oh, well, that's okay," I retreated. *Easy, Ann*, I told myself. *She sounds frightened. Careful now!*

I softened my voice to a gentle plea. "How about a—a—phone number. Can you just give me your phone number—in case we get cut off?"

"Well, I guess I can. . . ."

I jotted down the number she gave me. It began with the area code of my hometown! My eyes stretched wide open, but I kept my voice calm. "Oh, thanks. And, can you tell me your name, please? I've been longing to know your name."

"My name is Mary Anne," she said, softly.

"And your last name?" I coaxed.

"Well, it's—it's Holly," she said at last.

"Mary Anne Holly. What a pretty name! Someone must have loved you a lot to give you that beautiful name. Oh, thanks for telling me that, Mary Anne. Thank you so much! You don't know how long I've wondered what your name would be. It's so good to know at last."

Gradually, the energy was beginning to flow between us again. I gave a silent sigh of relief. *She's very timid,* I told myself. *If you want this to work, take it slow and easy.* I thought of a "safe" question to ask her next.

"Well, what else would you like to tell me about yourself?"

"Um, I can tell you what I look like," she said, brightening.

"Oh, yes, I'd like that."

"Well, I have long blond hair and hazel eyes and I'm about five-seven."

"Wow! You sound beautiful," I said. But a warning flag went up: how in the world had she turned out blond? "Let's check your birth date and place," I said.

The information she gave me was correct.

"Where did you find my name?" I ventured next.

"In an old issue of *People Finders* magazine," she replied.

I lifted my eyes and stared at the philodendron leaves, layered, one over the other. "Oh, yes, I remember! I ran an ad in there a couple of years ago." My body started to tingle again. "God, I can't believe this is happening." I breathed in slowly through my nose to allow the miracle sink in before continuing. "So what are you doing with yourself these days, Mary Anne?" The thrill of saying her name made me prickle with pleasure.

"Well, I graduated last year from Valley University," she volunteered.

A wave of wonder washed over me. "From Valley University? That's where *I* went to college! What a crazy coincidence!"

"Gosh, it really is!" she giggled.

"And do you still live in that area?" I asked, already knowing the answer.

"Yes." Her voice expanded again. "After I graduated, I got a job on campus taking care of young children. My major was social work. And I do volunteer work, too, with abused women."

I told her about my connection with the town and that my mother and my brother Fred still lived there, and that both of them knew about her. Then I asked where she was raised.

"Oh, back where I was born. My dad teaches college there."

"Are you musical?" I asked as another little test.

130

"Oh, yes." She spoke with a lilt. "I played the flute in high school."

"The flute?" A warm glow spread through my body. "That's what *I* always wanted to play. But my parents wouldn't let me. They thought the breathing would be too hard on my heart. I had to play clarinet, instead."

I told her that our whole family was musical. Then we chatted on about this and that for thirty minutes or more. Eventually, I asked her what the agency had told her about me. It didn't match what I remembered telling them . . . but, I told myself, they'd probably lied to her. "Well, maybe I'm someone else's daughter," she ventured at one point, but we both giggled at that. Finally, I tried again to get her address.

"Mary Anne, I'd really like to write to you, to send you some pictures. Are you comfortable enough yet to give me your address?" I asked it gently.

There was a long pause. . . .

"Mary Anne—Mary Anne . . ." I called out.

Then the line went dead.

No! No!, my heart screamed. My inner cry dropped down a long, dark tunnel and shot straight through my soul. Love and anguish froze into vapor as the vibrations died away.

Then, as usual, my mind took over.

My hand scrambled for the note pad and my finger punched out the numbers she'd given me. It was ringing. *Come on, Mary Anne. Answer it!* I prayed. But the phone just rang and rang. *Maybe I misdialed*, I told myself. *Quick. Hang up. Dial again.* I selected each number, one by one. Again it rang . . . and rang . . . time after hopeless time.

I surrendered the receiver to its cradle. *Damn! I got it right that time! Why won't she answer?*

Or could it be something else?

I ticked off a list: I could have written down the wrong number. (Logical explanation, but I was sure I had been careful.) This could be the right number but she's not answering. (She could just be scared right now. I can try again later.) She could have *given* me the wrong number. . . .

The possibilities rolled around in my mind. . . . Then I jerked my head to the left, eyes flaring: *maybe she gave me the wrong number, and we DIDN'T get disconnected. Maybe she hung up on me!*

My breathing grew tight. I could feel my trust in Mary Anne steaming away. I put my head down and massaged my temples. I couldn't let go of hope just yet.

Well, maybe she'll call back . . . if not now, maybe later.

Then I dialed the regional operator. "Do you have a listing for a Mary Anne Holly," I asked in a tight voice.

"No one by that name," came her reply.

I slammed down the phone, jumped up, and paced past a round-backed wooden chair that sat beside my desk. I turned toward the French window that framed my philodendron and gazed out. The traffic light was changing. I watched while northbound traffic screeched to a stop and eastbound traffic scooted across the intersection onto the expressway ramp. A dull red car with a rusty spot on its side careened around the corner and headed north just as the light changed back.

You blew it! Scared her away! Why did you have to go and ask her for that address again? Dummy! You were too damn pushy! Are you ever going to learn not to be a pushy bitch? You threw away your one golden chance here. How are you going to get another one? Huh? Serves you right for not letting her go at her own pace.

I sighed. Gradually, a space cleared in my mind. I turned and walked back to my desk while a benevolent part of me made a suggestion. *Write down all the clues she gave you before you forget them.*

A few minutes later, I was holding a long list. I filled my lungs with air and let it out slowly. Something clicked inside. *She'd called me collect.*

I expanded my chest again, and when I released my breath this time, the tension whooshed out. She wanted me to find her. She'd left me a trail. Besides, my brother Fred lived near her and had worked as a people-tracer, not long ago. He'd help me find her. It was just a question of time.

I stacked my unanswered correspondence into neat piles and logged out of my computer; then I stood up and flipped the switch. The dull buzzing sound fell silent. I shuffled over to the corner near the laser printer, where I keep my coat and briefcase.

My life had been rolling down a smooth, paved road before 3:00 that afternoon. But now, it had slammed to a stop before a gaping hole. I was staring straight into the raging flood of my grief. Years ago, I'd learned how to ignore it. Except on her birthday . . . and holidays . . . or times I passed a dark-haired child on the street. It was such a fearful place, so thick with secrecy and shame it could sweep you away. But now, that torrent of grief and unexpressed love was welling up all around me. *I had to find my daughter,* or drown.

I struggled into my coat, slung my briefcase over my right shoulder, and headed for the front office. "Alice, I'm going home early," I announced, keeping my upper lip stiff and my eyes averted. I pulled open the heavy outside door. As it banged shut behind me, I bounced down the marble steps and angled over towards St. Paul Street, heading south for Mount Vernon Park.

It was crisp, late March, and new white buds were bursting open on the flowering pear trees that lined the street. I walked three blocks under a fairy canopy of delicate white flowers, inhaling the aroma of new life. Then I turned up a steep cobblestone street, past a row of large brownstones on the right and an arm of the park on the left. The towering trees, still leafless, did not yet block the sunlight. Park fountains stood empty, benches unoccupied.

I hurried past them all to the middle of the park and then turned north. Ahead, in a raised flower bed as big as a room, was the sight I'd come to see: a legion of golden daffodils standing at attention, in full, erect bloom. The air around them throbbed with proud yellow.

I plopped on a nearby bench to absorb the beams of color, while my soul feasted again on the memory of Mary Anne's call: the tingling ecstasy of a dream fulfilled . . . her soothing words of forgiveness. I remembered our connection . . . how our souls had touched and vibrated with love. However briefly, I'd sipped the joy of completion with Mary Anne, and its taste was sweet. Her call was a priceless gift. And no matter what the outcome, I would always be in her debt.

I squeezed my eyes tightly shut in a promise to myself: *I will find Mary Anne. No matter why we were disconnected, no matter whether she's my daughter or not—I'll befriend her. Perhaps I can help heal her like she helped heal me today.*

Little did I know what an arduous task I was setting for myself that unforgettable day.

18 - Detective Work

My car motor hummed along steadily in the pre-dawn stillness. Nippy air seeped in through two inches of open window, carrying with it the trill of bird songs. In the eastern sky, the sun was rising, red. It shimmered behind a steamy veil of clouds like a half-remembered dream. Ever upward it inched, into a pale pinkish-yellow sky. Low-lying bands of blue clouds seemed, for a moment, to strap it to the horizon. But then, it slid free and ascended, solid and orange, into a clear patch of sky.

Eight days had passed since the call from Mary Anne. Like the horizon, my mind was clouded with confusion. Could I emerge some day, confident and glowing, like the sun now hanging in the eastern sky? At the moment, it seemed impossible.

Voices from sleeptime were still arguing in my head: "You have no right to intrude. You signed away your right to know," the angry voice carped. "But she sought you out. She's frightened. She needs you. Go to her," the gentle voice urged. "You do this for love. Nothing is bad if you do it for love."

A car whooshed by and then something beside me rustled. It was Renate, my youngest, nuzzling her head a little farther into the pillow she'd wedged next to the window. Her golden red hair framed a fine-featured face. China smooth skin stretched over her delicate, freckled nose, sweeping eyebrows and small chin. Sixteen and a junior in high school, already. We'd spent the last few days traveling, shopping for colleges. Her lips parted and closed, then she twisted her head again and settled back into a deep sleep.

She and Ned had been so supportive the night I'd rushed home with news of Mary Anne's call. I'd called brother Fred, too, of course, and had even dashed off a short letter to the adoption agency asking them if Mary Anne Holly was my daughter. (They might or might not reply, but it was worth a try.)

In the days that followed, Fred had checked for Mary Anne's driver's license and combed the alumni records office, but, so far, he'd come up empty-handed. She must have lied about her last name. Undeterred, we'd devised another plan.

A little after 10:00 a.m., I pulled into the parking lot near a recently constructed three-story red, brick building, the site of the abused women's center, where I thought Mary Anne might be a volunteer. When I switched off the motor, the whooshing silence sent shivers of fear through me. *Was this illegal? What if we didn't find her? What if we did?*

Renate stretched her slender arms. "Are we there yet?" she asked, spreading a yawn all over her face. Her watery eyes blinked shut before I could answer "yes." She groped near her feet for her leather purse and rummaged through it for her brush. Soon her glossy hair was crackling to brisk, downward strokes.

I scanned the parking lot nervously. "Fred should be here somewhere," I mumbled. The sky had clouded over and a chill breeze rattled the budding trees that guarded the building in front of us.

Then I heard a vehicle door creak open behind us. A tall, broad, young man with a dark beard and mustache stepped out of a green pick-up truck. He had my dad's narrow shoulders and concave chest. He slammed the truck door and began walking our way, while Renate and I scrambled out to meet him.

He extended his arms over his prominent belly and enfolded us both. "How ya guys doing?" My head only reached to his chest. I buried it in the warmth of his vest and inhaled the sweetness of hemlock and wood fire. *It feels safe here. Can he protect me? Keep me from failing?*

Then I pulled back, shivering. I spoke in a low tone, forcing the words out over a lump in my throat. "Just how is this going to work, Fred?" I stared out over the parking lot, turning my face so he couldn't see my tears.

Fred slipped a hand on my shoulder and gave it a squeeze. "No problem. Just bring Renate and follow me," he said, starting towards the building.

Stop this mind chatter. He's a pro at this. Relax and leave it to him, I lectured myself. The breeze combed through my hair as I scampered across the macadam after him and Renate.

When we reached the building, Freddie pulled open the glass and steel door. We checked over the list of tenants, printed just inside on the left; then we summoned the stainless steel elevator and rode it to the third floor. Less than a minute later, the door slid open in a single, smooth stroke and the three of us stepped into a fluorescent-lit hallway, carpeted in gray.

The guard jerked his head up from his book and squinted at us. His jaw tightened. He raised a hand to the bill of his hat, where a silver badge gleamed, before shuffling to his feet. "May I help you?"

Renate and I stood by mutely, hands at our sides, trying to look mild and pleasant. Fred stepped forward with an easy smile and did all the talking.

"Hi. Isn't it a great day? You must know my friend, Buddy Jones. He does this kind of work, too. Hey, my sister here is in town for the day and we have a problem. . . ."

About five minutes later, we reboarded the elevator. After the door slid shut and the cable was humming downwards, Fred winked and handed me a scrap of paper. It contained the address and phone number of someone named Mary Anne Bird who volunteered at the center. My heart pounded. We had a fresh lead.

As soon as we were outside, Fred told me the rest of his plan: he would go home and make some calls. If he could find this girl's driver's license, we'd have her description and birth date. Renate and I could go to the library and check college yearbooks. Then he gave me confident wink and turned to go.

I waved. "See you later." My face glowed hot with excitement, and yet my stomach felt like it had dropped 50 floors in half a second. I stood, white-faced, and stared off behind him until Renate touched my shoulder. When I looked into her clear eyes, the corners of my mouth began lifting in an uncertain smile. Then I slipped my arm around her waist and we walked back to the car in silence.

The search at the library had been fruitless, but I thought it was time to tell my mother about the call from Mary Anne. "Mom, I need to talk to you about something," I bravely began later that afternoon. But then I had to stop and swallow hard. My hands were freezing cold.

Mother shifted her green, upholstered recliner to the forward position, retracting the footstool. Her eyes darted up to search my face, and then they narrowed. Her chin tightened. I tugged at the gray, brocade rocker, where I was about to sit, pulling it around so I could look at her more directly.

A simple thing. Why is this so hard?

It felt like she was in a separate room from me. And the room was guarded by a heavy door. And the door had been sealed off for 23 years. I pulled, but the knob slipped in my hand. I tugged and heaved with all my might before the latch jerked loose and the rusty hinges slowly creaked open. Cobwebs hung inside the room; dust lay thickly on everything. Time had stood still.

You feel like a little girl in here. You're afraid the wicked old witch will get you. Pictures of the past. Shake them off!

Outside, a crow cawed twice. I glanced out the window toward one of the tall hemlock trees that towered beside Mother's A-frame vacation house. The sweet, woodsy smell of her cookstove fire saturated the room.

When I turned back to face Mother, I saw a different person from the one I'd known then. She'd suffered a lot in 23 years: my father's death, my heart trouble, her own health problems. Then, too, she no longer needed to be a "perfect mother" or "perfect wife." Her thin white hair puffed out around her strained face. She sat quite still, shoulders hunched forward like a wounded animal in hiding. *What you're going to say isn't half as bad as what she must be thinking. Spit it out!*

I swallowed hard. My heart thumped against my chest. "Mom . . ." I continued, unsteadily. "I know we haven't talked about this for many years, but I wanted you to know . . ." (I looked down at my lap and said the rest very fast) ". . . that I've been looking for the daughter I gave up for adoption." *There. It was out!* I cringed and held my breath.

Her eyes and chest expanded, and she rattled out a reply, as though she'd had it stored and ready for a very long time. "Oh, that was such a bad time for us. You and Billy were in college and Fred was still little. I had all the problems of adolescence and childhood to deal with at once. . . . I just couldn't have coped with another child."

When I heard her say that, my mouth dropped open. It was almost an apology!

"No—no, Mom. It's okay. I never wanted you to keep my baby. I think we did the best thing we knew how to at the time."

We paused, astonished with each other, our faces still tense. The first exchange had gone well. We sat for a moment, just listening to the tick of the cuckoo clock. Then I picked up with news from the present . . . the call from Mary Anne . . . how Fred and I had spent the morning.

She retreated into her chair. Her face clouded. She might feel guilty about giving the child away, but the sudden appearance of a flesh-and-blood granddaughter would pose a few problems. What about her friends and relatives, who didn't know anything about this? All that shame and disgrace! She was slipping away. How could I bring her back? I wanted her to like Mary Anne!

I leaned forward and looked into Mother's downcast eyes. "She was so sweet to me on the phone, Mom," I said, making my voice steady and mellow. "She thanked me for not aborting her. I was so touched by that. . . ." Mother looked up. When her eyes filled with tears, I knew we had reconnected.

She spoke as if from a dream. "Yes, I'm very glad we didn't do that." Grabbing a sharp breath, she added, "She does sound like a lovely person."

There was another long silence, but my blood was pumping, warming my hands once more. Three caws pierced the air.

"Well, what are you going to do now?" Mother asked carefully.

I filled her in on our plan. "And I may try to call her," I added. I got up, leaned over the green upholstered chair, and reached to hug her. "Thanks for listening, Mom. So glad we can talk about this again."

She sighed. "Yes. So am I." I let her hold me in a long embrace before I slowly pulled away.

I opened the sliding glass door and stepped out onto her wooden porch. Nearby, was a path to my parents' original cabin, where Fred now lived. I shuffled along over last year's damp, brown leaves, drawing in the sweet smell of hemlock to cleanse my system. All the while, the conversation with Mother turned over and over in my mind.

I'd never thought about *her* losses before. But it was true: she'd lost her first grandchild . . . had had to deal with the threat of social disgrace . . . alienation from me. In her view, I had betrayed her value system. In my view, she had shamed me. And we had both lost. A draw. What now? I wondered.

Fred was still on the phone when I walked in. No driver's

license. Nor had he been able to find her father teaching at a college in the area where I'd surrendered.

"Why don't you just try calling the number we got?" he urged.

I blanched. "Fred! How could I do that?"

"Well, you know what her voice sounds like, don't you?"

"Yes . . ." (How could I forget?)

"Well then, just give her a call, and if someone else answers the phone, you can hang up."

That sounded reasonable, but my hand was shaking so much I mis-dialed twice. Finally, I got it right. My heart fluttered; I held my breath, waiting to hear her soft, timid voice again. But, alas, there was no answer.

"Her birthday was two days ago. Maybe she went home for the weekend," I told Fred, dropping the receiver like a hot rock.

No more calls. I'd send a letter instead. But not right away. First, I needed to know if this person was the right Mary Anne. Maybe someone at the center could give me a description. I had to have more to go on than a name on a scrap of paper.

I had another idea, too. I'd write the agency again: "The girl who called me last week may have given me the wrong name. Is Mary Anne Bird my daughter?"

A week later, I received their reply: "Mary Anne Holly Bird is not the daughter you seek."

19 - Body Cleansing

The sweetness of early June hung in the air. Barbara's luscious, blue-rimmed white iris spread open in the sun, soaring proudly above their tall, flat, pointed leaves. I paused on her front walkway to imbibe their perfume. A creeping, purplish green ajuga with spikes of blue flowers spread between the iris. Elsewhere, random rocks set off the clumps of white-striped green hostas and regal ostrich ferns. White and pink impatiens, caladiums, coralbells and miniature pink roses splashed color everywhere. I reached up and pressed the doorbell, but my gaze lingered on the garden's pleasing harmony.

When the door opened, Barbara invited me in with a warm hug. My masseuse was a trim, muscular woman whose age was impossible to guess. I knew she'd just celebrated her fiftieth birthday, yet she could have passed for twenty-five.

"How's your search going, Ann?" she asked as I stepped inside.

I sighed and tossed my briefcase beside the little L-shaped couch tucked inside the dining room wall. "Oh, Barbara, it's not going very well."

I plopped down. My eyes wandered across the room to where an antique, carved oak sideboard stood. Barbara's current art project, a patchwork quilt-in-progress in orange, purple, pink and yellow, was draped over a dining room chair. An arrangement of cut iris from her garden, anchored in dark blue marbles in a clear glass bowl, graced the cherry diningroom table. I chuckled at her "crazy geometry" placements, patterned after the puzzles she'd been designing in her spare time. Cheerful color and beauty. Barbara's home was always full of that. It was just the oasis I needed today.

I sensed her standing close by, waiting for me to continue. "She gave me a name we can't trace, Barbara, and my phone bill hasn't come in yet," I said, still staring across the room. I finally looked up at her. "Did you know the phone company won't give you any information about your bill unless it's a police emergency? So that means my big leads are a wrong name and phone number I don't have. I had really wanted to find her before we go to Ireland in July, but I'm afraid I'm stuck for now." I turned away again and froze my face to stone.

The couch cushion bumped up as Barbara seated herself beside me. "I thought you were going to call the abused women's center."

When I looked over, her brow was creased. "Well, I did, but I didn't get much from them. They're too worried about the security of their people. Talked to the director a couple of times. She agreed to help me, but she never did. She said she'd ask around . . . but they have fifty volunteers and she's away a lot. I don't know. I guess I'll just wait for that damn phone bill." I picked at the stitching in a pillow that lay between us on the couch.

"Should be in by now, don't you think?" Barbara asked.

"Certainly *should* be. It's been over two months. I told the accounting people to let me know, but they probably forgot. I'll have to check again tomorrow."

Barbara touched my shoulder. "Boy, I really hear your frustration," she said. "What's your family have to say about all this?"

That was one place, thankfully, where there weren't any problems. My face must have brightened. "They've been great. Really supportive. Even my mother's excited, in her own quiet way."

It was time to start our session. I'd been going to Barbara for over ten years and always got more than my time and money's worth on her massage table. Naturally, the massage cleared tension from my muscles, but Barbara and I used it to clear my mental house as well. I had learned from my reading that, in an ultra-relaxed state, you can talk to your subconscious mind. Also, whatever your subconscious mind *believes*, it will create in your life, sooner or later. So, I used this time to program my subconscious to believe in my "hopes and dreams."

"What are you 'intending' for today?" Barbara asked lightly.

I shut my eyes and imagined my higher self looking down at my life. "Barbara, I want to be reunited with my daughter. I want to find the courage to pursue this search, wherever it may lead. And I want to find out the truth about Mary Anne's call. Can we 'intend' for that today?" I asked, looking up.

Barbara's black, curly hair framed her small, sharp-featured face; her dark eyes sparkled back at me. "You bet ya," she said with a wink. "Why don't you go on upstairs."

I left my briefcase behind on the couch and skipped up the steps to her studio. It was a tiny room with the massage table in the center and a large mirror on the right-hand wall. I undressed, hanging my clothes on the hooks behind the door and slipped face-down onto the table, pulling the flannel sheet over my backside. The massage room contained a bookshelf, packed with two rows of books on anatomy, yoga, massage, and holistic medicine. At the far end, was a large window with lowered louvered blinds, and beside it stretched a large poster showing the bones and muscles of the human body. A small vase of tiny pink roses and blue ajuga flowers sat on the window sill. I lay there listening to the birds twittering outside. Then I tried to block them out and concentrate on my "intention."

A few minutes later, Barbara stepped into the room. She shuffled plastic cassette cases and then clicked a tape into her tape player. Soon, the sounds of flute and harp floated through the room. I heard the rapid rubbing together of palms. Next, Barbara would dip her fingers into a jar of almond-scented massage cream. I waited, my skin tingling at the heat of her approaching hands. Soon, the cool, soothing cream glided her strong hands across by back in large swirls. Barbara kneaded my shoulders first; then pulled her middle finger deeply down the channels on either side of my spine. Tension fled from my body. I breathed deeply . . . expanded . . . held . . . slowly released. "I will be reunited with my daughter. . . . I will be reunited with my daughter," I repeated to myself. I was slowly dropping into a bottomless space . . . through my subconscious . . . into the universe. Over and over, Barbara stroked and pulled the pain out of my shoulder and back muscles. I groaned with relief.

But when she began working on a spot just below my right shoulder blade, my muscles tightened and resisted. Barbara used her thumbs and prodded into the muscle, slowly, thoroughly. I watched her work with my mind's eye, amazed when a gush of grief escaped my eyes. Tears flowed out of me each time she pressed a certain spot, though I felt no physical pain. I couldn't explain my reaction. It had never happened before. But sorrow was leaking out of me. I just lay there, like a hollow rubber doll, as Barbara pressed and tears oozed out.

"Barbara, I feel such sadness there," I finally gulped. "It's just below my right shoulder blade. Feels like a big knot of sadness."

"That's okay," she reported. "Lots of people cry up here.

Unexpressed emotions get stored in bodies and massage gets into those places. Just let it come out. It's okay."

I soaked the sheet I lay on with silent tears of pity for the naive young girl I had been . . . tears of grief for the baby I'd never held. While Barbara squeezed the sadness out, it reminded me of how I used to press water out of my hollow rubber Betsy-Wetsy doll. I would fill her up through the little round hole between her cherub lips. Turn her over. And squeeze her pink rubber body until the water spurted out the hole in her bottom. Squeeze, squeeze until it was all gone. . . .

After dinner and a hot shower at home, I made the quick trip downtown to hear the symphony. Safe in my perch in Box B, I rolled my chair forward and leaned my elbows onto the curved wood railing. They'd be playing Mahler's Third tonight! I looked down and studied the stage. *Will I hear another message?* I wondered. *What about my search?* The magic of Mahler's First last March seemed so far away and hopeless now.

I stared down at the stage. The musicians were still wandering in. Brass players, with mutes and mouthpieces. Woodwinds, with a horde of reeds and small, weighted chamois, to be tucked somewhere close at hand and pulled through the instrument to remove moisture later. Near the back wall of the stage, the tympani player tapped on his drumhead. He adjusted the screws on the rim, leaned over, tapped again. Seated string players sawed away at tricky runs. The flutist and first oboe practiced a duet. Trumpets and French horns noodled, adding to the peaceful cacophony. Then the stage lights shot up, the house lights dimmed. Music ceased; whispers died away.

The concert master walked on stage to light applause. He bowed to the audience, turned, and pointed to the oboe. A loud, level "A" sounded. Woodwinds and brass blew, then twisted the necks of their instruments, and blew again, until the pitches matched. Then the strings . . . playing, listening, adjusting pegs, playing, listening again.

When they were finished, a hush spread over the hall. Then, the conductor strode out, a short, energetic man with dark hair, thinning on top. He acknowledged the audience's applause, then turned and picked up his baton. Looking intently at the French horns, he swept both arms through the air. A moment later, we were all living in the timeless mystery of the music as eight horns pealed out a bold theme in reply.

The fanfare charges through the silence like a sudden shock of light. But soon, the fresh theme is mired in a swamp of low, plodding sounds. Fog seeps in and darkness creeps over everything that moves. It's as if the light has been quickly muddied with the shadow of sadness. I see a figure, groping blindly through the fog, weighted down by defeat and lost dreams. A solo trumpet raises a cry of despair. The horns answer. A string tremolo rises below like a chorus of women crying.

Everything fades into silence, and then, as if from heaven, comes a sweet theme, high and fresh with new life, innocence and childhood's joy. But soon the heaviness, the sadness, returns, ached out now by a solo trombone. He rails on insistently about his vision of life, until the fog lifts again, and I find myself in a clear-aired mountain village. Young people are prancing a small-stepped, circle dance. Brown braids bounce on white peasant shirts; blue eyes blaze with energy. And then the dancing stops.

I turn to look out over the mountain landscape. There floats my dream, but the weight of the world is there, too . . . always . . . one, then the other. The two themes begin to parody each other. They turn surreal and dance with each other in accelerated confusion.

The opening repeats: the horn fanfare, the plodding despair. A mournful trombone tells once more of life's sad tragedy and unfulfilled dreams. And then a quiet march begins. It builds and builds . . . to riotous joy. It picks up each theme and embraces them all, working each one into the glorious tapestry of life, itself.

After a pause, the music grows quiet and contained, and the new melodies send my mind drifting away. "What the Flowers Tell Me," the program says. I shift in my seat and listen politely. But then I close my eyes and try to watch the notes bouncing around like dancers on the stage. But soon, I drift down into a slit between the worlds, where I can almost touch last night's dreams. They float by, just out of reach. If only I could connect with them again. I chase, but they slip away, like Eurydice, down a long, dark tunnel. I look after . . . and the next thing I hear is the peal of bells.

"Bimm, bamm; bimm, bamm." I blink my eyes open to see a boys' chorus on stage with women singers, and somewhere in the back of the orchestra, chimes. It sounds like angels singing a joyful song. But then, a contralto solo sings her part in a minor key. She despairs before God about her sin. But the angels reply, "You must not cry . . . Love only God at all times. Thus you will attain heavenly joy." And then the bells bimm and bamm away . . . to silence.

Low strings now take up a full, slow, quiet, transcendent theme, as if they, too, know about God's love. High strings join in. I close my eyes and see a peaceful meadow, shimmering in pre-dawn mist at the moment when light begins to brighten the eastern sky. A beam of light crooks a finger over the horizon, and that steady, growing light reveals the serene perfection of life: bare spaces of dirt and rock, a carpet of grass and wild flowers, clumps of tall trees with limbs reaching towards a sky now streaked with orange and yellow.

A solo flute threads serenity through the scene, pulling behind her a soft but regal trumpet. Irresistibly, that trumpet marches forward and is joined by his brass brothers. Then strings flood in, and winds, gradually opening a gap in the universe.

The sun rises. Its gleaming light burns away the veil of illusion that hangs between the world and it. I behold it in awe: all-knowing, all-encompassing love. Its warmth embraces me, fuses me to it. I quiver in ecstasy as the timpani pounds, strings shimmer and the brass ascends . . . until we are all one with love.

Enveloped by the rapture of the music, I see my lost daughter, beaming warmth to me like the sun embracing a frozen traveler.

That's what it felt like when I talked to Mary Anne, I remember, tingling all over. *And that's the message. I must continue my search, no matter what!*

The following day, I dug through the black filing cabinet upstairs in the accounting office. Yes! The March phone bill had finally come in. My heart thumped hard in my chest; my eyes began to water. I flipped through the blue and white printed sheets, holding my breath until I came to it: Friday, March, 24, 1989, 3:05 p.m., a collect call, thirty-eight minutes. I closed my eyes in a prayer of thanks, then let my eyes rove over to the second column. There it was in black and white: HER PHONE NUMBER.

20 - Diversion

The bus bounced out of Headford and turned north towards Shrule, Kilmaine, Ballinrobe and Ballina. At last, Clare and Galway were behind us; we had made it to Mayo. Low-laying, black, peat bogs lined the road. Another foot of peat had been hand-sliced, brick by brick, from the earth this past May. After cutting, the peat was scattered to dry on the land bridges that crisscrossed the bog for all of June. Now that July was here, it would be collected in gunny sacks some sunny day, and hauled home on tractors. A neat pile of fresh turf would soon lean beside each cottage to keep its cookstove burning through another dark, cold winter.

The low hills, ribbed with stone fences, rose behind the bogs. Treeless and pimpled with stones, they provided meager feed for the cattle, who had to graze by twisting grass and weeds from between the rocks. For generations, Irish farmers had slogged through the marshy land in tall, black Wellingtons to pile the stones into low fences. Many boundaries were needed, for each farmer owned but a single piece of bog land, along with a few postage-stamp fields on the lower slopes and others in practically worthless high meadow land. True, the land was poor; yet, there was a stark, unchanging beauty here, and, oddly, I realized, it felt like home.

Tears in my eyes, I turned to Ned to tell him . . . but there was no need for words, for his eyes were glistening, too. He took my hand and squeezed it gently.

Ned's mother had been born and raised on one of these stony hills. The crumbling stone walls of her family's two-room thatch-roofed cottage still stood in a bare and windy spot overlooking Lough Conn. There hadn't been enough food to feed all five children, so three had been sent away. A boy had gone to England; a girl to Scotland; and Ned's mother, to America.

She'd come to the States as a maid in the 1920s, eventually marrying a young widower with Irish roots. She raised his two children and bore him seven more, and then died an old lady with a small sum of money in the bank. Ned's share was paying for this, his sixth and my third, trip back home.

We'd come to see his Cousin Willie, of course, Mom's sister's youngest boy. Willie would be wearing two sweaters and a dirt-spotted vest and his dark hair would be obstinately sticking out of his gray cap, but his face would be wide and beaming. The cottage door would be standing wide open behind him, the collie would be panting at his side, and he'd be shouting, "Neddie and Ann is home! Welcome! Ye are most welcome!" He would shake our hands, pat our backs, and clutch us in deep, heart-felt hugs.

That's what meant so much to me about my family in Mayo. They welcomed me; accepted me exactly as I was. They had few worldly goods, but the people here loved me and rejoiced in my company. No wonder it felt like home to me.

The bus let us off in Foxford, an old mill town on the Moy. We could walk home from here. We stashed our baggage in the back room of our nephew's pub, to be collected later, and set off on foot, over the bridge and down the narrow road that led to Stonepark.

Willie's house was set in a valley between an ancient two-stall stone stable and a new, tin-roofed, concrete block barn. It was a modest, four-room dwelling with cement-block walls and a linoleum floor. Constructed in the early 1920s when the government had parcelled up the land, the house was carefully whitewashed every few years and was affectionately referred to as "The White House."

"Neddie, Ann, get up by the fire," Willie insisted, once we were safely inside. Perpetually damp and cold, even in summer, the Irish weather had no doubt created the first rule of Irish hospitality: offer the guest the seat by the stove. We smiled broadly as we proudly took the places of honor, in sturdy, wooden chairs, smoothed by decades of wear.

"My home is ye home," Willie began eagerly. "Now, make yeselves comfortable. This is ye holiday, and I'm honored that ye are spending it with me. Whatever ye wish, we will do it!" He looked over expectantly, awaiting our reply.

Ned explained that we'd already done all the "running around" we cared to do and we had come to Mayo just to relax and visit.

"Very well. Tat's beautiful," Willie said, as he would have to any suggestion we might have made. He rattled off a list of possible chores as I looked around the room.

The furnishings were spare. Beside me loomed the old cookstove, radiating its perpetual turf fire. In the middle of the room stood a Formica table, surrounded with scratched, but sturdy wooden chairs. A battered sofa hugged the front wall, facing a china closet with its curious mixture of plates, cups, and glasses and drawers full of utensils, fresh eggs and butter. Behind the wooden doors at the bottom were stored packages of bread, cookies, and other makings for "tea." Beyond the door to the back hallway hid a small kitchen, complete with an under-the-counter refrigerator, a gas-fired hot plate, and a large sink, spotted with grime. The toilet was in the unheated room farthest back the hall.

"Would ye like to help me bring in the peat? It's been cut and drying for weeks now," he said.

I looked to where he sat on the couch. He was bending forward, eager, with a impish twinkle in his eye. "Sounds great, Willie," I said, innocently.

"Well, now, the solicitor will have to watch himself," he added with a sly grin, reminding us all of our previous visit during May, a few years before. It had been turf cutting time, of course . . . but cutting turf had proved to be hard work! Ned had begged off one day because of "tennis elbow," and had suffered much kidding ever since.

We all laughed and bonded once again.

The days with Willie flew by quickly. We helped him gather eggs, tend cattle, collect turf. And Ned and I took long walks down country roads, filling our lungs with the sweet smell of cows and new hay and the turf smoke that curled out of every chimney along the road.

With every breath of country air, with every smile, with every slow-paced day, I cleansed my body of cares, tension, and old guilts. I needed to make a clear space in my life for my new daughter, Mary Anne.

On our last full day there, I sought solitude on the hill behind Willie's. It was a fine day, with warm sun and a stiff breeze when I set off in my wool shirt and hiking boots. Up the stony path I plodded—past neighbors' houses, past barking dogs, following, finally, a narrow trail where the farmers led their cattle on foot, with sticks and curses, to stony, marshy fields on top of the treeless mountain. When the trail ended, I picked my way past fences and through the boggy ground, to a spot I remembered from when I'd brought my girls here, some years before. Together, we'd looked down over Lough Conn, an undeveloped lake front full of marsh plants and ducks and an occasional wooden rowboat tethered to a stone on the shore.

This afternoon, I was the only human on this wind-swept hill. Willie's dog Breadman, who had made the climb with me, darted across the hillside, following the scents of small animals. Cattle, grazing at a distance, paused when I approached. I sat on a large boulder and looked over the peaceful valley. To my left, the lake sparkled as sun reflected from it. I could trace the glistening water's path, down the river Moy to my right, into the Bay of Killala and out to the Atlantic Ocean. In the distance, stood the Mountains of Mayo.

Below me, I heard the Dublin train chugging its way to the nearby market town of Ballina. The cuckoo called, and a bee buzzed by me into the prickly yellow Scotch broom that bloomed nearby. The ground was carpeted with purple heather, growing between the rocks. God's rock garden. I drew a deep breath of the sweet air.

Oh, if only I could bring this bliss home with me. I couldn't stop thinking about my search for Mary Anne. The phone bill had provided an important lead, but hardly instant success. After many tries, someone had finally answered the phone, but it was a middle-aged woman, not my young, soft-spoken Mary Anne.

"Is Mary Anne there?" I had asked lightly, quaking inside.

"No. May I give her a message?" had come the formal reply.

"Please ask her to call Ann," I had said, as calmly as I could manage. "It's long distance, and she can call me back collect. Could you tell me when she's expected back?"

"It's hard to say. She's in and out," the woman had replied.

"Well, thank you anyway. And I do appreciate your giving her my message," I had said, trying to sound both casual and courteous.

And so the waiting game had begun. Though my calls were never returned, I did manage to gather some important information. First and most importantly, someone named Mary Anne did live at that number. Second, Mary Anne must be old enough to be independent, and possibly, she lived with a boyfriend or elsewhere some of the time. Third, I guessed that the people who always answered the phone were Mary Anne's adoptive parents. This meant that Mary Anne had lied to me when she told me they still lived in the city where I had surrendered her.

The people who answered the phone were always guarded. One time, however, I'd gotten a last name, and this had allowed me to find their address in the phone book. The phone was listed to a man, no doubt her adoptive father. Not only that, the house I was zeroing in on was exactly a block and a half from the house where I'd been raised. Lots of coincidences!

The breeze suddenly stiffened and brought me out of my reverie. Scattered clouds were moving in. Though it was still bright, I felt chilly. Drawing my hat over my head, I crouched down as far out of the wind as I could. Then I took out the writing tablet and pen I'd carried up with me.

"Dearest Mary Anne," I began. "I'm on a beautiful hillside in the West of Ireland, feeling very much in touch with nature. . . ." I poured my heart out, telling her how much her phone call had meant to me and how much I longed for the chance to connect with her. When I had captured my heart on paper, I folded up my letter and tucked it away in my pocket. Then I rubbed the kinks out of my legs and hiked back down the hill to Willie's.

When I got home a few days later, I mailed my letter and waited anxiously.

I received no reply.

21 - The March

I picked up the flier from my dashboard and read it for the fifteenth time: "August 5, 1989. 10:00 a.m. Washington, D.C. Rally for Opening Sealed Adoption Records. Meet at the Holiday Inn in Rosslyn, VA. Show your support for adoption reform. March with us to the Lincoln Memorial."

I folded it up, put it in my shirt pocket, and returned to staring through my windshield at the building in front of me. *Can't go in too early: don't know anybody. Can't be late: they'll leave without me. Hope this is it.*

A sea of cars already filled the parking lot: yellow, green, red, black, white, blue—sedans, pick-ups, compacts, vans. A black sedan pulled in beside me. When its doors opened, three people stepped out onto the hot pavement and moved downhill towards the main entrance. I waited for them to reach the door; then, steadying myself with a deep breath, I got out, locked the car, and followed the others.

A trim man in white shorts stood in the red-carpeted lobby calling directions to his assistants while greeting newcomers. His face lit up at the sight of the people in front of me.

"Hi, Bill, Sally, Mary! Great to see you!" he said, extending both his arms and catching them all in a quick embrace. "Welcome. Thanks for coming. Over that way," he gestured, nodding his gray curly locks to the left.

I followed the group into a large ballroom full of people who were talking, squealing, and hugging. Balloons filled the air. Buttons and new T-shirts declared: "Open Hearts: Open Records," "Reunited and Whole At Last," "Where is my Mommy?" on everyone I passed.

I stood out of the way by one of the T-shirt tables and looked around the room. A young woman with shoulder-length brown hair looked familiar somehow. I squeezed through the spaces that opened and closed in the shifting mass of bodies between us. When I reached her, I touched her shoulder. Her head turned, and she swished her long straight hair to one side. Now her face, framed with brown bangs and a green headband, tilted toward me; her hazel eyes searched my face.

"Ann?"

"So it *is* you!" I exclaimed. "We had lunch together once. Remember? Sorry. I forget your name."

"I'm Laura. Sure. You, me and Eileen, at the Harvey House. Two or three years ago, wasn't it?"

"Right." Meeting them had made me feel like less of a freak. But they had seemed so far behind me at the time. "So, what are you doing here, Laura?"

"Old times, partly. Used to do political demonstrations in the '60's. Besides, I met my daughter a few months ago!" Her whole face crinkled in a smile. "Oh, Eileen found her son, too. Last year, I think."

Heat flushed through me and I exhaled sharply, as if someone had shoved a stick in my chest. *You arrogant jerk!* I lashed out at myself. *You "better-than-thou" asshole! You decided not to keep meeting with them because you felt so superior, and now they've both accomplished what you're still only wishing for.*

She must have wondered at the blank expression on my face, but when I finally looked back up at her, she continued in a cheery tone. "So, have you found your daughter yet?"

I opened my mouth to answer, but a voice boomed through the loudspeaker. "Okay. We're ready to march. Please move toward someone holding a sign with the name of your state. Some of you can carry the placards that are over against the wall. Let's go!"

The crowd began to swirl in many directions all at once. Laura grabbed my arm. "Come with me," she said as we moved toward the Maryland contingent.

The loudspeaker voice began the roll call: "Alabama, Alaska, Arizona, Arkansas, California. . . ." At the front of the room, people were filing out. Five minutes later, Laura and I were jostling out of double-glass doors. The wall of sweltering heat hit us hard.

"It's 102 degrees out here!" someone shouted back to the long line of people still pouring through the doors. "Let's heat up Washington some more and tell them what we think!"

"No more secrets! No more lies! We want ALL our family ties!" "Adoptees have the right to know. Sealed records have got to go!" "What do we want? Open records! When do we want them? Now!" Next, we sang the first two phrases of "We Shall Overcome" with our

153

words: "We Want Open Records . . . today." And then back to the chants.

I felt the sweat dripping off me in little rivulets, trickling down my back, between my breasts. I fanned my face with my free hand and then wiped the sweat off my forehead.

"They would pick the hottest day of the year for this," I groused to Laura. We were to plod a mile or two down the shaded walkway along George Washington Memorial Parkway, then head out into the blazing sun crossing the Potomac on the Arlington Memorial Bridge, and finally, on to the Lincoln Memorial. Along the way, Laura brought me up to date on her life.

"My search was really easy," she began. "I was so lucky. Two summers ago, a few months after my daughter turned eighteen, I got up the courage to contact the adoption agency. I asked to leave a letter in my file for my daughter. Would you believe, they said 'yes?'" She looked up at me and wiped her brow. "Not only that, but the social worker who handled the case originally was still working there. She called me back to say they'd help arrange a reunion if both sides wanted it!

"I was so shocked, I didn't know what to say right then. But, later, I called her back and told her, 'Okay.'"

I shook my head incredulously and related the short version of my tale of adoption agency woes.

"It took them three months to locate the family," Laura continued. "When the social worker called to tell me she'd found them, she asked me to come in for a personal interview. I remember trying to read Jane's name upsidedown on her file."

But a year had passed before Laura had found out the name or met her daughter. The contact had come at a bad time. The adoptive parents were going through a divorce and Laura's daughter was having some problems in school. But Laura and the social worker kept in touch and, little by little, Laura learned more about the adoptive family. She learned of Jane's case of mono that summer and of her later recovery.

In February, 1989, Laura's daughter turned twenty.

"I wanted to send her a birthday card. Didn't know just what to choose, so I ended up selecting one of those, 'Thinking of you' cards.

Something dumb. Wrote a little one-line note. 'I've been thinking of you and if you'd ever like to meet me, I'd be really happy.' Gave it to the social worker without asking if she'd send it or not.

"Three weeks later, I'm going through my mail and here's this big manila envelope packed with photos. No return address, but a short note signed, 'Love, Jane.'

"As I'm shuffling through everything, my eleven-year-old daughter Krissie passes by and asks what I'm looking at. I must have looked kind of strange standing there with tears rolling down my face, but I couldn't even tell her the truth. I told her they were pictures of the daughter of one of my friends.

"When I finally did get up the courage to tell her later, I'll never forget what she did. She just jumped up and down with happiness. She said she'd always wanted an older sister."

I smiled and looked down at the sidewalk sections slipping by. "I know what you mean. I was afraid to tell my kids, too. Did manage to do it when they were around 10 and 12. They were very sympathetic, actually. Asked a couple of questions about why I gave her away. Then they wanted to know what I was making for dinner.

"How was your husband about it?"

"Well, he knew about Jane, but I didn't talk to him about my search. My feelings were too twisted up. He found out when I got the package."

I looked at Laura. She was gazing down at her feet. "So tell me about Jane," I said, trying to cheer her up.

While we made our way toward the Lincoln Memorial, Laura told me about her first meeting with Jane and about how she'd explained the circumstances of the surrender: the quickie marriage that didn't work out . . . the pressure to surrender from her husband, his parents, her parents . . . how her dad had committed her to a psych ward for depression to insure she'd surrender . . . the alcoholism afterwards. "But I finally got myself back in school and decided to study law," she concluded. "I think I chose it just because I'd been pushed around and hurt by the system so much."

I was looking down at my feet, ignoring the sweat dripping off my brow. "So are things working out between Jane and you?"

"I hope so. She always waits for me to call. Probably feels some

155

torn loyalties. But she's so much like me. In a bad way, too: it's hard for her to talk about her feelings."

"How do she and Krissie get along?"

"Just fine. That's been great."

"Well, Laura—are you happy you found her?" I asked slowly, looking up again.

She glanced over to catch my eye. "Oh, yes! But I'm so afraid of losing her. I don't know when or if that will ever go away." She turned and shook her head wistfully.

The crowd ahead of us was swarming around the Lincoln Memorial by then. A few people scurried towards the popsicle vendors. Others draped their sweaty bodies across the steps leading down to the large reflecting pool. Laura and I followed and settled ourselves up near the top row of steps. The trim, curly-haired man, whom I'd seen in the lobby before we started, walked over to the microphone and gave it a few trial taps before he began to speak.

"Hello, everyone. Thanks again for coming. I'm Joe Soll, leader of the first *annual* March on Washington for Equal Rights in Adoption."

The crowd responded with hoots and wild applause.

"We all know the pain of lost connections. Some of us, like me, don't know who we are, have never laid eyes on another human being who resembles us. Some of us are crushed under the weight of worry or guilt over a surrendered child. Some desperately need medical information for their adopted children.

"And when they ask their adoption agencies, what are they told?

"'No! The records are sealed. You have no right to know.'"

Eyes flared all around us; people in the crowd nodded and whispered to each other.

"Well, *I* say we have *a RIGHT* to know the truth of our lives. We have *a RIGHT* to know who we are." Joe's voice grew still stronger. "And so do these people who have walked with me all the way from New York City to Washington, D.C."

The crowd roared as he motioned fifty people forward. They formed two lines, flanking him, and he introduced each in turn. Some of them stepped up to the microphone to speak.

A birthmother told about waiting for 27 years to search for her son, and then finding him in a grave, the victim of a freak accident that had happened when he was fifteen months old. The adoption wasn't final when he died . . . yet no one had told her of his death. And when she searched, the agency had lied.

Another birthmother recounted how, unknown to her, her son had been damaged at birth. She had tried to reclaim him from the adoption agency at six months of age. And, even though he was too disabled to be offered for adoption, they told her nothing about her son's condition and they sent him to an institution, rather than give her back custody.

There were stories in which the searcher found abuse or death—where medical information could have saved a child's life. On and on they went. My head was throbbing. I could take no more, so I stood up and started wandering toward the popsicle vendors. Laura followed me.

"So what about you?" she asked me again, once we reach the shade. "Have you found your daughter?"

I shook my head, trying to clear it of negative thoughts. "What? Oh, yeah." I replied. "My daughter? Well, I *think* I've found her. Anyway, I should know for sure by next weekend. I came here today looking for advice. You see, it's kind of a strange situation. . . ."

I told her about the phone call and about the flurry of excitement that had followed. By the time I finished my story, we were both licking the wood of our popsicle sticks. The speeches were over and the crowd was beginning to break up. We stood to leave.

"Do you know anyone from Pennsylvania who might be able to help me with searching, just in case this 'Mary Anne' is not my daughter after all?" I asked Laura.

Laura pointed out someone she knew who might be able to help me. I ran down and introduced myself to Sonia, an adoptee with black wavy hair and a perky smile. I explained my story briefly and scribbled her phone number on the back of my flier about the March. When it was safely stuffed back in my pocket, I waved goodbye to Laura and began the trek back to my car.

Many disturbing thoughts were still rumbling around inside me. What did this all mean? And what in the world would next weekend bring?

22 - Cul de Sac

The following Saturday, I was at Mother's, pacing the floor. *Do I have to wait till 11:00? Or can I get away with calling earlier? It is Saturday—they might be sleeping in. Better not. God, I hope they'll be home. What if they go out before I call? I* **have** *to reach Mary Anne somehow.*

It was just Mother and I in the A-frame in the woods, and she was back in her bedroom. All I could hear was the tick-tick-tick of the cuckoo clock on the dining room wall. Meanwhile, I felt a million needles poking and jabbing at me under my skin.

Oh, to hell with it. I'm calling now.

I set my jaw, plopped down on the chair beside the phone, and carefully punched out the number, one digit at a time. On the third ring, a familiar woman's voice answered.

"This is Ann Hughes. I'm here from out of town today and was wondering if I could come by and ask you a few questions about a phone call I received last March that was made from your phone. I also have a letter I'd like to drop off for your daughter, Mary Anne. Will you be there in an hour or so?" I tried to sound calm, yet my body was shaking, my heart nearly paralyzed with fear.

"Okay," she replied. "We should be here this morning."

A wave of relief swept over me. I'd never expected it would be so easy. "Thank you. I'll see you soon." *She didn't even give me a hard time,* I marveled to myself. *And somebody's home. What luck!*

I ran to find Mother. "Will you drive?" I asked. Soon, we were on our way to Mary Anne's—me riding in the passenger seat—exactly the way it had been on that long-ago day when I signed the surrender papers.

Since that fateful day, we'd been like two wrestlers, squared off in a bitter struggle. The fight was always the same: whose value system would prevail? For decades now, we'd slammed each other to the mat with shoves and dirty kicks, scratches, eye pokes—fought with every force we could muster. We both bore bad bruises from sorrow, deep gashes from distrust.

What does it mean that she agreed to go with me today? I wondered.

We drove along in heavy silence. I studied her face. It told many tales. Her eyes beamed excitement: her first grandchild, found at last. But her set jaw betrayed her terrible fear: people will find out her daughter had a child out of wedlock—as if she herself were responsible for allowing disgrace to fall on the proud family name.

Well, I can help her work through that, I told myself confidently. *That's all distorted thinking on her part. She's not responsible for my conduct, and besides, I know that old shame will be blasted away by joy when we reclaim Mary Anne.*

Still edgy, I watched my brave thoughts about Mother slowly recede, like a departing wave. Then, with a thunderous crash, my own misgivings surged to the fore.

My dream last night: "The Execution." What did it mean?

I had dreamed of a large-scale execution. It had taken place on a bridge. I was there with other condemned souls. They were all being shot, one by one. I knew I was not supposed to be shot, but there was "another me" that had to die. Wearing a thin shift, she quaked pitifully in front of me, trying to hide from the executioners. I talked to her gently, explaining to her that there was no escape: she had to die. She could kill herself or be shot like the others, and it would be better for her if she could just accept it. She looked at me with deep, deep sadness in her eyes, but finally she understood. Then she hoisted herself up onto the bridge wall and bravely let herself slip into the black waters. I stood on the bridge, watching, as her body disappeared. There was a tiny splash and a few ripples in the dark water. That was all. Then the executioners walked off the bridge, and I was left standing there.

I shuddered. When I looked up again, Mother was turning onto the street where we'd lived so many years ago. She drove past our old house, the one with my father's studio and band rooms built into the basement. We went one block, turned, went half a block more, and parked in front of a split-level house, attractively landscaped with grown trees. I'd walked by that house hundreds, and probably thousands of times, returning home from school. It was right across the street from my best girlfriend's house. Now, I gazed in awe. Just to think: that familiar spot could hold the answer to the two questions that had been on my mind for over twenty-three years: "Where is my daughter?" and "Is she okay?"

There was nothing I wanted more than to walk up to that house and find out the truth. And there was nothing I wanted to do LESS! *How am I ever going to start talking to these people about this? What will their reaction be? Will they deny the whole thing? Will they be hostile? Will they feel threatened by me? Will they tell me what I need to know?*

The barrier of fear between me and the people on the other side of that door felt like a wall of fire. But my need to know the truth was stronger. I felt like the girl on the bridge, and like her, there was nothing to do but jump. My mind and emotions were frozen in fear. Nonetheless, my legs dutifully obeyed the command of my higher will. I got out of the car and walked up the sidewalk. My cold hand stretched out stiffly and pressed the doorbell.

Pleasant chimes sounded. It was the same chime-tune that had rung at our house, just around the corner. I strained my ears to hear approaching footsteps. Finally, the door opened, and a somber, middle-aged woman stood on the other side of the screen door. Her dark hair was pulled back in a bun.

"Yes?" she said in a familiar voice. She looked me over carefully.

"Hello. I'm Ann Hughes. I called you earlier. I wonder if I could come in and ask you a few questions about a phone call I received last March that was made from your phone."

Hesitantly, she opened the screen door and let me in. A dark-haired man of medium build stood in the foyer, his glasses in his hands. They escorted me past a family room where two teen-aged boys played, and into their sunken living room.

I was pleased to see a baby grand piano in the room and to hear classical music playing on the radio. A rich library of books surrounded their tasteful furnishings. I smiled and breathed deeply. This was exactly the type of adoptive home I had hoped my daughter would be raised in. They must be cultured, educated people.

I had pleaded with Mrs. Day to place my baby in a home like this! Since the father and I were both college-educated, I felt sure my baby would be intellectually gifted. She would need educational advantages. I had told them that.

Now I drew in a deep breath. "I'm sorry to disturb you," I began. "Thank you for inviting me into your lovely home. As I said, my name is Ann Hughes. You know, I was raised right around the corner from here. My dad was the high school band director here for

160

many years. You may have known him. He died in 1975."

Can I bond with them in some way before I start asking questions? Maybe I can talk about things we have in common. I don't want them to see me as an adversary.

They admitted having heard of my father, and marvelled with me at the irony of my having lived so close by. When they seemed a bit more relaxed, I moved on to my big question: the call made from their phone last March by "Mary Anne Holly."

A worried look passed between them.

"I'm a birthmother," I confessed quietly, after a short pause. "I surrendered a daughter for adoption in 1966. The girl who called me said she was my daughter. I've been hoping to be reunited with her for many years now." Tears filled my eyes. "Please, can you help me?" I implored softly.

The father spoke first. "We are adoptive parents," he began, clearing his throat.

My heart cracked open with relief. *Yes!* I thought to myself. *I have the right people! Everything is going to work out! Joy jumped inside me, up and down, up and down.*

"We have two adopted sons, whom you saw coming in," he continued, "and an adopted daughter, Mary Anne."

Yes! I said to myself. *A match!*

"Our boys are twins, and they have never showed any interest in finding their birthparents, but Mary Anne has always been obsessed with finding her birthmother," he explained. Then he took a deep breath and looked away. "Mary Anne undertook a long and arduous search for her birthmother some years ago. She was quite persistent and resourceful, I must say."

Yes! She IS my daughter—just like me, I was thinking to myself.

". . . and she found her birthmother last year. Unfortunately, she was in a mental institution." He paused then, and looked at me. Heavy sadness weighed down his eyes.

WHAT? My own eyes grew wide. My heart stood still.

Then, taking another deep breath, he went on, while my eyes slowly filled with tears. "Her birthmother was in a mental institution, suffering from schizophrenia," he sadly repeated. "Mary Anne contacted her mother there early this year, but the mother rejected

161

her."

"Yes," his wife joined in, picking up where he'd left off. "Mary Anne couldn't accept the rejection of her birthmother. After all the effort she had gone to . . ."

"Oh," I murmured, stunned by the blow of disappointment, I responded as if in a dream. "I've heard that some birthmothers never get over giving their children up. I've heard it can drive them insane. And I know how very deeply Mary Anne cares about her birthmother. She told me she thinks about her and has kept presents for her since she was little. Rejection must have been a terribly cruel blow for such a sensitive person. Poor Mary Anne."

Her father spoke carefully. "That's when she started making the phone calls to birthmothers. She had some *People Finders* magazines and started calling women who'd placed ads there."

I blinked slowly and sucked in air. The puzzle pieces fit now. My blood began to flow again. "That's where she said she found my name." Now I knew why she'd called; why she'd lied; why she hadn't answered my calls or my letter. "Poor Mary Anne. How is she by now?"

"Well, she seems to be coming along," said her father. "We were quite concerned, of course, especially with her mother being schizophrenic, that she may have inherited mental problems, herself."

"Naturally. Where did she get the name 'Holly?'" I inquired, still reluctant to let go.

"That was her birth name," explained her mother.

I understood full well the tragedy of a missed birth connection. What more was there to say? I stood at last. "You have been more than kind to tell me all of this." My face flushed with gratitude as I looked back and forth between them. "Thank you so much. Without this, I would have been walking around in the torment of not knowing."

They stood, too. "Several women called here," her father volunteered, "but you were the only one to actually track us down."

A smirk of pride spread across my face. "Maybe I'm learning to be a good detective. I'm persistent, anyway!" I turned to the mother. "Please give Mary Anne my love," I said, reaching deep into her eyes. "Her phone call was so healing for me. Just to know that an adoptee would want to know her birthmother—and that I could be forgiven for surrendering her. That did wonders for me. I don't for an instant regret that she called me. I'm just sorry for her pain. I hope she'll be okay."

We exchanged long looks. I hoped they could know how truly grateful I was for their candor.

I bravely yanked up the corners of my mouth and regarded them fully one last time. "Thanks again for talking to me. Good luck to you . . . . " (Slowly, I backed off.) "I just hope my daughter was raised . . ." (my voice began to crack) "by folks a nice as you." I turned away then. My face was contorted, my eyes were filling with tears, but I made sure to keep my gait steady.

It was dark and cool in the house, but outside, bright sunshine and oppressive heat blasted me with confusion. What they said made sense, but was it really true? I wondered. How could I be sure they weren't just jealous adoptive parents trying to keep me from my child?

But then, I replayed the scene in my mind and remembered the profound sadness in the eyes of the adoptive father. No, they'd told the truth.

I looked up, and there was Mom, sitting in the front seat of the car, patiently reading her magazine. My ever-faithful mother, waiting for me . . . . I brushed the tears out of my eyes before I opened the passenger door and slipped beside her.

"How did you make out?" she asked carefully.

"It's the wrong girl," I said with dull sadness. And I retold the sad tale as we drove home emptily.

23 - Spiritual Resources

The sharp twittering of ten thousand cicadas pricked pinholes into the black silence of the moonless night. Renate and I walked single file. Renate, in front, fixed a dim flashlight beam on the ground; I shuffled along behind her, through layers of old leaves, stumbling over submerged roots. Ahead, Fred's porch light spread a golden umbrella of light. Soft laughter leaked out of the cabin windows. When we stepped into the clearing, a soft breeze brushed my bare legs, suddenly bristling them with goosebumps.

We tramped up the open wooden staircase, and Renate pulled open the door. A cozy room of shiny, bare log walls gleamed back at us. A few dishes stood in the sink; toys littered the living room floor, and the hum of the hot tub motor told me where everyone was.

"Out here," Fred bellowed over the sloshing of water and a round of giggles from my niece Jennie. I looked down at my feet and scuffed off my shoes.

"Hey, grab yourself a soda if you want one," Freddie's wife Sherrie called out amid another burst of high-pitched squeals.

The refrigerator door sucked open behind me. "Want one, Mom?" Renate asked, reaching inside.

With a deep sigh, I shook my head "no," then tossed my towel on a chair before heading out to the porch.

Two sets of shoulders and heads stuck out of the frothy, gurgling tub. Fred looked ten years younger since he'd shaved off his winter beard, and Sherrie, a foot shorter than her husband, was sporting a new hairdo of tight, brown curls. They occupied opposite sides of the tub. I slid between them and sank in up to my neck. Steam invaded my nostrils. I twisted my body so the water jets would pulse onto my shoulder and back muscles. Little Jennie slithered her wet tummy over the edge of the tub and swam into her mother's lap. Then she shot a splash at her dad.

He raised his hand to block the spray. "Hey, Kiddo, stop it now," he said before turning my way. He spoke gently. "Mom told us what happened."

Soda in hand, Renate joined us. While her slender form disappeared into the bubbles, Jennie squealed and kicked toward her, water wings bobbing. Renate's free hand reached out to catch her. I wiped some drops off my face and crouched a little lower, letting white foam lap into my ears. My stomach was churning again.

Sherrie shook water out of her springy curls. Her deep-set, blue eyes searched my face. "We're really sorry things didn't work out." I looked up and gave her a little sigh. She and Jennie had the same short, broad forehead and upturned nose.

"Are you going to be okay?" my brother asked.

I stared blankly in his direction. "Sure, I'm fine," I said.

Everybody tried to comfort me: "It all happened for the best," they all said. Even my mother—seldom the optimist—agreed after she joined us later. In my mind, I suspected they were right, but a thick, black curtain of grief had smothered the life out of me. I lied, claiming to be "fine," but I sat among them like a shadow, not really there. My chest felt caved in. I hunched my shoulders and bent forward, trying to hide the ugly hole of mourning that was gaping in my middle. I just kept breathing and waited for the pain to pass. . . .

The next afternoon, I was back in my living room, perched in the bentwood rocker. Our grandfather's clock was ticking relentlessly and I was scraping my slippers back and forth on the floorboards in time with the strokes of the rocker. Scrape, scrape. Rock, rock. Tick, tock-tick, clacked the clock, a little off-beat. I tried to keep the two rhythms in time. Perhaps it would help keep the walls from closing in on me, as it seemed they might.

I knew I had to mourn my loss before I'd feel better, so I'd gotten away from the "cheering up" at my brother's house as quickly as I could. But now, alone with my sadness, I could feel the panic rising. My heart was beating fast and my breathing barely moved my chest. My mind was twirling in a wild tail-spin:

I love Mary Anne. We connected. She's so gentle and forgiving. Why can't she be my daughter? I feel so lost without her in my life. What do I do now?

But another part of me yelled, *Enough!* I stopped rocking the chair, though the clock still tocked its slightly uneven beat. The stern voice continued. *You can't just sit here and let this disappointment crush the life out of you.*

I lurched out of the rocking chair and began pacing the floor.

The voice was right. I had to do something. But what?

My eyes swept from one end of the room to the other, registering the brick fireplace we never used, Ned's wrinkled leather reading chair, the empty L-shaped couch, the glass coffee table with its wrought-iron dragons seething underneath, the *Science of the Mind* magazine sitting on top of a pile of books. . . .

My eyes stopped and stared at the magazine. Wasn't that where I'd seen an ad for something called the Ministry of Prayer? Wasn't there a phone number you could call, day or night?

I grabbed the magazine and riffled pages, scanning until I found the ad, boxed at the bottom. "We're here for you. You are not alone. In prayer 24 hours a day"—and a Los Angeles phone number. I drew in a large breath and let it out slowly.

But you don't believe in that silly stuff. You've never asked anyone to pray for you, part of me scoffed.

Oh, shut up, another voice argued. *You need something and you need it now. It might help, and, if it doesn't, no one will ever know you called. Why not give it a try?*

So I limped stiffly into the kitchen and plopped myself down on the wooden stool by the wall phone. The legs of the stool screeched across the linoleum.

Now what? I asked myself.

The narrow kitchen walls, cupboards looming, seemed to be bulging inward, ready to crush me. Yes, I had to do something. I closed my eyes and prayed for courage. Then I picked up the phone and dialed.

The phone rang twice before a deep, soothing voice reached out to me. "Ministry of Prayer. How may I help you?"

My stomach flopped like a beached fish. I fidgeted on the stool. "Well, I don't really know." I grabbed a short, quick breath. "I've never called here before and I'm not sure what to tell you." I paused. "All I know is that I feel horribly sad. I can't shake it off and I don't know what to do to make it go away."

"Why don't you just tell me the problem," he prompted.

I told him about the surrender, about Mary Anne's phone call, and about what I'd found out over the weekend. But it all came out like a weather report. And while I rambled on, an inner voice began to wail like a siren: *This is your life you're talking about, you idiot. Don't waste this opportunity. Tell the truth!*

Finally, something released inside me; I closed my eyes, cupped my left hand around the phone mouthpiece and spoke directly into the little holes. "I feel so guilty," I said, my eyes filling with tears. "I feel horrible that I relinquished my daughter when she was born. I know that must have caused her excruciating pain." A scene flashed before me. A helpless infant, alone in the world . . . her hopeless cries . . . her despair at being abandoned by the mother whose body she'd shared. Then I remembered all the times I'd thought about my child, worried about her, beat myself up about what I'd done. "It's caused me a lot of pain, too," I admitted. My throat constricted then, so I had to squeeze my next words out of a tiny opening at the very top of my throat. "I don't know why, but I've always lied about that."

The corners of my eyes were wet, but, at least, it was out. My mind had gone numb and blank; my body trembled.

"Let us pray together," said the gentle man on the phone. His steady voice rose and fell, pointing out that I was "one with the Life Force"—and that I could "release the past to the past." While he spoke, I squeezed my eyes shut and traced his words onto my soul. When he finished the prayer, I took a deep breath. As I released it, I let the poison of negativity drain out of me. "Thank you," I whispered, and then I softly hung up the phone.

I just sat there staring into space for a second, before an unexpected wave of emotion rose up inside me. I ran to grab a tissue, but it took a fistful to sop up the flood that followed.

I collapsed on the couch and cried for my baby and all babies deserted by their mothers. I cried for the emptiness we have all suffered. I cried for the way we needed each other, children and parents, alike, and for the pain of our not knowing each other, and for the impossible tangle of laws and secrets and destinies that block our reunions.

When my sobs subsided and I could breathe freely again, it was as if a weight had lifted. I was free. Remembering his words, "Release the past to the past," I let my eyes fall shut, scrunched myself down into the couch and slid a pillow under my head. Then I bobbed up to pull a wool afghan over me before drifting off, blissfully unaware of the jolt that would be hitting me next.

167

24 - A Fresh Start

"Hi, Ann. My name's Louise." The caller was probably in her 30's; excitement bubbled in her voice. "I'm calling about the letter you sent to our adoption support group," she said, flipping the pitch of the words up at the end of her sentence.

I struggled to catch her meaning. Yes, I'd sent a letter at Sonia's suggestion. But three weeks had passed without a word. August was nearly over; frankly, I'd given up hope.

"I just found out about it yesterday," Louise chirped. She'd been grocery shopping . . . bumped into a friend . . . the friend had mentioned my letter . . . remembered the date I'd asked about, March 30, 1966.

March, 1966? Zing. An arrow had flown to its mark. "May I make the call?" Louise had begged her friend.

I started lighting up like a Christmas tree. Was this my Spiritual Mind Treatment at work?

I thought back to my call three weeks ago to the Ministry of Prayer and the powerful meditation I'd done later that day. People used Spiritual Mind Treatment to heal illness and find jobs. Why couldn't I use it to locate my daughter? I'd sat on the couch, with my back straight, and followed the instructions:

> First, affirm that God is everywhere; therefore, God is in you. So, you are one with God. Being one with God, you can do as he does: create your future by using the Law of Mind. Form follows thought, so, visualize what you want and give thanks as if it already exists. The Universe will then begin shaping matter into the form you hold in your mind. It's an automatic response, so all one needs to do is to wait and trust that the results will show up. It's the power of Thanksgiving that sets the Law in motion.

I'd breathed deeply and closed my eyes. A vision had formed: it was me, embracing my daughter, absorbing the warmth of her chest, her heart beating next to mine. I inhaled the scent of her dark, shiny hair. *Miracle of miracles, we're reunited—together again after all these years. Thank you for helping me find her—for making my dream come true. Thank you.* I shouted silent praises to the Universe, and they echoed back to me in waves of joy, that washed up and down inside me. *Thank you. I'm so grateful. Thank you,* I repeated again and again, until the waves subsided into glistening ripples.

With a deep breath, I'd sent my prayer flying to the Light, then opened my eyes and stretched. A tickle in the back of my mind said, "It's okay to help God along a little." That's when I'd called Sonia and heard about how to contact the adoptee support group. She'd suggested sending for my hospital records, too. So I'd done both.

And now this call. On a Friday? At the office? Thoughts of Mary Anne slinked by like shadows.

Louise launched into her tale. "I'm an adoptee, myself—I've been searching for my birthmother for thirteen years. I was placed through the same adoption agency as your child. I've begged them—pleaded with them—to help me. Once, I sat in their office all day and cried, but they wouldn't even talk to me. The courts are no better. They're all fascists here! They've done absolutely everything in their power to keep me from finding my birthmother."

I smirked and cupped my chin with my free hand. *Plenty of times I thought of going up there. Glad I didn't waste my time.* Hope spiraled downwards.

"That sounds rather discouraging," I said.

"Well, it is, but I have something else I wanted to tell you about," Louise said. All at once, her mood brightened. "The reason I was so excited about your letter is that I have an adopted sister who was born March 26, 1966, just four days before your daughter. She was born in the same hospital and adopted through the same agency."

I gave a little snort and tilted my eyebrows. "Really?" The dates didn't even match. I'd already had one false find. I didn't need another.

She paused a second before charging back in. "I was wondering if she might be the daughter you're seeking. I certainly wouldn't put it past this adoption agency to alter someone's birth date by a couple of days," she added temptingly.

I furrowed my eyebrows. "But how could they possibly do something like that? A person's birth date is sacred."

"Oh," she spat out, "I think they'd do *anything* to make it impossible for adoptees and birthmothers to find each other!"

My chair squeaked as I shifted back in it. "Well, what's your sister's coloring?" It wouldn't hurt to ask a qualifying question or two—just in case.

"She has an olive complexion and very dark brown, almost black, hair," came Louise's reply. "It used to be curly when she was little."

My heart stopped; my voice faltered. "My daughter was dark at birth." I straightened my posture and began scratching words on my note pad. "What else can you tell me?" I ventured. "Is your sister at all musical?"

Her reply gleamed back like sparkles of light. "Yes, she is. She took piano lessons for quite a while. And she's very bright! She's always been a top student. She went to Valley University."

I scribbled it all down. My heart was racing.

"Really? My other daughters are excellent students, and *I* went to Valley University." (So had Mary Anne.) I put my pen down. The room seemed to twirl. "Oh, Louise! What if this were really true?" I felt myself being swept downstream by a powerful current of hope. "What else can you tell me about her? What's her name? How is she? How has she been?" The questions came tumbling out.

"Well, my sister's name is Clara," Louise said, slowing her pace. "She had a pretty rough childhood, but she just got a great job last year with a big manufacturing company. She's their production manager."

My heart jumped again. "Production manager? Part of my job is managing the production of books." My words started bounding out ahead of me. "I've always been quite analytical, very organized."

"Oh, that's Clara, all right. Very organized," Louise waved a flag of pride. "She can figure out the most efficient way to get things done. They really like her at her job. They gave her a promotion already. She's taken charge of her whole area."

While Louise rattled on, I took a deep breath and let it all sink in. Could I possibly get this lucky twice in a row? *So* unlikely, yet, how could I dismiss her call out of hand, when all these things matched? I'd been careful not to give away the answers, but Louise had piled one right response atop the next. Didn't that defy the law of probability? Shouldn't I find out more?

But there was something I wanted to go back to . . . something she'd said earlier.

"Louise, what did you mean when you said Clara had a tough childhood?"

Louise heaved a little sigh. "This is a sad story," she warned me. She lowered her voice. "My sister Clara was physically abused by our adoptive mother when she was young."

Her words gored me. *Physically abused? That was my very worst fear. How could it have happened anyway? How unfair!* My stomach clenched; my mind was too blistered to reply.

"Our mother had been a very sweet lady," Louise explained, "but soon after we got Clara, she became mentally ill and started physically abusing Clara. I tried to stop her, but there were a couple of bad years. Clara's much better now, but she still carries some emotional scars from what she went through."

I had to say something. "I'm so sorry," I murmured. A deep silence lay between us.

"I think finding her birthmother would be a good thing for Clara now," Louise offered quietly. "Our adoptive mother's been dead for a few years."

She paused for my response, but the story she'd related was still ringing in my ears like a tolled bell. I swallowed and forced my lips to move. "She had a rough time, didn't she?" I could hear Louise breathing, but she didn't reply. I sighed and picked up my pen, rubbing my thumb back and forth over its smooth barrel. *Come on, Ann,* urged voices in my head. I swallowed.

"I'd like to help her, Louise, whether I'm her birthmother or not. It sounds like Clara could use a sympathetic mother figure." That said, I felt lighter.

"And, hey, we might even have a match. If not," I bantered, "we sure have a lot of strange coincidences here! We'll need to verify this somehow, though." My mind flashed a to-do list: Call Sonia. Write to the agency with this new name. Talk to Linda to see if what I'd just heard matched the astrology chart I had.

I explained what I'd just been through with Mary Anne and that I'd already been planning to travel up her way the following week. I promised to call her back soon. . . .

When I hung up, joy was still rushing through me like clean, bubbling water, but, little by little, it all ebbed away. By the time I got back from lunch, the river bed was parched and dry and a steamroller was maneuvering on my chest, flattening me into a caricature of myself. Work was impossible. All I wanted to do was cry.

I left the office at two and headed home to dig out the affirmation the Ministry of Prayer had sent me in the mail. I read it to myself again and again: "I am a cherished and loving expression of God. Today I consciously release the past to the past as I practice love and appreciation for myself and others. I think and act with confidence."

Show love and appreciation for myself? How am I going to do that? I hung my head and let my mind go blank.

Then, I knew. I grabbed my writing tablet and went out on my back porch to enjoy the sun.

The late-summer chirping of cicadas came and went in waves. My goldfish pond was abuzz with bees hovering over a few waxy, pink water lilies. Water iris leaves spiked up nearby. They hosted blue dragonflies, whirring from perch to perch like pencil-thin helicopters. In the pond's center, a yellow water lily stood erect with a pale fringe of petals flaring out around a deep gold center. Outside the pond, garden boxes of shrubs and flowers spread a crazy quilt of purple, pink, yellow, orange and white. A gray catbird perched on the copper birdbath beyond, dipped its beak cautiously for a drink, and then flipped water over its back. Our neighbor's wind chimes tolled in a sudden, leaf-tickling breeze.

My cold, heavy guilt and sadness seemed strangely out-of-place here, next to the dance of the warm breeze. I took out my pad and pen. It was time to write to Clara.

How do I connect without raising false hopes? I asked.

The answer drifted into my consciousness on a butterfly's wings. *Write to her as a birthmother to an adoptee friend.*

So, I sat in the sun and composed my letter out of the dark mists of my soul. I reassured Clara that a birthmother never forgets her child. I related the twisted tale of my pregnancy . . . the affair in

France . . . my parents' reaction . . . my fear of being an unfit mother. And I told her how my pregnancy had changed my life . . . led to counseling and a new outlook. I described my baby's appearance and my own. I also mentioned being able to pick up objects with my double-jointed toes, a trait passed down from my father. In closing, I offered to help her search.

When I put down my pen, I felt peaceful again.

. . . I'd forgotten all about that scared, lonely girl from long ago that I'd just described to Clara. I'd forgotten how inexperienced, how unwise and how guilt-ridden she'd been. . . .

Why am I still condemning myself? I did the best I could at the time. Maybe I'm not the criminal I've been making myself out to be.

Slowly, my thoughts drifted back to Louise's phone call, to all those bizarre coincidences. . . .

Could this be the miracle I'd been hoping for?

25 - Skirting the System

The following Friday, I bolted back down the narrow hall to Linda's office and planted myself on the couch. Before she had a chance to finish closing the door, I was already launching into my tale. Leaning forward with my elbows on my knees, I chattered on about my encounter with Mary Anne and the recent phone call from Louise.

"Isn't it bizarre?" I said, finally looking up. "Clara actually *could* be my daughter. At the moment, there's nothing to contradict it. I wrote to the Agency last week, asking if we're a match. Of course, they'll probably lie." I twisted my hands together. "Don't you think they would, to cover up the abuse?"

There was a scratch at the door. Linda nodded and got up to admit her dog.

"My friend Sonia suggested blood tests. Isn't that a great idea? We'll see. I'm going to meet with Louise first, next Tuesday. Maybe we can spot some physical similarities."

I paused, breathed deeply, and slid back on the sofa. Ti-Ti had flopped at Linda's feet and lay there, head down, like a shaggy, white dust mop. Linda shifted in her wing-backed chair.

"You've certainly been busy on this project, Ann," she said. "How can I help?"

I told her I wanted to know if the life story I'd heard about Clara matched the chart I had for my daughter. Linda's square jaw bobbed and set her oversized earrings to twisting under her ears. The little silver stars were tinkling softly when she sat down beside me on the couch. Together, we leaned forward and puzzled over the chart.

Pointing to the lower half of the wheel, she began her analysis. "There's a definite possibility of child abuse here: Saturn in Pisces in the fourth house. The fourth house rules early beginnings, personal foundations ('childhood'). Saturn represents limitation and discipline; its position usually shows where there's a serious life problem. Pisces is often a self-sacrificing, martyring energy; so, Saturn in Pisces in the fourth house can add up to abuse in childhood."

My forehead furrowed. My heart thudded against my chest. *Does that mean abuse would have been her destiny whether I'd kept her or not?*

I wondered.

Linda was still absorbed in the chart. "She has a south node in Scorpio in the first house," she continued. "That's another indication of turmoil in early life in matters like ego, personal survival, and self-concept." She looked up at me then, her eyes deep pools. "Her life task is to find serenity and confidence in herself. When you begin life with a lack like this, it helps you to value and seek what you don't have."

She returned to the chart, sliding her finger to the side. "Her north node falls in the seventh house. That means she has lots to learn about relationships. I'd be surprised to find her married at this young age with this kind of seventh house."

Linda glanced over at me. "Is she married?" I shook my head "no." "How old is she? Twenty-three?" I gave a quick nod.

"Well, she'll probably work this out later in life, but it will be a tough area for her," she said.

"Anything else, Linda?" I asked, though everything was starting to jumble together.

"Well, she has Scorpio rising." Linda rubbed her chin. "That should make her very mysterious-looking and secretive. She should be the kind of person who keeps pretty much to herself."

"I'll look for that when I see her picture."

"And I think we talked about her Moon in Cancer last time: she should feel very sensitive to and close to her mother."

I sighed and looked over at the snoozing dog. "Her sister says she was quite devoted to her mother in spite of the abuse."

Linda raised her eyebrows. "That's Moon in Cancer. . . ."

When I got home from Linda's, a fat envelope from the hospital was waiting for me. My face broadened with satisfaction when I ripped it open. At last—four pages of faded records, *proving* that, on March 30, 1966, I had delivered a baby girl. So, I hadn't imagined it all, as it sometimes seemed.

In faded print, I read my doctor's long-forgotten name. His image flashed before me . . . kind eyes and a red bow tie. Next, I saw my father's name. That had been long ago, when he was in his prime. I remembered his narrow shoulders, his broad middle . . . the dark hair, thinning at the temples, combed straight back . . . full lips and clear, steady, blue eyes.

Our old address jumped out at me from the line below . . . the stone house with the circular drive. And there was my once-upon-a-time weight . . . (I weighed now what I'd weighed then, pregnant!) . . . eye and hair color, blood type. I paged back through two sheets describing my labor progress . . . when my water broke, how many centimeters I was dilated; all of it had been faithfully logged over the twenty-six-hour span, along with blood pressure readings . . . and then, on the very last page, the date and time of my baby's birth.

I blinked my eyes. *Damn! I had her time of birth wrong. That's going to change her chart.*

I made a mental note to mention that to Linda, while I proudly tucked my records away in the section in my search notebook reserved for "official documents." The very first one. I drew in a slow, deep breath, and, with its release, warm satisfaction cruised through me. I'd reclaimed a piece of my missing past. I felt good about that!

I'd make a copy to show Louise next week, too. . . .

I skimmed along the interstate the following Tuesday morning. Gray clouds insisted on hugging the horizon, but I was guided by the sun that blazed in my heart. The last ten days had dragged past, and, finally, I was on my way to see Louise.

I'd never before returned to the city where Jennifer was born. I approached, now, on an interstate highway that hadn't been built twenty-four years ago. The old town had a slick, modern look. A few street names sounded familiar, but that was all. It seemed only vaguely possible that I'd ever been there before.

I followed Louise's directions, proceeding north to the small town where she and her siblings had been raised. When I got off the interchange, my heart sank. Such a boring little town. It reminded me of the town where my dad was raised . . . so dull that I'd spent my time there walking up and down the streets, past the old ladies sweeping the sidewalks in front of their tidy homes . . . past the general store and the filling station. "Fun" was poking around old churchyards and swinging at the school ground. A dark-haired child wobbled down an empty sidewalk on a two-wheeled bike. That could have been Clara fifteen years ago. I sighed. So much for the "cultural and intellectual advantages" I'd asked for. I'd have to be content with the fact that she'd made it to college.

I pulled into Louise's driveway off the main street, a little way out of town. The pavement wound around the back of a two-story, brick, detached house. A flower garden ringed the yard. A small, trim woman in her mid-thirties popped out of the back door just as I was getting out of my car. Louise was casually dressed, like me, in shorts and a knit shirt.

"You must be Ann." She stepped forward and shook my freezing hand. "Please. Come in."

I followed her into the kitchen, a tidy space with yellow, ruffled curtains and gleaming, new wood cabinets. Children's toys were neatly put away. She offered me a cold drink, and then invited me into a small family room which adjoined the kitchen. I slid carefully into a soft couch. Louise perched herself in an upholstered chair opposite me.

A knitted afghan, folded on back of the couch, caught my eye. I pointed. "Did you do this?" I asked, to break the ice.

"Yes, I did." She smiled proudly and took a sip of her soda.

"It's very nice. I knit, too." I set down my drink and felt my hands begin to lose their nervous coldness. "I learned to knit when I was at the home for unwed mothers."

I cracked a smile. It was okay to talk about "it" here—my forbidden past. I pulled out the hospital records that proved that I wasn't an imposter. Louise looked them over and then carefully passed them back to me.

"Let me show you a picture of Clara when she was a baby." She reached over and picked something up from the table next to her. "We have this from when Clara was about ten months old," she said, leaning forward to hand me the precious slide.

When I took it from her, my hand was shaking. I squinted and held it up to the light. But I couldn't see it clearly. So I walked over to the window at the side of the room. I tipped the slide first to the window and then to a nearby light bulb. *How can I tell if it's her?* I bit my lip and slowly maneuvered the tiny image so I could see it clearly. I could barely make out a smiling little girl with curly, dark hair standing in a play pen. Could it be my daughter?

I groped for the memory of my dark-haired baby in her hospital bassinet, but it kept receding down the dark tunnel of long ago. I rubbed my forehead and sighed.

"Well, maybe. I really can't say for sure." I plodded back to the couch, balancing the slide by its edges and turning it one way and then the other.

"I'm sorry to say we don't have too many pictures of Clara when she was a little girl because our adoptive mother was so sick," Louise apologized. "But I do have this picture of her when she graduated from high school."

She passed over a 5"x 7" photograph in a silver frame. It was a close-up of a face that made my heart stop.

Louise saw me freeze. "What is it?" she asked.

"Oh, Louise," I gasped. "I think this could be my daughter." For an instant, I had seen Claude's broad face smiling back at me.

I haltingly told Louise about my two French lovers and how my daughter resembled the second one, Claude, when she was born. Soon, she knew all about my first marriage and my current life, too. After I'd finished, she began telling me the long, sad tale of Clara's childhood.

Louise had been the oldest of four adopted children. Clara was thirteen years younger, and there were two boys in between. Their father, a top executive for a major defense contractor, worked long hours, and his wife had stayed home to raise the children. The adoptive mother had always been an attentive, gentle woman. But the year after Clara was adopted, everything changed.

"In 1967, my mother became pregnant for the first time," Louise said. "But when her baby was a few months along, the doctors removed it from her womb."

She paused, while I sat, frozen in silence, struggling to understand.

"Her child was surgically aborted because of an Rh-factor risk," she explained, her lip trembling.

"Oh, that's awful." I twisted my head away to shut out the horror while shudders ripped through my body.

When I looked back at Louise, she was staring straight into my eyes. "Our mother was never the same again after that. Mentally, she cracked." A vat of deep pain had opened in Louise's face and she allowed me to see her feelings. For the flick of an eyelash, our souls mingled.

Then, she continued on in a flat voice. "Most of her wrath fell on one-year-old Clara. We older kids were all off at school, and Dad was off at work, so much of the abuse was unwitnessed, I'm afraid."

"But, one morning, as I was getting ready to leave for school, I saw Mother hitting Clara's head again and again against a headboard. I was afraid for Clara's life, so I went in and screamed at Mother. I pummelled her until she stopped." She paused to catch her breath and wipe a tear out of her eye. "When I finally got to school, I was shaking and hysterical. So, they took me to the office and questioned me. I broke down and told them about the abuse and begged them to help me."

She gave me a quick summary of what happened after that. The school had contacted both the adoption agency and Louise's father, trying to intervene. But the agency did nothing . . . and her father had waited until Clara was three or four before having the mother committed to a mental institution. Unfortunately, much damage had already been done to Clara by then.

Once the mother was hospitalized, Louise became Clara's surrogate mother and raised her as best she could. Their mother had taken her own life about three years ago, and Clara herself had attempted suicide after that. But that bad time was in the past. Clara had recovered, successfully completed college, and, just a few months ago, had accepted a great job offer in Massachusetts. She was living there now with a female friend from school. It seemed she was on her way at last.

Louise smiled wearily and took a sip of her now-watery soda. We sat in silence, wiping the tears out of our eyes.

"Thanks for saving Clara's life," I murmured.

Louise gave a little shrug and then told me she knew somebody who worked in the hospital. Maybe her friend could get my baby's medical records. Perhaps there we could find a clue that would tie Clara to Jennifer. She also promised to tell Clara about our visit and ask her if she wanted me to call.

My heart was beating fast. Everything was coming together. I reached in my purse and pulled out the letter I'd written to Clara that day by the pond. Louise read it though and said it sounded fine. She'd find Clara's address for me. We hugged each other and agreed to talk in a few days.

When I pulled out of Louise's driveway and turned back onto the main highway, the car seemed to float. I felt lighter than I had in years.

26 - Buried Burdens

By late afternoon, I had breezed off the interstate onto a cracked, concrete two-lane. On either side, majestic maples defined the roadbed and dappled it with shade. The ripe scent of late summer edged the air that whistled in my window. But soon, the road bumped over railroad tracks and wound past clapboard houses, spattered with mud—"company houses" they called them years ago, when their yards sported clotheslines and kids' toys and when steel mill smoke choked every form of life.

But things were different, now. The smoke was gone; the men were unemployed.

The road twisted up a steep slope and past my ex-mother-in-law's church, back on the left. Then, just down the hill on the right, stood the "beer garden," favorite hang-out of that good-for-nothing Benny. I pushed down the pedal and sped by.

What a poor excuse for a father-in-law that man used to be! All he'd do was blow smoke in my face and ask me to sit on his lap. I wonder what she ever saw in him. He must have sweet-talked her or something. Maybe she fell for the candy and flowers he brought in the beginning. She'd always said he had a kind heart, but I could never got past the noxious smell of smoke and stale beer.

A few miles past town was the turnoff to Adrian's mother's house. Familiar landmarks appeared to guide me . . . a house, a sign, a cow pasture. Soon, I spotted her house, incongruously set on a landscaped hillside overlooking a dairy farm. Rhododendrons, pine, and birch trees filled the space at the bottom by the road; a rock garden climbed up the bank behind the house; and on the back hill, a young pine forest sprawled on one side and an orchard on the other. It was Adrian's design, constructed twenty-five years ago, and he and his mother, together, had pampered and pruned each plant ever since. The result was spectacular.

I pulled in front of her two-car garage and gave a quick beep-beep. A second later, a familiar old moon of a face appeared at the porch window.

Adrian's Mom, Margie, was a strong, big-boned woman of Flemish stock, born in the second decade of the Twentieth Century, a few years after her parents had immigrated to America from Belgium. All eight children had helped work the farm. Now in her mid-seventies, Margie suffered from many physical complaints, but she was always helping others, rather than feeling sorry for herself.

By the time I had grabbed my bag and slammed the car door, she'd managed to throw her arms around me.

"Hi, Mom," I squeezed out, in spite of her tight embrace.

"Hi, yourself, Kiddo," she said, her faded blue eyes giving off sparks. "Golly. It's good to see you! You're looking great."

"You're looking great, yourself, for an old lady," I kidded her.

Her face crinkled into a grin. "Hey, Brat! You're not getting any younger yourself, either," she rejoined, clasping me around the waist. We walked up the garden steps arm in arm.

My first meeting with Margie had been seared in my memory. It was the spring after I'd surrendered Jennifer. Wedding plans were in the air, but I had yet to meet any of Adrian's family and was worried sick that they wouldn't like me.

I was quaking in Adrian's apartment, decked out in my finest dress, when Margie strode in wearing a pants suit. "Are you Ann?" she boomed. Then she'd flung her arms around me in a bear hug and declared, "We love you, darling. Any girl my son loves, I love her, too." And that was that. No tests. No trials. It still brought tears to my eyes when I thought of it.

She'd taught me a great lesson that day: love accepts people unconditionally. And Margie had never wavered in her love for me. Even through the awkwardness of my divorce and re-marriage, she'd always been there for me and her grandchildren. But I'd never told her about Jennifer. *Today, I will*, I resolved as we strolled up the steps together.

After dinner, she led me on a garden tour. We inspected the sprawling tree wisteria in front of the house and the pines and birches below, which needed thinning. We checked the rhododendrons for swelling flower buds and agreed they'd be dazzling next spring. She tallied the season's take from the vegetable garden. When we'd worked our way back to the house, we settled into a chair swing near the rock garden. We sat there, pushing the swing back and forth, listening to its steady creak-creak. The sun steadily slipped behind the hill. All the while, I was trying to force my voice over a very large lump in my throat. Finally, when the colorful sky began to fade to a pinkish blush, I began speaking in a thin voice.

"Mom, there's something I want to tell you about that happened to me a long time ago," I stumbled. "You never knew about this, but I have another daughter, a child I had out of wedlock a year or so before Adrian and I were married. Adrian has always known."

Her rough, warm hand tenderly clasped my smooth, cold one. "Oh, Honey. I'm sorry for you. Do the girls know?" she asked.

"Yes. They've known for a long time," I said quietly, squeezing her hand. I pushed myself onward. "I wanted to tell you this, Mom, because I've been searching for my daughter. As a matter of fact, I think I may have found her." Quickly, I told her about my meeting that morning with Louise and the earlier episode with Mary Anne. I sighed deeply when I finished. Twilight was setting in and the frogs and bugs were tuning up for their nightly twitters. The swing continued to creak steadily back and forth.

"That's quite a story," she said. She smiled and looked me in the eye. "I'm glad you could tell me about it."

The air between us seemed to vibrate. I kept silent and continued rocking. Margie said something about the abuse Clara had suffered, and then she looked away into the darkening sky.

"We were all beat as kids," she began. "Our father, the Old Belgian, would come home drunk and mean. We used to run away, but he'd lock us out of the house until morning. Many a night I spent in the barn or huddled under the steps." But her mother had been the sweetest and kindest person on earth, and they'd all survived somehow. (Of course, the chance to get out of the house had no doubt influenced her early marriage to Adrian's father.)

Yes, Margie was reconciled to the past, except for one thing. Her father had cut off her dream of education. She could never forgive him for that.

She straightened up and her voice took on a bitter edge. "Ann, I was the best student in the eighth grade. My teacher even went out to my house and begged my father to allow me to go to high school. I thought it was all set. My mother made me a new dress and everything. I had my hair braided and my new dress on and was ready to walk out the door to go to high school when my father stepped up to me and said . . ." She curled up her lips and put her hand on her hip in imitation . . . "'You girl. You no need school.'" Her nostrils flared and her eyes blazed. Those two stubby sentences had shattered her dream.

"He slammed the door in my face, Ann. And that was the end of it. . . . Oooh," she shuddered and shook her head. Her voice grew husky. "I was the best student in the eighth grade, but he said, 'You girl. You no need school!' and that was that."

By the time she'd finished her story, the sky was black and her eyes were sad and impotent. I saw that, for her, that day sixty years ago was as fresh as yesterday. I leaned over and squeezed her cold, dry hand. The swing ground to a stop.

Suddenly, in the moonlit darkness, I thought I could see a long parade of suffering souls. Margie and Clara and all those who had suffered physical abuse limped along, wounded, brandishing sticks. Clara's adoptive mother and Margie and all those who had lost their precious dreams groped along the path, blind and lost. Louise and I were there, too, along with all who had set standards of perfection for themselves. We lay in the mud, wallowing in guilt over things that had turned out in ways we couldn't control or predict. It was like a scene etched by Blake for Dante's *Inferno*.

Are we cursed to always bear these burdens? I wondered. Are all of us like Margie? Will our wounds never heal? Or can some of us heal and walk away free?

If we hold onto our hurts, where, exactly, do they go? Do we tuck them away in our kidneys, our backs, the foot, the hands, the eyes? Margie had major health problems in all those areas. Were they related to this unresolved anger toward her father? Also, why had the kindest, most generous woman in the world been stuck in two unhappy marriages, the last one to an alcoholic?

Questions, questions . . . I held my head high and breathed in the night air. Sure, it was scary and risky for me to deal openly with my past. But, possibly, it was far more dangerous *not* to deal with it.

I made it home the next day, and by evening had fallen back into one of those dips life gives you, after the rise, to let you learn the lesson all over again.

"Ned, if only I hadn't given her up, none of this would have happened. I'm afraid Clara won't like me. I'm afraid I'll mess up our

184

relationship," I lamented over our dinner out. A candle flickered and threw a shadow over Ned's drawn face. He stretched his hands across the white table cloth and rested them on top of mine.

"Why do you feel that way?" he probed.

I withdrew my hands and sat up, twisting my head around to make sure the waitress was out of hearing range. "Because I'm such a louse and a screw-up." Out came a whole tirade of harsh self-judgement that sat heavily in the air between us.

Ned leaned forward. His eyes, those wide-set, probing, heavy-browed eyes, looked at me steadily. "You know, it sounds like you're being unreasonably hard on yourself."

I could see the waitress sashaying across the tile floor with our salads. I sighed and sat back, silent, while she served us. I knew he was right. After all, I'd done the best I could at the time.

"Okay," I said just before I picked up my fork and stabbed it into a gleaming leaf of spinach, "I know what I'm going to do." I poked my fork in my mouth and then jerked my napkin to the table.

"I'm going to write all my negative thoughts down on this napkin, and when we get home, I'm going to burn them and flush the ashes down the toilet." I smirked with pride. While Ned dug into his salad, I fished my pen out of my purse. "It's called 'purge affirmation,'" I explained. "I just learned about it last week in Linda's class."

And so I scribbled down all those harsh judgements on the thin, bumpy surface of the napkin. When I got home, I lit a candle in our darkened dining room and put the napkin in a metal dish. I touched the candle flame to the napkin and watched as it curled and blackened. When the venomous thoughts were a fragile black shell, I crushed them and flushed them down the toilet. I envisioned the ash flowing down the sewer pipes and out into a river somewhere. They'd be swept away into the vastness of the ocean some day. I wasn't going to let them ruin my future with Clara.

Late that night, I wrote another letter to the Agency. "I know about the abuse Clara suffered," I told them. "I don't hold you responsible. Please tell me truthfully if Clara is my daughter. We're going to proceed with blood tests to make sure," I added, just to let them know I held a trump card. I sent Louise a copy of my letter. Then I went out of town for two days.

When I got home, a letter from the adoption agency was waiting for me. "I thought I'd let you open this," Ned said. He looked at me solemnly. My hands shook as I tore open the envelope. My eyes swept down to the sentence in the middle of the page: "With regard to your recent inquiry, we are sorry to inform you that Clara ____ is not the daughter you seek."

My throat burned: "'Not the daughter I seek?' How *dare* they lie to me like this?"

27 - Blood Tests

The car's blower whimpered into silence when the key clicked off. I stared over the steering wheel at the windshield. The rain seemed to drum down even harder now, and steam was creeping back over the glass. With one hand, I fished for the sheet of paper I'd tossed onto the passenger seat; with the other, I rubbed a clear spot out of the corner of the window. My eyes shifted between the paper and the view outside. "Four-story, red brick building . . . arch windows . . . a green awning. Yeah, this is it," I muttered to myself.

I glanced down at the clock built into the tan dashboard. 8:55 a.m. "Okay. Let's do it."

Clutching my briefcase, I unlatched the car door. A cold spray misted my face, but I widened the opening enough to unfurl my umbrella and hop out. I slammed and locked the car door, then skipped over a swirling rivulet and squished off toward the lab, my heart beating in time with the pounding rain. I reached the shiny, green awning a moment later and pulled open the heavy glass door. When it sucked shut behind me, a grin spread across my face. I was safe, at last, on an island of truth that floated far above the sludge of adoption bureaucracy.

After a three-week whirlwind of phone calls, it was now September 20. I looked through the window at the darkened sky and watched it all flash by again, like a silent movie. . . . First, my throbbing rage over the letter from the agency; next, Sonia's repeated suggestion about the blood test, and a rekindling of hope; then, the call to Louise. . . .

She started laughing when I read her the agency's one-sentence letter. "I think they're lying. Why don't you do that blood test?"

"Okay, Louise, but I'd like to talk to Clara, first."

"Okay. Call her," she said.

It sounded simple, but my stomach had turned over. "I'd feel funny doing that. Shouldn't I send her my letter first?"

So, I had . . . then waited eight gut-clenching days for a response. When I started pacing in tight circles, I broke down and called Louise back.

"Hi," she answered. "Clara got your letter. She likes you."

My heart had broken open with relief. Tears leaked into the corners of my eyes, even now, thinking of it.

"She's open to taking the blood test. She wants you to call her."

Why did the thought of calling still stab me with fear? I poured myself a mug of hot tea and walked around the house twice. Finally, I went upstairs and perched myself on the edge of our bed. One by one, I punched out the numbers on our upstairs phone. Then I pressed the receiver to my ear.

"Hello!" lilted a friendly, female voice, over the reggae music rippling in the background.

"Hi . . . ah . . . this is Ann Hughes. I'm calling for Clara," I stumbled. "Is she there?"

"Sure. I'll put her on. One moment please."

I stopped breathing while I waited for a hand to pick up the phone. At last, a quiet, unsure voice reached out for me. "Hello. This is Clara."

I shot out of the gate like a race horse with his tail on fire, blabbering about the picture I'd seen at Louise's, the negative report from the agency, and the news that blood tests could prove the truth. Finally, I stopped to swallow, and then slipped her my burning question: "Will you take the blood test with me next week?"

I held my breath.

"Sure," she agreed.

I tucked her reply safely away in my head, and rattled on: they'd send her a kit Tuesday. She should go to her doctor that night and have him send it back by overnight mail. I'd give my sample the following morning. The data would be analyzed and we'd have a result in ten days.

All that was fine with her, too.

I sighed aloud. My heart started pumping again; slowly, the tension melted out of my forehead.

"Did you get my letter?" I asked.

"Yes. And I thought it was funny when you said you could pick things up with your toes, because I can do that, too," she giggled.

"Really?" My ears were buzzing. I shifted forward on the bed and swallowed hard. "You can pick things up with your toes?"

"Uh-huh. I used to pick up kitchen towels like that, when

Louise and I would do the dishes at home. And didn't you say something about a high arch? My feet have that."

I kicked off my slipper and slid my foot nearer, scrutinizing it. My voice quivered. "Do you have a funny bump on your foot below your little toe?"

She paused. "Yea. . . ."

"Clara, how about if I draw an outline of my feet and you can see if yours match? . . . ."

I know I must have looked ridiculous hopping around in my bare feet, dragging a pencil point around my foot. But, who cares, when your future happiness is at stake and everybody with answers is slamming doors in your face. I got two decent outlines, jammed them in an envelope, and mailed them off the next day. A few days later, I called Clara back.

Her voice jiggled with excitement. "I stood in them with my bare feet. My feet are smaller than yours, but the outlines are identical. My roommate Belinda thinks so, too."

Beams of joy had shot through me. I'd stomped the floor and whooped for joy. We were a match, by golly! We'd do the blood test Wednesday, and, by the end of September, I'd be able to prove it!

Outside, lightning splintered the sky with jagged streaks of light. I jerked out of my stupor at the crack of thunder that followed. Rain was pelting the green awning, swishing down the sidewalk in a bubbly tide. A door knob clicked on the inside wall. I turned around to see a receptionist in a white lab coat.

"Mrs. Hughes?"

My heart thumped. "Yes."

"We're ready for you now."

She led me down a brightly lit hall, past several offices, to a reception area, where she weighed and interviewed me. I presented my check for $250.00, and, a few minutes later, was escorted to a padded, reclining table in an adjoining room. Soon a nurse entered, carrying two empty blood vials and a sign with my name and case number, which she asked me to hold at chest-level. She snapped two Polaroid pictures and then labeled the two vials.

"Did they do this to Clara, too?" I asked, trying to envision her visit to the doctor the night before.

189

"Yes," she said crisply. "We always do it the same way. Now just relax." She tied a rubber hose around my upper arm and fished for a vein. I wrinkled my face and waited until both vials were filled with dark red liquid. Afterwards, she escorted me back to the receptionist.

"We haven't received your daughter's blood yet," the receptionist noted, "Usually, it's here by now. Please call us back at noon to be sure it came in. Ask for me. My name is Mrs. Cartwright."

By the time I left, the rain had slowed to a drizzle and so had my fears . . . for the moment.

Five tension-packed weeks later, on Friday, October 20, I had Mrs. Cartwright on the other end of the phone again. Another mix up? I nearly throttled the receiver when I heard what she was saying!

First, there had been the problem with the blood kit. Clara had received it a day late, so the testing couldn't start until Thursday. Then there was the puzzling first test result: 28.28% probability. That meant Clara was *probably* my daughter, but they couldn't say for sure without an extra test, which they would run for me at no charge.

"The new test brings your probability of a match up to 57%," Mrs. Cartwright had reported two weeks ago.

"Does that mean for sure we're mother and daughter?" I was fighting a battle in my chest, with hope rising on one side and caution pressing down on the other. Finally, I'd asked to speak with the lab technician, himself.

"Well, let's say, most likely you are," Mr. Brown had replied.

My voice was taut. "Please understand. This is vitally important to me. I need to know with absolute certainty. What's your very best professional opinion?" Maddening!

"Well, these results do look very promising, Mrs. Hughes," he said warmly, zipping a thrill up and down my spine. "I'd be inclined to say there **is** a match here, since this result eliminates about 99% of the population. But there are other ways to produce these commonalities. The only way you can know for sure is to run a DNA test."

"A DNA test? Isn't this test kind of like that?" Were they giving me the run-around here?

"No. We did an HLA test." He explained that an HLA test was

quicker and cheaper to perform and completely accurate *if* you have the blood of the father, mother, and child. However, the DNA test was the only test that could tell parentage 100% when you have the blood of only one parent. "But, it's a very complicated procedure. Even with the work we've already done, it will take another two weeks to complete."

"Another two weeks?" I whined. My eyes had shot over to the calendar. October 6 . . . two weeks would be October 20.

"Yes. It's extremely complicated. Oh, and, I'm sorry to tell you, but there will be an additional expense, too. It will cost you an extra $200.00."

Another $200.00! That would run the cost of this caper up to $450.00. I sighed and tried to calculate what bills were due. There was my older daughter's college tuition to pay. Maybe I should just be satisfied with this "probably." What were the chances we'd be getting any correlation at all if she weren't my daughter?

But what if you're wrong? My heart sank.

"Will it give me 100% certainty?" I asked one last time.

"Yes. I promise you, it will."

Something had prodded me from inside. "Okay. I want the test. Please start it immediately. I'll be down with a check at lunch time."

Two more weeks! Clara and I were anxious to meet, but now we'd have to wait until the end of October. And it would have to be then, because my weekend calendar was full of rehearsals and concerts to sing for months afterwards. I could fly up on Friday night, October 27, and stay through Sunday, or we'd have to wait until January. Clara and I had talked it over, and then I'd bought a non-refundable ticket.

But, today . . . Friday, October 20 . . . my wait was supposed to be over!

"No, I'm sorry, Mrs. Hughes," Mrs. Cartwright was explaining a second time. "Your DNA test results aren't due in until October 30th."

My body rattled and shook like a combustion engine about to explode. "What do you mean October 30th? That's Monday a week! Mr. Brown told me he'd have the results today."

Her voice was calm, but firm. "No, I'm sorry, Mrs. Hughes. The

DNA analysis takes three weeks, not two. It's a very complicated procedure."

I glanced over at a blank wall as a wave of sadness drained through my body. "May I please speak to Mr. Brown?" I sighed in defeat.

"Surely. I'll be happy to connect you," Mrs. Cartwright replied, polite and efficient, as always.

Mr. Brown apologized. He'd been in error. The test did take three weeks, and nothing could be done to hurry it up. However, preliminary results would be ready sometime Saturday morning, October 28th. He'd be in the lab that morning, and I could call. He could tell me something, around 11:00 a.m.

My brain buzzed. Maybe I wouldn't have to put off my trip, after all. I could just fly to Massachusetts Friday night, then call and get the results Saturday morning. It was a little risky, but, all things considered, it seemed like a good plan.

28 - Getting There

The airplane motor rumbled beneath me in the darkened cabin. I pressed my face to the tiny side window and felt its cold smoothness on my cheek. Clouds pillowed the plane; all was dark below. The uneasiness I'd felt all week was still twisting inside me. I snapped open my seat belt and jockeyed one of my carry-on bags out from under the seat. *Photo albums. They weigh a ton.* I reached for the journal that stuck out of the side pocket, then booted the bag back under the seat.

I flipped to my entry for Friday, October 20 . . . "Found out test won't be done for another week. Big fight with Ned over whether or not to go to Massachusetts. He says, no, wait. He's worried I won't be able to handle a negative result. Thinks I'll be leading Clara on if I go. Told him I'd be careful about that, but what difference did it make where I was? Bad news would be upsetting wherever! The real question was: was I going to give up my ticket and my chance to meet Clara before January? Besides, how could the test be negative? I'm going. Sent her our family history book today, too."

"Monday, October 23. Huge pain in my right shoulder. Can hardly move my arm. Started Saturday. Worse today. Will get massage tomorrow. Wednesday, I'm going to see Linda and talk about the trip."

The refreshment cart bumped through the aisle. I waved them off and bent back over my journal.

"Wednesday, October 25. Massage yesterday didn't help much at all, but shoulder feels better since I talked to Linda today! She says the shoulder represents Virgo. In my chart, my Moon (emotions and 'mother' energy) are in Virgo in the Twelfth House. Since the Twelfth House represents my unconscious mind, limitations and karmic past, that means my ability to mother and feel emotions has been blocked in past lifetimes or by my unconscious mind.

"This is supposed to be a time when I can liberate myself from these emotional blockages. But she says, to do it, I'll have to give up my Virgonian perfectionism, my need to control everything, and my obsession with having everything go as planned. The amazing thing was, when she said all that, I got the shivers and something released in my damn shoulder.

"Sure is queer to go to an astrologer for a pain in your shoulder, but it worked for me today. Linda says your soul insists on growth, and when you go against that, it zaps you physically. She told me to go to Massachusetts and enjoy myself. If the tests turn out positive, great. If not, I can still have a nice weekend and probably do Clara a lot of good, too."

The cabin lights dimmed. I took a deep breath and closed my eyes. The deep droning of the plane bored through my solar plexus. *"Enjoy yourself. . . ." Sure,* I sneered, *that's easy for Linda to say. She's not the one living it. I hate not knowing what's going to happen.* When I opened my eyes and looked around, I could see only one dark figure seated across the aisle and a few heads silhouetted in front of me. Was I alone in some kind of twilight zone? The constant vibration of the plane's engine was the only sign of life. I shook off my fantasy and flipped to a fresh page of my notebook. My pen began to wobble across the page:

"Friday, October 27. On my way to meet Clara . . ."

A heavy weight pressed down on my chest. I could hardly breathe, but I forced the pen onward.

"Pampered myself this afternoon. Long lunch. Walked around the art museum. Ned took me to the airport. Promised him I'd be okay, no matter what. But why do I feel like crying all the time?"

I put my pen down and leaned my head back on the headrest. Then I closed my eyes and replayed last night's dream:

It's night, and I'm driving my car down a divided highway going south, when I suddenly realize I want to stop at a shopping center I've just passed on the other side of the road. I do a U-turn and head back.

A minute later, two police cars zoom up behind me, blue lights flashing. At first, I think they're coming after me about the U-turn. But when they scream past, I figure there must be an emergency somewhere ahead.

Soon, I turn off the highway onto the steep access road that leads to the shopping center. The lot looks quiet. I pull into a free space near the front and get out.

"Get down!" people shout at me from somewhere in the dark. I crouch between some parked cars, but a man in a black leather jacket has spotted me. He's toting an Uzi machine gun. I freeze in horror as he approaches and starts blasting away at me. I'm sure he'll kill me, but when I get over my fright, I find I'm okay. His bullets have only nicked me.

Then another assassin appears. He stands even closer and unloads his gun directly at me. He shoots me in the head, in the chest, everywhere. I'm positively riddled with bullets. I know I'm a goner this time. The shots knock me down . . . my flesh stings, the world spins around. I lie there, thinking I'm dead, but, gradually, my senses return. I stagger to my feet and rub my arms. When I look at the bullet holes, they're mere pin pricks.

The gunmen are gone, so I walk up to the mall to register a complaint. But the cops are busy with real problems, and they ignore me. Eventually, I realize I might as well go home. . . .

The low drone of the plane crept back into my awareness. I stared, unfocused, at the chair back in front of me. What could it all mean? A heavy weight still pressed on my chest. Slowly, I turned my head and peered out the window. We were descending. A city of a million twinkling lights loomed below. "My daughter Clara's city," I whispered to myself. A shiver wriggled through my body. I squeezed my eyes shut. "Thank you, God, for this incredible gift of reunion with my daughter." I squeezed out a few more tears, enough to make my nose start itching. Then, the plane wheels bumped on the ground, and I was lurched backwards when the engines roared into reverse. By the time I blinked my eyes open, the terminal gate was approaching.

The cabin lights flicked on. Mumbling began as people stood, stretched, climbed into the aisles, clicked open storage bins and shouldered their luggage. Finally, the line of bodies began shuffling off the plane. I wiped my eyes and released my seat belt buckle. Then I leaned over to unwedge the carry-ons. When I stood up, I hoisted a bag to each shoulder and bumped stiffly down the aisle.

As I approached the bright terminal, I squinted out over the buzzing crowd of faces, searching for Clara. But before I could spot her, I felt a hand on my shoulder. A large black girl with a broad smile greeted me.

"Hi! I'm Belinda, and this is Clara. You must be Ann."

I turned toward her in surprise and then saw a short person with wavy, dark hair standing at her side, glancing up at me. Was that Clara? Why was she so short and stocky? I'd expected Claude's daughter to be someone much taller.

"Hi, Clara!" I clutched her in an awkward embrace. "Forgive me for being so nervous. I cried most of the way here," I confessed.

"That's okay. We're nervous, too," Clara said in a husky but friendly voice, still looking down.

The two of them led the way to the baggage claim, and that's when I noticed Clara's limp. There was something about it that was deeply familiar. . . . I'd seen that very same limp in Paris, when I'd walked behind Jean-Michel. My heart sank; my mouth went dry.

"Louise didn't mention your limp, Clara. Are you okay?" I asked from behind in as flat and steady a tone as I could manage.

Clara glanced back once, but kept walking. "Yeah. I'm fine. Had it all my life. Might be something wrong with my back or something. I don't let it stop me, though. I go running every day."

My heart was hurting; I massaged above my breast. That dirty rat, Jean-Michel! I took a deep breath and tried to shake off my disappointment as we slowly made our way through the buzzing crowd to the baggage claim section.

Keep things on an even keel. Don't lead her on, I reminded myself. When we reached the luggage carousel, we stood there awkwardly, not knowing what to say.

"May I use your phone in the morning to call the lab?" I ventured at last.

Belinda turned to face me, her dark eyes full and liquid. "Sure. No problem," she answered in sing-song style. "Clara and I both have to work tomorrow morning. You can sleep in, and we'll be back around 12:30 or 1:00."

Her easy manner, her slight accent . . . "Are you from the Caribbean, Belinda?" I asked.

"Yes. From Jamaica." Her eyes sparkled. I glanced over at Clara, who stood nearby, looking at the floor.

After my luggage came through, with still more photo albums, we set off in Clara's car. Belinda drove. I sat in the back. They treated me to dinner at the local Red Lobster. I gave Clara the gift I'd chosen for her, a pair of tiny pearl earrings. All evening, we stared at each other and tried to make a connection. I gave her some sketchy family history, but mostly we talked about the present: my work, her work, small talk. No rush. We'd have the rest of our lives to get to know each other.

At one point, I reached over to feel her hair. It was coarse and black. She said it had been curly with a reddish tint when she was a kid.

"Well, that could be," I told her. "I carry a red recessive gene. My daughter Renate has red hair."

At last, we gave in to our fatigue and headed for their apartment in a complex across town. Once inside, they helped me drag my suitcases into Clara's room. Clara paused to say goodnight. Then she grabbed her stuffed lamb and headed off for a sleeping bag on Belinda's floor.

I closed the door and looked around her tiny room. On the walls, a close-up poster of Michael Jordan "hanging" and another of the Chicago Bears football team spread on two adjacent walls. Above her bed hung a blue and white college pennant. A small bookshelf held mysteries, animal and sports books and Clara's collection of stuffed animals. Soon I turned off the light and changed into my nightgown. I settled under a heavy pile of blankets, hoping for sleep. But a thick silence closed in around me and besieged me with disturbing thoughts. *I like Clara. She's friendly. Just has a hard time expressing herself. It will probably take a while to get to know her. I'll be patient.*

I turned over and tried, once more, to sleep. But this time, a huge lump of disappointment bulged under me. *Don't be a fool. There's no way Clara can be Claude's daughter. She's short like Jean-Michel. They even have the same limp. Damn!*

Angry thoughts shadow-boxed in my mind. *I guess I had to tell myself that back then. It was pretty stupid not to consider the other possibility.* My stomach twisted in frustration. *Why am I going through all this for HIS daughter, anyway?* I heaved a sigh. *What about the child I thought I had with Claude?* Tears invaded; I mourned her loss.

As the night crept by, I made my peace with Jean-Michel. *After all*, I finally told myself, *he did give me a child, the most priceless of gifts. And what really matters is that Clara's MY daughter. I don't care WHO fathered her any more!* Deep in the night, I sighed my acceptance and sank into a restless sleep.

29 - Moment of Truth

It was still dark outside when Belinda's alarm had buzzed, but I was careful not to get up. I lay there listening as a door swished open and another banged shut. The toilet flushed; the shower sputtered on. Later, while the hair dryer droned away in the bedroom, the ritual was repeated. A little after 6:30, two sets of feet shuffled down the hall. The front door opened and closed. Then, quiet settled back over the apartment like a heavy layer of dust.

I lay there for hours, listening to the rise and fall of my breath . . . to bird chirps . . . rolling rubber . . . and the sound of dusty silence swirling around me. Every once in a while, I cracked my eyes open to catch a glint of sun pouring through Clara's blinds. I'd doze off, wake, check the clock, doze off again. At 9:30, I scrambled to my feet.

My chest was already tight. I slipped into the shower and let the warm water cascade over me. I sucked in curls of steam, wallowed in its comforting tat-a-tat. Afterwards, I blow-dried my hair, donned loose jeans and a flannel shirt and wandered out to the kitchen to fix myself a cup of coffee.

Everything was set out for me on the sparkling, white countertop. A jar of instant coffee, a spoon, mug, sugar. I put the tea kettle on to boil and looked around the tiny alcove. The tall cupboards seemed to be whispering strange messages just out of my hearing. I poured some hot water in my coffee cup and headed out of there.

Setting my coffee on the side table, I lowered myself onto Clara's thinly padded couch. The digital clock beside the phone read 10:10 a.m. I sat there staring, until it flipped to 10:11 a.m., pause, flip . . . 10:12 a.m. . . . pause, flip. . . .

I rose and paced to the window, scanning the sculpted lawn below. It was littered with fallen leaves. I fixed my gaze on a row of spikey flame-red bushes that lined the base of the apartment building across the way. Expressway traffic whined in the distance. I turned away from the window. The red family history book I'd sent Clara lay accusingly on the dining room table. I grimaced and headed off toward the huge exercise bike near the door. I climbed on the metal monster and pumped a few times, then dismounted and plopped back on the couch. My heart was racing. I rubbed the knot of tension in my chest and stared at the square, red bar pattern on the clock.

Only 10:19 a.m.? What the hell! Get a hold of yourself!

I chugged down the rest of my coffee, returned my mug to the kitchen and scurried back the hall to Clara's room. I rummaged through my bag for my *Science of the Mind* and then flipped through the Daily Guide section while stumbling back to the living room. Finally, one caught my eye: "Right Action Prevails In My Affairs."

> Therefore I say unto you, What things soever ye desire, when ye pray, believe that ye receive them, and ye shall have them. *Mark 11:24.*
>
> Realizing there is a Law of Good that governs my affairs, I loose every thought of doubt, fear or uncertainty and accept the good that I desire, here and now. Knowing that the Law of Good not only knows how to create, but must contain within Itself all the details of its own creation, I let go of every thought of outlining and accept the perfect answer today. . . . I declare that I move into a greater sphere of action and life with complete certainty, calm confidence and limitless trust.

I breathed deeply and let my shoulders drop. A gentle wash of relaxation spread through my body. *Good,* I thought. I kept my head down and concentrated on more Daily Guides and then two articles. Finally, I looked up. The clock read 11:03 a.m. That old tightness began to stretch across my chest again, but I knew I could handle it now.

I fumbled for the slip of paper where I'd written the lab's number and my telephone credit card number. I tried to imagine Mr. Brown, in his white lab coat, perched on a stool, bent over a microscope. He'd be sitting at one of those long, black tables with a built-in sink.

I dialed and waited, eyes wide.

The phone would be on the wall. He'd have to get up and walk past a row of benches, past a jumble of bubbling test tubes. Computers and fluorescent lights would be humming in the background. His nose would be tickling from the dirty-socks smell of live cultures that hung in the air.

Please be there. Please answer, I prayed.

After the third ring, a smooth baritone voice answered, "RH Lab."

"Hello. Mr. Brown?" My hands were freezing by now, and my body shook, but I tried to hold my voice steady. "This is Ann Hughes. I'm up in Massachusetts. You said I could call this morning for my DNA test results." My heart pumped fast.

"Oh, yes." He paused. I held my breath. "I'm sorry to tell you this, Mrs. Hughes." His voice sounded measured. I felt myself go numb. "I know you wanted a positive result, but Clara is not your daughter. Two of the necessary indicators do not match up."

A powerful force kicked me in the stomach. I doubled over, light-headed. "You're joking, right?" I gasped. The feet. The red recessive gene. The limp. The astrology chart. My mind shifted into overdrive while tears tingled in my eyes. "This test has to be wrong. I'm up here with her now. She has a limp just like her father." My voice was hard and desperate.

"No. I'm sorry," Mr. Brown affirmed. "It's the truth. She can't be your daughter. We might have had some doubt with only one indicator not matching, but in this case two important ones don't match up. I'll have a written report out to you next week."

An inpenetrable wall bumped up against my nose. I mashed myself against it, but nothing budged. "Okay . . . thank you, Mr. Brown," I squeezed out with my last ounce of control. My paralyzed hand slowly lowered the receiver.

Like a helpless stick swept downstream, I swirled into a floodtide of sorrow. *How can this be? All the matching clues . . . How's Clara going to feel? How can I hurt her like this? Where does this leave me?*

Empty. Back at zero again.

I wept, and wept some more . . . raging rivers of tears. When the heaving subsided, I blew my nose and wiped my eyes, Slowly, the room came back into focus and my eyes widened with a new thought. *Maybe I should just keep this to myself! I can pretend everything's okay. Would that be so bad? Clara and I could help each other heal. We don't have to be related.*

"What about your *real* daughter?" an inner voice asked. "There's another daughter out there somewhere, your daughter by blood. If you live this lie, you'll never find her. She'll never know you care. She needs you, too."

My mind went numb with confusion.

"Look inside," my inner voice said. "You know what to do."

"Where?"

Then, I remembered: that place deep inside . . . at the center of my being. I closed my eyes and visualized a circle of warm, golden light, whole and complete. *Please show me the way*, I prayed.

It felt as if a gentle but firm pair of hands clasped themselves around my waist. "Tell the truth," a deep vibration said. "You must tell the truth."

Gradually, the vision faded, and, when I breathed and stretched, calmness had cleansed me like a new wave wipes smooth the trampled beach. My numbness receded, and I started to vibrate with aliveness. I stood and walked to the window, again riveting my eyes on that row of flame-red bushes, then I looked up and surveyed the sun-sparkled medley of colors that dressed the distant hills. . . .

Forty-five minutes later, I was staring into Clara's broad, innocent face. She'd arrived home a little after 12. Sitting in the chair in front of the window, she seemed to have a strange blue halo, the way the clear sky framed her head. She was asking about my morning, being carefully to avoid any reference to the test.

"I found everything I needed," I assured her. "Thanks for giving me your room last night. You and Belinda have been so nice to me." Tears formed; I flicked my eyelids down to hide them. Then, pushing past a solid block of dread, I took a deep breath, raised my head, and forced my leaden jaw to move.

"I've got some bad news for you, Clara," I began, the words low and heavy. She looked at me directly for the very first time. I couldn't begin to hide my sadness. I swallowed and plowed ahead.

"I'm not sure how you're going to take this after all you've been through, but I called the lab this morning, and they say we're not a match." My lower lip trembled. "I'm so sorry, Clara," I squeezed out.

She flinched and then recovered herself immediately.

I sighed, trying to flush away some of my tension. I went on to explain what Mr. Brown had said about the two indicators and was careful not to mention my private hope that the tests were wrong. She continued staring at the floor, motionless. Silence rang in my ears while I waited for her to respond.

"It's okay," she said, at last, in a husky voice. "I can take it. I'm a rock."

I rose slowly, my muscles aching to hold her.

"Come here and let me give you a hug." She walked toward me and I pressed her short, square body to my chest. Her warmth penetrated me. When I opened my eyes, a shower of yellow leaves was tumbling down outside. I gave Clara a final squeeze and felt calmer, somehow, when I let her go.

"Well, at least I won't have to bore you with all those awful pictures," I joked, wiping my eyes.

"Yea," she said, still looking down but cracking a crooked smile. "We can just relax and enjoy the rest of the weekend." She glanced up briefly. "Here, I should give you back the stuff you sent me." She sidled over to the table and handed me the family history book and my hospital records.

I tucked them under my arm. "Clara, I want you to keep the little pearl earrings I gave you last night. Those were for *you*. I hope you'll remember I love you, whether you're my daughter or not."

A look passed between us. I breathed in, slow and deep. Somewhere in the back of my mind, I heard the crash of surf and the cry of gulls. My nostrils flared and my heart pounded in the rhythm of the waves . . . where one rushes forward, then dances retreat on little foam feet . . . to be gobbled by the next wave . . . and the next.

30 - Re-Grouping

I pressed my face to the tiny, scratched windowpane and watched the ground rush by. But when the force of gravity began pushing on my solar plexus, I closed my eyes. By the time I blinked them open, the earth had grown smaller and was tilting. We were turning south for Baltimore, leaving Clara and Belinda behind. Another wave of loss washed through me.

Below, suburban houses (empty pools set in back yards like sapphires), stood in neat rows on curved, tree-lined streets. The neighborhoods were strangely peopleless, like a builder's masterplan. Beyond the city, a once-boundless tract of fall color had been separated into parcels by fields and highways. Vehicles moved along the asphalt ribbons like convoys of ants.

As we flew upwards into the thick, puffy cloud fields, I remembered how two-dimensional—how flat and painted—the clouds had looked from earthside just yesterday afternoon. . . .

We'd set off in a giddy mood yesterday—Clara, Belinda and I. We'd driven across town to collect a carry-out lunch of Jamaican food. Then we'd dodged flies and bees to eat it in the park. After lunch, we'd hiked a needle-strewn path through a pine woods and discovered a large, sunny meadow with a duck pond. Each of us had spread out in a separate spot of grass. I'd sat in mournful silence at first, watching a few flat clouds drift by, while some ducks squabbled and preened near the pond. Then I'd leaned back into the delicious-smelling grass, face up, and closed my eyes over puddling tears.

The sun blazed orange on the inside of my eyelids, and its warmth penetrated my every pore. *Heal me*, I prayed as I surrendered to its radiance. *Bake your heat lamp into my body; renew my wounded spirit.*

I drifted off into the space between the worlds and listened to the counsel given by the ducks and the birds. The gentle grasses caressed me. The full, fertile smell of fall, wafting in on a soft breeze, sated me with its perfume. Then I felt my inner voice speak:

You did the right thing when you told Clara the truth.

A broad smile of satisfaction spread across my face. My body pulsed with harmony. Yes, I'd done the right thing. And now I felt like I had in the dream: I'd been shot, but not injured. I imagined looking down and seeing myself lying there in the grass. *You're fine.* I told myself. *Somehow, everything will be okay.*

A moment later, there on the back of my eyelids, somewhere in the orange glow, I began to see Spirit's perfect plan. I slowly went over everything that had happened in these last few months: Mary Anne's call, tracking her down, forgiving her; accepting Clara, the blood tests, telling the truth. *Everything* had been a test! And I'd passed with flying colors!

All this time, they'd been preparing me, testing me. I'd learned something about myself at every step. I'd grown stronger from each challenge. Suddenly, my insides lit up like fireworks on the Fourth of July! This whole journey had been a cosmic trial! My face broke wide open in a grin. YES! I was going to find my daughter! They wouldn't have put me through all this if I wasn't going to find her!

Tears of gratitude trickled down my face. What a beautiful game they'd created to teach me all that stuff. I opened my eyes. Flat clouds were scooting across the sky. I had no idea how. I had no idea when. But, from that moment on, I *knew* I would find her. . . .

Now, my airplane was skimming over a deep fiord of snowy clouds. Like endless icebergs, they spread below me in trackless splendor. How different clouds looked from this higher view.

Turning downward, the plane swam through a soup of white wisps, and soon, familiar landmarks appeared: the mighty Chesapeake Bay, the sprawling Sparrows Point steel mill, then the city's sparkling new Inner Harbor area, with brick walkways, green-roofed shopping pavilions and museums. The ground tilted again as the pilot banked the plane south to the airport. In a few minutes, he touched down on the runway. As we taxied to the gate, I realized how much shorter this trip had seemed than the one to Massachusetts the previous Friday evening.

A familiar figure in worn blue jeans, a tweed sport coat and a gray, felt cap leaned against the wall at the terminal gate. I'd called Ned briefly on Saturday to give him the news. His wide-spread, sad eyes were fixed on my approach.

"Hi, Darling," I said, giving him a long hug. "Look, I know you're worried about me, but don't be. I'm fine."

His ruddy face still twisted with concern. "I was afraid you'd be all upset."

"I know. Wasn't easy," I admitted with a sigh. "But, really, I'm fine, Clara's fine. *Don't worry.*" I told him about our foray to the park Saturday afternoon.

Squeals erupted near the gate ramp. I turned to see a knot of eight to ten people—a family group with children. They held brightly colored, heart-shaped balloons that floated gaily above their chatter. It looked like someone was having a happy reunion.

I closed my eyes and sighed.

Ned glanced over at the scene behind us, then stared down at his feet. Remembering my mission, I motioned to two nearby seats and set my carry-on bags on the floor.

"Look, there wasn't any harm in meeting Clara," I argued. "I have a new friend now. It was good for both of us. So, the tests came out negative. At least there were tests we could take. Fifteen years ago, where would we have been?"

Next, I told him about my leave-taking that morning. I could remember Clara's car lurching to a stop before the U.S. Air entrance to the terminal. . . .

"I'll get the luggage, C.B.," Belinda had chirped as we all sprang out of the car.

"C.B.? What does that stand for?" I asked.

She grinned and shuffled her feet. "Oh, that's my nickname. C.B. Clara Bess. Get it?"

"Bess . . . what a pretty name . . ."

We stepped up on the sidewalk. I hugged Clara and told her what a marvelous human being I thought she was. We laughed together over our bee-plagued picnic and the walk in the park. Then, my face grew long. "I'm sorry the tests were negative, Clara. I would have been proud to claim you as my daughter." My voice dropped to a whisper, then caught. "You know, any birthmother would." I recovered myself and smiled. "I hope you'll find your real birthmother someday," I said, feeling the tweak of jealousy.

Clara smiled and then fixed her eyes firmly on the sidewalk. "Any adoptee would be lucky to have you for a birthmother, too," she said. My throat swelled up and shivers slid from head to toe. I reached out and held her to me one more time.

After final goodbyes, I waddled inside, a carry-on pressing down on each shoulder and a weighty suitcase in my hand. Somehow, though, the luggage felt lighter than it had on Friday. After the glass door slid shut, I turned back. My friends Belinda and Clara stood side by side waving at me. I waved back, then moved away quickly, before my face crumpled with tears. . . .

The gate area where Ned and I sat was deserted by now. Even the reunion group with their heart-shaped balloons had moved on. There were clusters of people far away, but around us, all was quiet and still.

"See what I mean, Ned? Don't you think it did us good to meet?"

He smiled a little at last. "Well, maybe. You don't seem as fragile."

"Well, disappointment isn't fatal. And here's something else: I know I'll be able to love my daughter, now—and I can trust myself to tell the truth, too."

Ned's hazel eyes were glowing with love. I stood and picked up one of my carry-on's. Ned picked up the other and put his hand on my free shoulder.

"Come here, you," he said, squeezing me in a big hug. "I'm really proud of you."

I inhaled his clean soap smell briefly and then pulled back. "Ned, God wouldn't have put me through all this for nothing, you know." My voice started cracking. I buried my head in the scratchy wool of his jacket. "I'm going to find her—I just had to learn to trust myself first," I mumbled to his shoulder.

Ned held me tight, and the warmth of his embrace spread through me. "I hope you're right," he said at last. His eyes were wet, and so were mine. We turned and fit our arms around each other's waists. Hips touching, we stepped off down the corridor, matching each other's pace.

* * * * *

We called it "Plan X."

Back on the phone with Sonia again. The dishwasher was churning nearby, and I clasped the receiver tightly to my ear so I could hear. I'd been careful to close the narrow louvered door between the kitchen and the dining room. This was secret stuff, "Plan X."

Well, I'd done all the easy legal stuff already. The reunion registries, of course. Support groups. Getting information from the hospital and the adoption agency (hah!). . . .

Now what?

Hire a detective? Tedious record searching? Give up? Or "Plan X?"

"Plan X involves deception," Sonia explained. "You'll need to use it in order to procure her birth certificate. But without your daughter's name, there's no hope of finding her. Truthfully, Plan X hardly ever works. When it does, it takes a long time. But there's always a chance."

A hole gaped in my stomach. *Lie? I've just been through this whole experience with Clara where the lesson was "tell the truth." Now, I'm supposed to turn my back on all that and lie?*

"Sonia, I hate to lie."

"I know. I do, too. But just think of the Dutch that lied to protect Anne Frank and her family in World War II. Think of the Quakers that lied to protect the black people moving north on the Underground Railway. Sometimes it's *right* to lie."

I cupped my chin and sighed. "If we had humane laws, we wouldn't have to do it this way, eh?" My eyes stared blankly ahead. "You're probably right."

"Well, whatever you do, *please, please* don't tell anyone about this. If they find out what we're doing, it will close the door even tighter for others who follow."

"Okay, Sonia. I promise."

The stool squeaked against the yellow tile when I stood. I opened the louvered doors and slogged towards the living room. TV noises upstairs told me I had the downstairs to myself.

Hardly ever worked, huh? Well, if I'm going to try this, it's going to work for me. I'll do a Spiritual Mind Treatment to make it work.

So, I settled myself on the couch, feet up, and closed my eyes. *I affirm that I am one with the Life Force and that the good I desire is now taking form.*

In a vision, a white, #10 envelope floats into my hands. It

contains my daughter's amended birth certificate. My fingers fly to rip open the flap, extract the document. I unfold its blue and yellow patterned paper, gritty to the touch, and run my fingers over the raised edges of the seal. There, typed in the middle, is her name. A shudder of awe runs through me. Her name! At last, I know who she is, I know what people call her! Wild joy charges through me.

"Thankfully accept that the good you desire is yours right now," I read.

Thank you! Thank you for giving me my daughter's name. Thank you for helping me find her. Thank you for the chance to make a difference in her life, as she has in mine.

"Release: Accept your good as already accomplished. Release your prayer to the activity of the Life Force, completely freeing yourself of concern."

When I opened my eyes, I was vibrating with gratitude. *Okay, I'll release it, but is there something else I can "do?"* I ask myself. Immediately, I got my reply.

"Yes. Do what Sonia suggested. And constantly visualize the envelope coming to you. Leave the rest to the Higher Powers. Forget about it and involve yourself in other things."

Then I remembered a passage I'd read recently in *Science of the Mind*: "We must hold before us a dream. . . . Once we step forward into our commitment, [the] means and methods [for success] begin to actualize in our experience."

31 - Trusting the Universe

The orchestra is already spread out on the stage, a hundred strong, testing their instruments when I step onto the riser and walk across the brightly lit stage. "Follow the person in front of you. No talking," we've been told. I'll be singing with the BSO Chorus tonight, and we'll be recreating the fall of ancient Babylon as told in William Walton's marvelous 20th Century cantata, Belshazaar's Feast. The warm-up cacophony of strings, winds, brass, and percussion covers up our shuffling as we thread our way onto the chorus bleachers.

The house lights dim. The orchestra tunes to the oboe's "A" and then grows still. Heels click across the floor—tonight's conductor enters jauntily, a slight, young blond with piercing blue eyes. He bows to polite applause and then turns to face us. His fine-featured face grows rigid while he waits for the canvas of fresh silence to spread before us. I breathe deeply. In my mind's ear, I can already hear the first note of the piece. At the thrust of the conductor's baton, the trombone rattles off a round of high B-flats, piercing the silence like a machine gun. Dense, black smoke seems to cover the stage. I squint, trying to see through its swirling mystery. . . .

"Thus spake Isaiah," chant the men in four-part dissonance . . . forcefully . . . ominously.

"Thy sons that thou shalt beget
"They shall be taken away,
"And be . . . EU-NUCHS . . .
"In the palace of the King of Babylon."
(Brows furrow in concentration; out comes a haunting growl . . .)
"H-h-howl ye."
(Shivers run up and down my spine.)
". . . h-h-howl ye, therefore:
"For the day of the Lord is at hand!"
Violins and violas tremble as the stark prophecy shimmers off to wait in the smokey background. Cellos and basses surge darkly below the tremolo, setting the mood for the next scene. I breathe deeply and put on my mask of sadness. It's heavy and solid, like clay.

I look down at myself. In my mind's eye, I'm wearing a coarse toga. Sweat drips between my breasts. I'm an Israeli captive marching into slavery. Dust fills the air; it coats my damp skin, sticks in my throat. Our procession approaches a grove of gnarled willow trees. Beyond is the Euphrates River. We stumble through the copse, leaving behind what we carry, and collapse in the soothing waters. Afterwards, we slump under the trees and sing a low melody that slowly writhes in pain:

"By the waters of Babylon,

"There we sat down: yea, we wept

"And hanged our harps upon the willows."

Low cellos rake heavy bows across thick strings. Sobbing winds pick up the sorrowful melody we singers leave behind and swirl it magically into the air. The pace quickens. Anger stirs in my breast as the music begins to pulse insistently. My jaw tightens:

"They that WASTED US

"Required of us MIRTH."

(Trumpets blare, drums spike our outrage.)

"They that carried us away CAPTIVE

"Required of us a SONG."

(Their demand:)

"Sing us one of the songs of Zion.

"Sing us one of the songs of Zion."

It's impossible! We knot our fists; our eyes flash. How dare they ask us to sing our sacred songs for heathen pleasure? They mock us and everything we call holy. The orchestra explodes; music jumps jaggedly, like hands thrown up in wild desperation.

"How shall we sing the Lord's song/ In a strange land?" we ask, our mouths puckered in bitterness. Gradually, our impotence deflates our anger, and our hopeless question drains into the abyss of the unknowable.

The scene is washed clean. A baritone solo speaks for us now, his words, formed in an unblemished space, deep within.

"If I forget thee, O Jerusalem/Let my right hand forget her cunning/Let my tongue cleave to the roof of my mouth."

His face glows with love. His ardor draws us all together, and our joint passion mushrooms into a glorious knot of remembrance. But our dream fades with the baritone's words, "yea, if I prefer not thee above my chief joy."

Now, our aching sadness returns. Low cellos and bassoons thump us back to the willow grove, where we lie in a weeping huddle once again. . . .

Then, the scene shifts again. Shrill trumpets and sharp drum beats recall an ancient prophecy: the city of Babylon shall be quickly and utterly destroyed. Jaggedly, we sing:

"Happy shall he be that taketh thy children/ And dasheth them against a stone,/ For with violence shall that great city Babylon be thrown down."

My skin prickles as we gaze into the misty future . . . to the time when these massive city walls and pagan temples will have crumbled. Someday, ghosts will walk these now-bustling streets, and Babylon "shall be found no more at all."

Now, we twist through the narrow cobblestone streets of the ancient city. The way is lined with cloth-draped vendors' stalls. The baritone's voice lists the city's merchandise: "gold and silver, precious stones, pearls, fine linen, ivory, precious wood, brass, iron, marble, spices, wheat, beasts, chariots . . . slaves . . . and the souls of men."

Brass and xylophone announce the glistening court of Belshazaar, King of Babylon. Full orchestra paints the scene: a high-ceilinged banquet room, a great feast for the king and a thousand of his lords. Murmurs of approval ripple through the room. The king, robed in red, sits at the head table, smiling and nodding. Young, narrow-featured, he sports a dark moustache; dark, straight hair peeks from beneath his glistening crown.

"Belshazaar, whiles he tasted the wine,

"Commanded us to bring the gold and silver vessels. . .

"which his father Nebuchadnezzar

"Had taken out of the temple that was in Jerusalem . . .

"That the King, his Princes, his wives

"and his CONCUBINES might rejoice and drink therein."

Our hands fly up to silence gasps of horror. Looks dart between us. Drink wine from our sacred vessels? Sacrilege!

"Then the King commanded us:

"Bring ye the cornet, flute, sackbut, psaltery

"And all kinds of music. . ."

The music thunders on. Belly dancers writhe; the guests swagger in drunken debauchery. We look on in powerless agony.

"They drank wine again."

(A freeze-frame shout of outrage):

"Yea! Drank from the sacred vessels!"

(Low brass blasts out a dissonant wall of sound.)

Abruptly, trumpet calls and drum fanfares bring us back to the great hall, where the king is celebrating his heathen gods. Triangles and cymballs, xylophones, trumpets, flutes, etc., flash a view of each god in turn: the God of Gold, Silver, Iron, Wood, Stone, and the God of Brass. "Praise ye, Praise ye," the revelers call out.

"After they had praised their strange gods,

"The idols and the devils,

"False gods who can neither see nor hear,

"Called they for the timbrel and the pleasant harp

"To extol the glory of the King. . . O King, live forever."

The music swirls and glistens into the splendor of Babylon.

An insistant rhythm summons us to retell the story of the feast in doubletime. Then, the baritone interrupts with a mysterious tale:

"And in that same hour, as they feasted

"Came forth fingers of a man's hand

"And the King saw

"The part of the hand that wrote."

A plodding bassoon and quivering strings weave a shimmering veil of mystery and drop it over the scene.

"And this was the writing that was written: 'MENE, MENE, TEKEL UPHARSIN'

A flute traces the mysterious words in the air, after which a solo trombone blats out a string of high B-flats.

'THOU ART WEIGHED IN THE BALANCE AND FOUND WANTING,'" the men's chorus translates.

"In that night," sings the baritone, his voice alone in the darkness, "Belshazaar the king was SLAIN."

"SLAIN!" all we on the stage explode with cymbal and snare drum accent. (Shock shoots through the auditorium.)

"And his kingdom is divided."

We Hebrew slaves break into a wild celebration, delirious with joy:

"Blow up the trumpet

"Blow up the trumpet in the new moon

"The trumpet in Zion."

We are free! Sing praises to God! Babylon has fallen! Alleluia!

Then we pause to pity the passing of the great city:

"The trumpeters and pipers are silent,

"And the harpers have ceased to harp,

"They cry 'Alas, that great city, in one hour is her judgement come.'

"And the light of a candle shall shine no more."

Then our wild dance of joy begins anew.

"Then sing aloud to God our strength:

"Make a joyful noise unto the God of Jacob. . .

"For Babylon the great is fallen. . .Alleluia!"

From the sheer force of joy, the music sweeps along at an ever-quickening tempo. As the pulse goes into one beat per measure, an incredible crush of sound—wind, string, voice, and trumpet fanfares—melds over a slow shimmer of gongs and orchestral noise. It's a long, slow ecstasy. Then, back in tempo, we charge forward with a hail storm of "Alleluia's" and are overtaken by a crush of brass-blown, string-scraped, cymball-crashing sound that ejaculates into a quivering climax. Even after the music ends, the sound rings on and on, completely filling the instant of silence . . . that's soon cut off by applause thundering back from the auditorium.

I stand, exhausted, shaking with emotion. I've *been* an Israeli slave. I've *felt* the hopelessness of bondage. I've carried a deep love for something lost. I've suffered the moral outrage of having my values violated by others; I've rejoiced in my captors' downfall and have pitied their fate. I've celebrated an unexpected triumph.

The music has stretched me. I'm deeper and stronger inside. By living these experiences, just now, on stage, my emotions have been primed. I'm ready for the next phase of my search for my lost daughter, Jennifer Lynn.

Part IV

Connections

That which we obtain too easily, we esteem too lightly. It is dearness only which gives everything its value. Heaven knows how to put a proper price on its goods.

— THOMAS PAINE

32 - Serendipity

My breath stilled, my body stiffened, and the image formed again in my mind's eye. The name, in dark print, seemed to shimmer just above the surface of the rectangular paper. I stared past it to the pale gold image ghosted in the background. It was an eagle-topped crest, bearing a ship, a plow and three shafts of wheat. Holding up each side of the crest, like bookends, were the pawing hooves of bridled stallions, one on each side. I tried to focus on the six words and numbers, typed on top of the pale gold crest in dark blue: "SUBJECT, BESS LYNETTE DAWN; SEX, FEMALE; 03-30-66."

That's my daughter's name. My real daughter. Not Clara, after all. Someone new. Bess. Wasn't that Clara's middle name? C.B. . . . Clara Bess? And the middle name, Lynette . . . I wonder if they knew I named her Jennifer Lynn. . . .

A warm glow spread across my chest, as it did every time I recalled that miraculous moment when her birth certificate arrived in the mail. I shifted in my chair and massaged the back of my neck; the scene dissolved. On my desk, now, lay that scratched-out list I'd been working through.

A lot of good it's done you to know her name. Seven weeks you've had it, and you still don't know if she's dead or alive. Seven weeks!

Not that I'd been idle! I'd been scurrying around a lot in those seven weeks. I'd reconnected some cold trails; I'd gathered some new clues; I'd made a lot of calls. But, so far, no results.

I'd hoped for instant success, of course. I'd hoped that one call to Clara's sister Louise in Pennsylvania would supply the phone number and address I needed. But when she checked the phone book for me, there was no one listed under "Dawn."

"Look them up in the Poole directory," my friend Sonia suggested later that night. "It's a great little resource that lists heads of families, spouses, and places of employment. Search the years around your daughter's birth."

I'd called the reference librarian the next day. "There's a David B. Dawn here in the directories for 1966 through 1970. Wife, Helen. Insurance agent. Nothing after that," he'd reported. I'd jotted down the Dawns' street address and the name of Mr. Dawn's employer, and set off to play detective.

It took a couple of calls, but finally I tracked down the company he used to work for. "Closed down that office. Moved out of town. Records confidential," was all they'd say.

Someone else in town must have known him, I reasoned. *Another agent?* By the next day, I found someone.

"David Dawn? Yeah, I knew him a little. I think he had a son and a daughter. He retired down south somewhere."

Retired in 1970? That would make them too old to be Bess's parents. Maybe they're her grandparents.

"Write to the people who live in the Dawns' old house," one of my authors suggested.

A week later, triumphant, I was reading their reply: "The Dawns retired to Florida. They had a son and a daughter who stayed in the area."

"Sure wish they had a phone listing," I grumbled, narrowing my eyes.

But I did have other resources. I'd sent away for a mailing list of all the Dawn households in the U.S. in zip code order. Meanwhile, a friend had checked to see if Bess had a Pennsylvania driver's license, and I'd polled elementary schools in the area.

No luck on either front.

When the list of Dawns came in, it showed a David B. Dawn in Florida. Hands shaking, I placed the call. An older woman answered.

"No, I never heard of her," came her reply. "But there was another Dawn in the area years ago, an army recruiter. . . ."

Should I trace that person? Should I call all 2000 Dawns on my list? This wasn't working. I needed her parents' names. What should I do?

I'd called Sonia back, of course.

"Bess's adoptive parents' names will be on the long form of her birth certificate. Now that you have the one, you can get the other without any problem."

The new document had arrived a few days ago. There, as promised, were her parents' names typed over the same pale gold crest.

"FATHER, RICHARD ALAN DAWN, 31; MOTHER,

MARY COWGILL DAWN, 31."

Good. They were mature people when they adopted her, and now there's another surname I can try to trace: Cowgill. They've probably moved away. But someone must be left . . . a grandparent, an aunt, a cousin. Somebody has to know these people.

I'd asked Louise to check the phone book again. Yes. There were nine Cowgills listed, and, today, I'd begun to make the calls.

"Sorry, we're new in the area. I never heard of them." "No, that's not our family. Sorry, I can't help you." Everyone had given polite answers, but, so far . . . only dead ends.

I rubbed at the back of my neck again. The lined notebook paper with the nine names and phone numbers, one scrawled beneath the next, lay there, flatly, on the desk. I cupped my hand to my chin and studied the sheet. Eight were crossed out already. William Cowgill was my last hope. A sigh slunk out of me. I reached over and punched out his phone number.

After four rings, an older woman's voice grated across the phone line. Her clipped greeting conjured up an image of puffy jowls, salt and pepper hair and a paisley apron over a plain house dress.

"Hello. Mrs. Cowgill? This is Ann Hughes. I'm calling from Maryland," I said, ignoring her unpleasantness. "I'm trying to contact a relative of mine who used to live in your area." I gave her the particulars and waited for her reply.

A pause spread between us. "Well, I never heard of them," she said at last, dismissal in her voice. *Oh, no! My last lead!* I felt the whoosh of a big door swinging shut. A swirling black pit gaped . . . then she sighed, "You should really check with my husband, though. He's the one who knows all about that stuff."

What was she saying? My heart stood still. Words wadded up in my throat. "Well, may I speak with him?" I choked out.

Her voice stiffened. "No, you can't. Not right now. He's outside fixing the car. You'll have to call back another time."

I beat a hasty retreat. "Thank you so much, Mrs. Cowgill. I'll try again tomorrow." As I hung up the phone, my eyes filled with tears. The last name on my list was now a long shot, and a dragon guarded the door!

My head began to throb. *What will I have to do next? Look*

through endless lists of courthouse records, old phone books, old newspaper clippings? Another surname list? Thousands of phone calls? Thousands of "no's?" Two brief days ago, I'd had a magical list of names, but, now, it had melted away to one thin hope. I packed up my desk and slogged home in a slump.

But the next morning, there was a zing in the air. It was Wednesday, February 28, my daughter Renate's 17th birthday. *I know it's going to bring me luck*, I told myself, hoping it might be true.

I went to work and kept myself busy opening mail and looking through book proofs until 11:15 a.m. Then, I placed my call. Mrs. Cowgill answered on the second ring. I tried to sound cheery.

"You said your husband might be able to help me find the Dawns when we talked yesterday. May I speak with him, please?"

Her voice thickened with suspicion. "Why are you looking for them?" she grumbled.

Out of my third eye, I beamed a mental spotlight. I envisioned it warming and brightening the room where she stood, phone in hand, talking to me. "I have a special invitation for Bess," I said, letting my light beam pulse away through the huge gap of silence.

At last, she cleared her throat. "Well, okay. I'll get him." I hugged myself with joy. *It worked!* "Bill, telephone," she called.

My heart pumped hard through the silence, but then a mellow voice reached out—"Hello? Can I help you?"—and my tension melted away. I'd known many people like him among my family history authors. He sounded almost 70. I pictured him wearing a plaid flannel shirt, with white hair, a leathery face and clear eyes.

"Your wife tells me you're interested in your family, Mr. Cowgill, and I'm looking for a young woman who may be related to someone you know." I gave him the particulars and asked if he'd heard of them. Then I closed my eyes and prayed for a miracle.

"Yes. I think I have," he replied. My heart must have skipped a beat. My ears started to ring. "I'm pretty sure they're the ones that moved to Canada."

Canada! No wonder they weren't in the phone book. No wonder I couldn't find a driver's license.

"The family history book is in the next room. If you can hold on a minute, I'll look them up for you."

A jolt shot through me. It ran through my arms and out my fingers, through my legs and out my feet. "What? You have a family history book?" My chest collapsed; my eyes filled with tears. The scene took on fuzzy edges, like a dream.

"Yes. A few years ago, a lady out in Minnesota published a book on the Cowgill family. It's over on the table. I'll look them up in the index for you."

My gaze blurred as I fixed it on my library of family history books. I pictured Mr. Cowgill, shuffling across the room, reaching out for the Cowgill book. Then I shot an arrow of thanks skyward. *My daughter's whereabouts will be revealed to me in a family history book. How perfect!* I shook my head in wonder as tears of gratitude trickled down my face. I reached for a tissue and dabbed my cheeks.

The receiver clattered back into his hand. "Yes, here they are," Mr. Cowgill reported between huffs. "Bess, Mary, Richard, and Thomas, p. 158."

"Could you read me what the book says about them?" I said, all cotton-mouthed.

He read me the whole entry. It was my Bess, all right. The date and place of birth matched. And now I knew she had a brother. And it said "adopted" after her name and her brother's name. *That's a relief. She must know she's adopted.*

"So, you think they moved to Canada, Mr. Cowgill?" I asked, trying to ignore the shivers that were still creeping up and down my spine.

"Yes. I held a big reunion here for the family just last summer," he said. "The Dawns didn't come, but Mary's sister did. She told us they lived in Quebec."

"So, you're a genealogist, Mr. Cowgill?"

"Well, sort of. It's my hobby," he chuckled modestly.

I told him about the work I did for genealogists and asked how I could get a copy of the book. He told me and then added, "You know, Bess's grandmother just died this past January. She was living in a nursing home near here." He mentioned its name and location.

My nose twitched. Another lead. "And who was looking after her?" I asked.

"Her daughter, Ruby. That would be Bess's mother's sister, who came to the reunion last summer. She's a widow who lives in this area. Her name is Lockhart. She works as a nurse."

I scribbled it all down and then said goodbye. "Mr. Cowgill, you'll never know how very much I appreciate this," I said, voice quivering. "Thank you from the bottom of my heart."

"Oh, you're welcome," he said. "I'm just glad this book was here so I could help you."

So am I. Thank you, Mr. Cowgill, and thank you, God, I thought to myself as I carefully replaced the phone on the receiver.

I sat in stunned silence for a moment, trying to digest the miracle. Then, when I could feel my blood pumping again, I shoved my chair away from my desk and sprang to my feet, spreading my arms and legs wide apart in a cheerleading pose.

"Hey, everybody! I found her! I FOUND HER!" I announced, sticking my head into the outer office. "Alice, Jane, Lisa, I found my daughter." Three heads turned my way, big-eyed, like startled deer. "*I found her!*" I shouted again, doing a little dance. "*Yes!*" I thrust my fist high in triumph.

I skipped back to my desk, grabbed my change purse, and then struggled to shove my arms into my winter coat.

"Hey, guys, I'm taking an early lunch," I shouted back over my shoulder. A few quick steps later, I skipped into the bright sunshine, a big smile plastered all over my face.

33 - Contact

That evening, I huddled by the lamp that glowed dimly in the corner of our bedroom. Panels of milky stained glass, fringed with strings of tiny, white glass beads, formed a tepee around the table lamp's molded brass pedestal. Its three brass feet perched daintily on the smooth slab of marble which topped the carved, cherry dresser, handed down to me from my mother's mother's mother.

I tugged open one of the top dresser drawers and pulled out two letters. I unfolded the thick one first, the one I'd composed in January, soon after discovering Bess's name. I'd liked it at first, but, now, it made me cringe. The lamp took on fuzzy edges as I thought back to last week, when I'd read it over again, trying to imagine her reaction.

She'd be a young adult now, living independently. What would it be like to get a three-page letter, out of the blue, from a half-crazed woman claiming to be her birthmother? A letter full of excuses . . . (which she calls explanations) . . . of why she got pregnant, why she gave me away. This is interesting: she says she's pulled herself together now and wants to make it all up to me. But who needs it? Why should I feel obligated to her? She gave me away when I really needed her. Now she wants *me* to fix everything for *her* and say it was all okay? Sorry. Not interested.

I folded the letter back up and threw it in the trash. *Boy, I'm glad I didn't find her right away.* A shiver of horror worked its way up my spine. *I would have sent it, too.*

That left me holding a single sheet of yellow tablet paper, handwritten, on one side, the letter my inner voice had coached me to write: "Remember, she has a Moon in Cancer. She's very sensitive, emotionally," it had told me. "Make your letter gentle. Be subtle. Be *non-threatening*."

I went to sleep with those thoughts one night, and early the next morning, the words of my letter had come to me in a dream. It was still dark outside when I got up, wriggled into my slippers, and rushed to the bathroom, clutching my yellow tablet and a pen. I sat on the toilet, hunched over to keep myself warm. With a dim light from the hall filtering in, enough for me to see, I transcribed the words from the dream. They merely told of her birth and the promise I'd made to find her someday.

> I have never forgotten about you, Bess. I love you and have always cared deeply about your welfare. I know there is much for you to forgive, but I also know that you have the sensitivity, the intelligence and the communication skills to work out anything you choose to. I pray you will be compassionate enough to work this through with me.
>
> I have learned much in the years since you were born, and it is my fondest hope that you will allow me to become your friend and ally. Please contact me if/when you are able.
>
> Love, your birthmother

When I was done reading, the light of the bead-fringed lamp slowly came back into focus. Calm had settled into my bones. But soon it was driven out by new, fretful thoughts.

What good is it without her address? Shall I try to get that from her aunt now, or wait until I find it out some other way?

I slipped my letter back in the drawer and stumbled around to the other side of the bed, fogged with uncertainty.

Ask for help, my inner voice rejoined. *Call Sonia.*

I grabbed the phone and dialed Sonia's number. Soon, I was babbling to her about my call to Mr. Cowgill and my good fortune in getting Mrs. Lockhart's address and phone number from the nursing home. All the while, I methodically traced three large triangular shapes on the pink notepad beside the phone.

"You have enough to find her now, Ann." The sound of children fighting was swelling in the background. Sonia covered the receiver and barked at her kids. "Sorry about that," she apologized. "Is Bess married?"

"Don't know," I put wings on my doodled triangles.

"Do you know what city she's in?"

I penned smiling faces inside each. "Yes." The lady who'd written the family history had confirmed that clue.

"Maybe you should just call the aunt," Sonia suggested. "You might be able to get Bess's address out of her if you tell her you're an old friend of Bess's."

"But what if she questions me?"

"You could always hang up."

"What if I get it and they find out later I deceived them?"

"Well . . ." Sonia excused herself to plead with the kids again.

My stomach was churning. I drew a big frame around my triangles while I waited for Sonia to come back.

"Sorry again. Where were we?"

"Once I get her address, Sonia, do you think I should write or call?" I wrinkled my nose and tapped on the note pad with the bottom of my pen.

"Boy," she hedged, "there are arguments both ways on that one."

I sighed. "I've got a nice letter all ready to send, but a friend of mine contacted by letter a few months ago. She found her son just before Christmas. Sent him pictures and everything. Five weeks later, she got it all back with a nasty note threatening to sue if she bothered him any more."

"Well, if you write, you'll be giving your daughter a chance to think about it before she responds. That's a good idea. Of course, *you'll* be going crazy, not even knowing for sure if she got it, unless you send it registered."

I grimaced. "And that makes it seem like something scary."

Sonia let my comment pass and then continued. "On the other hand, if you call, you'll be able to see her reaction for yourself without waiting. But it could be a terrible shock for her, depending on her frame of mind."

"You're really shooting in the dark with this stuff, aren't you?" I drew a big "X" through my triangles and started blackening them in. "I don't know what I'm going to do, Sonia, but thanks for being there." I mumbled good night and crumpled up my doodle.

I went downstairs to fix myself a hot drink. Soon, the fragrance of Sleepytime tea seeped through the kitchen. *Don't call Bess's aunt tonight. You're too wound up. You'll blow it. Wait a day,* my inner voice said as I spooned in some honey. The spoon scraped slowly back and forth on the bottom of the ceramic mug.

But, I hated to wait. When something needed to be done, I liked to charge in and do it. Be bold. Get it over with. It might be impetuous, but it got things done.

Heart pounding, I picked up the phone and dialed.

But the hand of God stayed me. There was no answer.

34 - The Call

The clock glared down at me from its perch on the den wall. Its black hands crept towards 7:30 p.m. The TV news droned on. Ned sat upright on the maroon recliner with the remote control in his right hand. Last night's bravado had evaporated. I heaved a deep sigh and scratched my head nervously.

Ned studied me and pushed the mute button. "Now what are you afraid of?" he asked, raising his dark, full eyebrows.

I twisted towards him. "Oh Ned, this is the most important call of my entire life. What if she hangs up on me?"

"Think positive. Visualize how you want it to be. And remember: you only want what's best for Bess."

"I know, but I'm *scared*," I whimpered.

"Look. Bess's aunt has worked as a nurse for 30 years. She won't be shocked by a story of unwed pregnancy. And you're no phone wimp. You talk to people on the phone every day. You make your living talking to people on the phone, for Pete's sake."

I chuckled nervously, thinking of the practice I'd had: fifteen years' worth. "You're right, Ned. Okay. I'm going. Wish me luck."

I stood at last and inched across the hall to our bedroom. Mrs. Lockhart's number lay on the bedside table. I picked up the phone and dialed. The three rings drilled into my brain like a dentist's bit.

"Hello," answered a female voice of the right age.

"Hello. May I speak to Mrs. Lockhart?" I said in my "friendly" voice. *I hope she doesn't think I'm asking for money.*

"Who's calling?" she asked cautiously.

"This is Ann Hughes. I'm calling from Baltimore." *That should make her curious.* I held my breath.

"This is Mrs. Lockhart."

Good. You got to first base. Keep going.

"Hello, Mrs. Lockhart. I'm hoping you can help me. I'm trying to locate your niece, Bess Dawn. Do you have her address, by any chance?"

There was a pause. "Why do you want it?"

I tried the line that got me past Mrs. Cowgill just yesterday.

There was a long pause.

My face grew hot. My ears started ringing. *It's not going to work this time. She's going to hang up on you. Quick, TELL THE TRUTH,* my inner voice screamed.

"Mrs. Lockhart," I pleaded, my words jumbling together. "Wait. I'm Bess's birthmother. I'm trying to contact her. Will you help me, please?"

Her voice had turned flat and suspicious. "Give me your name, address and phone number."

A thin sliver of hope knifed through me. *If she were completely opposed, she wouldn't be asking me this,* I kept telling myself. When I had finished, I remained silent.

"Bess has given us much joy," Mrs. Lockhart said at last.

I closed my eyes and let the relief surge through me. *Oh, thank God. No more horror stories.*

The words rushed out. "I can't tell you how wonderful it feels to hear you say that. I found another girl, and she'd been abused. I'm so relieved to know Bess's okay . . . that her family loves her. . . ."

Like a kid in a toy store, I wanted everything at once. "What does she looks like? Does she still have dark hair and a dark complexion? Is she pretty? Is she big or little? Is she musical? Is she married? What does she do? Where does she live?"

Mrs. Lockhart picked her way through the questions cautiously. "Well, I'm not going to tell you where she lives except to tell you that she lives far away—out of the country. But I will answer some of your other questions."

Fair enough. She just confirmed Canada for me, and I already know the city, so I needn't press further. If only I can get her last name. She's being very protective. I need to move more slowly.

"Well, can you tell me if she's married?" I asked.

"No, she's not. She still lives with her parents. She's attending graduate school."

Wonderful! Let her be in control all she wants. I have everything I need now. She and they will feel more comfortable if they know where I am but think I don't know where they are. This is perfect. It'll give them some time to get used to me. I'm glad I did it this way, I congratulated myself.

"What's Bess majoring in?" Now I was anxious to flush out the answer to my old unresolved question: who is Bess's father?

"Nursing administration. She's getting her master's degree," Bess's aunt reported proudly.

An interest in nursing equals medical student, I deduced. "You must be really proud of her. What was her major in college?"

"Oh, something scientific. Micro-biology, I think it was."

An interest in science equals medical student, I tabulated. "And is she short or tall—small or large?" I held my breath. This was Claude's last chance.

"She's a tiny little thing—about 5' 3"—very pretty and kind of mysterious looking," her aunt told me. The puzzle pieces had quickly fallen together: Bess's father had to be Jean-Michel. No question. And it didn't upset me in the least, anymore. I smiled and sent the Universe my thanks for giving me the practice session with Clara on that one.

One more thing I needed to know. I took a deep breath. "Mrs. Lockhart, Bess's father walked with a limp. He may have had curvature of the spine. Has Bess ever had any trouble with her back or anything like that?" I went rigid waiting for her reply.

"No, not that I know of."

A mass of tension slid out of me. It was time to tell some of my story. I explained I'd gotten pregnant overseas as a college student, that my family had considered the pregnancy a disgrace, and I wasn't prepared to raise my baby alone.

"Oh, I've seen plenty of that here at the hospital. It's a sad thing," she murmured, collapsing the distance between us.

I kept on pressing forward. "I had agreed to the adoption before Bess was born, but when I saw her for the first time . . . (you know, Mrs. Lockhart, you have children of your own) . . . I couldn't just walk away from her altogether."

I took a deep breath and closed in for the finish. "Now that she's an adult, I believe she has the right to know about her medical history and about the genealogy of her birth family. That's why I'm trying to contact her, Mrs. Lockhart. That information is her birthright." My eyes slowly filled with tears. "Can you understand what I'm trying to say?" I waited for her response.

It was clear and forthright. "Yes. I do."

"I wrote her a letter. May I read it to you?" I asked. There was a connection between us now. It was pulsing.

"Sure. I wish you would."

I dashed over to the dresser and pulled out my one-page letter. Then, I ran back to the phone and tried to read it, but each word burned in my throat. I stumbled through it like a barefoot pilgrim traversing hot coals. Faith, alone, led me forward. By the time I had finished, the woman on the other end of the phone was my ally and my friend.

We continued chatting for another 20 minutes or so. There were many common threads among our families. My father and Bess's father were both teachers. Like my parents, the Dawns had loved their children well and had modeled high standards for them to follow. My chest was full and warm by the time our talk ran out, Bess's Aunt Ruby had become *my* Aunt Ruby, too.

I explained again that I didn't want to disturb Bess's life or the life of her family. I just wanted them to know that I cared, and I wanted to be there to answer any questions Bess might have.

"I'll call my sister this weekend coming," she promised. "I'll call you back next Wednesday night and let you know what she said."

That sounded perfect. I thanked her again and said goodnight. I let my hand rest on the receiver a moment. *Two magical phone calls in two days!* I must have been glowing when I pushed open the door of the den. Ned quickly muted the volume on the TV.

"So, how did it go?"

I twirled around playfully, and then settled down in my favorite corner of the couch. I pulled a multi-colored afghan over me. It had alternating stripes of aqua and lime green, orange and purple, hot pink and orange, etc. It was the one I'd started knitting when I was pregnant with Bess. I wrapped myself in its wool warmth and told Ned the whole story. And when I finished, I made an announcement.

"I don't know exactly where Bess is yet, but I know she's okay. And that means that tonight I can go to sleep knowing *all* my daughters are safe and sound." I grinned from ear to ear.

35 - The Waiting Game

When I hold my goggled head out of the water, I hear the squeals of playful children echoing off the walls of the vast indoor swimming pool. When I put my head under the surface, with only my snorkel tube sticking up, all that comes through is the magnified sound of my own breathing. I kick steadily toward the magical world which looms ahead: the deep end of the pool contains a coral reef.

I slide carefully between two masses of elkhorn coral that guard the entrance. Beyond them to my left, I glimpse lacy pale-yellow sea fans and magenta sea anemones undulating in a gentle current. An easy kick of my flippers glides me past the gate of coral. I breathe deeply, gradually blending into this mysterious garden of exotic sea flowers and colorful fish.

Little white-striped orange clown fish hover in symbiotic safety among the beckoning tentacles of a violet sea anemone. Beyond it, a school of little blue damsels darts between coral branches. Moving in concert, the fish skillfully weave their azure shapes between the coral's old white limbs. All the coral is tipped with wriggling new growth. Orange, fuschia, and gold, it lightly scrapes my leg as I brush by. Near the bottom, a lemon-yellow parrot fish, striped lime-green and pale purple, hides by a rock. As I pass, he slowly swims on, moving farther into the maze of coral. I follow, fascinated.

Suddenly, my body jolts with pain. A spear point hurled from somewhere ahead in the darkness has pierced my right shoulder. Danger lurks. Frantic, I twist myself around and kick back towards safety. There's another whoosh from behind, and a strong, heavy body overcomes me, forces me to the bottom of the pool. I sink, and my air tube gurgles. At first, I hold my breath. But when I can hold it no longer, I say farewell to life and take two huge gulps of water. I should be drowning, but, instead, the gulps of water have refreshed me like air. I can breath the water, so I'm going to live. When I look around, my attacker has vanished. . . .

My eyes slowly opened and panned my darkened bedroom. The white panels of stained-glass on the brass-footed lamp reflected the moonlight. I tried to rub the dream's salt water out of my eyes. *The coral wonderland is my search for Bess. But who's trying to drown me?*

The answer flashed: "Could be her parents."

Puzzled, I wrinkled my face and slipped back into dreamtime.

This time, I'm hiking along a narrow parapet on a cliff overlooking the Hudson River in New York City. I'm with my young nephew. He keeps running in front of me and hiding. *Oh great, another dream about searching for Bess,* I think to myself lucidly. I chase after my nephew and find him crouching behind a rock. But soon, he disappears. I hope this is just a game and that I'll soon find him. I run back and forth from one end of the parapet to the other, but I can't spot him anywhere. At the far end of the walkway stands a slim stone tower with narrow steps that wind down to the city street. Did he run down the tower steps? I scramble down, shouting his name. But I suddenly realize I'm calling out the wrong name.

"I can't remember his name. I've lost him forever," I wail. Frantic, I ask people standing on the city street below, "Please—have you seen a small young boy?"

A woman from my office is standing by the tower. "Don't worry," she tells me in a slow drawl. "He'll show up." She looks away, coldly.

I awoke for good then. It had been nearly two weeks, and I still hadn't heard back from Aunt Ruby. When we'd talked March 1, she'd promised to call me back Wednesday, March 7. On the eighth, I'd sent her a short letter, along with my letter to Bess and a letter of thanks for Bess's parents. I also sent copies of my hospital records and Bess's birth certificate, showing matching times of birth.

That was a week ago, and I still hadn't heard a thing. But I'd been getting messages from elsewhere. Like the Saturday night Aunt Ruby had said she'd call her sister. I couldn't forget that scary dream:

I'm a passenger on a commercial flight. The nose breaks off the airplane as we're making our approach for landing. It's like a scene from a disaster movie: much confusion, but miraculously, almost everyone gets out alive. The baggage compartment has been ripped off, however, and the luggage is spread to the winds. Luckily, I've only brought one small bag, and it's still on my shoulder when I walk off the plane.

When I get inside the terminal, I try to call Aunt Ruby to tell her I'm okay. But I'm not able to call because the phone dial is broken. When I put my finger in the dial hole, it spins around loose.

My stomach tightened, as it did every time I recalled that dream. What could it mean? There was no way to know for sure what had happened, but I couldn't shake the disturbing feeling that SOMETHING HAD GONE WRONG IN CANADA.

But what?

Did Aunt Ruby get cold feet and not tell Bess's parents? Did Bess's parents react badly? If so, had anyone told Bess about me?

Oh my God, maybe she doesn't know I'm trying to contact her.

That night, I made myself dial Aunt Ruby's number. *I'll just ask if she got my letter.*

No answer.

When I reached her the following evening, I thanked her for the talk we'd had two weeks ago.

"Well?" was her chilly reply.

"Did you get the envelope I sent last week?"

Her voice had a hard edge. "Yes, but I haven't opened it yet."

My eyes widened. "You haven't opened it yet? Why not?"

"Well, it snowed here and I haven't had time."

It was like trying to pull answers from a stone. My stomach churned. "Did you call Bess's parents?"

A one-word reply. "Yes."

I ground my teeth together. "What did they say?"

"They'll be getting back to you." She wouldn't say more.

I told her exactly what was in the envelope and asked her to please forward everything to Bess and her parents. "I might do it when I get around to it," she replied.

I hung up, my stomach tied in knots. *For sure, something's wrong, but what? I've lost my ally. Now what do I do?*

Wild-eyed, I looked around the kitchen. Dishes stood dirty in the sink; pieces of cat food were strewn across the countertop. A pile of phone messages littered the free-standing cupboard where I kept my dishes. The inside of my toaster oven was littered with burned crumbs.

A thought zinged into my mind: "Clean up the kitchen. When you order your physical space, your mind and emotions will get clarified, too. And all that clear thinking might just ripple out to others."

I shrugged my shoulders. There was a certain logic to that. True, there was a difference between me and them, between physical clean-up and mental/emotional clean-up, but my physical space was the one within my reach. I could always clean up the kitchen and hope it would work on more than one level. . . .

The following Sunday morning, I sat with the rest of the church choir in our spot on the back church balcony. The pipe organ case blocked my view of the service that rattled on below. Around me, in Gothic splendor, rose filigreed white arches spanning two-story, salmon-colored walls. I closed my eyes, shutting out the perfect architectural symmetry, the balanced colors. Then I breathed in deeply and tried to remember how to send light.

> First, ground yourself. Pull the earth's energy into you by taking in the color brown or green. Imagine a cord coming up through the ground into your feet. Imagine it running through your whole body, keeping you attached to the ground.
>
> Now take in a few deep, cleansing breaths.
>
> Next, protect yourself. Imagine a white light that starts at your feet and then spirals around you. Wrap your whole body in a cocoon of white light, extending to 7" above the head and terminating in a point.
>
> Now imagine the color you want to use and fill your body with that color. . . .

I drew in the color violet first—the light of love, peace of mind, higher self. It gave off a light, gentle vibration that felt like the tinkle of wind chimes. When it filled me to bursting, I shot it out of the top of my head in an invisible stream that gushed into space.

I rushed to wrap Bess in a cocoon of white light like mine. I couldn't imagine her face yet, so, like a blind person, I patted the light around her with my hands.

Then I chased after my stream of violet light and found it glistening like fairy dust somewhere in space. I pointed it towards Canada, and soon it was touching the top of Bess's white light cocoon. I felt it pour through her blood, tickling her with a soft ecstasy of warmth and delight. I bathed her in the warm thrill of violet love until the color slowly faded, like a winter sunset.

Next, I breathed deeply and filled myself with yellow, the light of confidence and clear thinking. It was clear, canary yellow, smooth to the touch, like a Lucite dowel, yet soft and gentle. It was the color of "all's right with the world" and "wisdom and right decision are mine." When it filled me entirely, I shot it out of my crown, across the northern sky, and arched it towards Quebec, where my daughter waited to receive it. It filled her, now, with the light of confidence—bright, clear yellow. Drawing in a river of air, I held it and pumped yellow into Bess; then, gradually, I exhaled, and let the yellow dissipate. . . .

I was sending Bess "colors." If the way was blocked for us to communicate in the usual way, I would try using the "collective unconscious" again.

I opened my eyes. The perfect proportions, laid out by a master architect one hundred and fifty years ago, were still present in the church's every line. My eyes rested on my favorite stained-glass window. Each matching panel contained a white-robed angel, floating tall, a long trumpet in one hand, the other raised to high heaven. Sculpted glass, in shades of blue and white, rippled the angels' robes and the sky above.

I closed my eyes. "Perfect angels," I prayed, "please help me send my message of love to Bess." I held my mind perfectly still, and, when I opened my eyes again, I knew I had to contact Bess myself. So that afternoon, I penned a note on a small card printed with a simple flower:

By now, both you and your parents should each have received a letter from me sent via your Aunt Ruby in Pennsylvania. I've decided to send this short note directly to let you know I plan to call you this coming Saturday (3/25), between 7-7:30 p.m. . . . I only want to hear the sound of your voice and have the chance to tell you personally what an important and invaluable part of my life you have been.

I enclosed a copy of my contact letter.

There, at least they'll have some warning, I told myself when I popped the card in the mailbox Sunday evening. *Six days should be enough time to get to Canada.*

That night I had another dream. I am giving Renate a driving lesson. We stop at a traffic light, but we wait there endlessly without getting the green light. Traffic passes before us in a steady stream. Eventually, I figure out that the traffic signal must be broken. We wait some more, and then the line of cars breaks at last. "Go!" I shout to Renate. She hesitates. "GO!" I shout again. She puts her foot on the gas, and we shoot through the intersection.

36 - Rocky Road

My head was pounding. My hand shook as I dialed the number. "Please, is Linda there? This is Ann Hughes."

"Oh hi, Ann. No, she's out of town today."

"Who's this?" My voice caught. "Is this Teri?"

"Yes. What's wrong, Ann?"

"Teri, I need to talk to somebody right away. Do you know anything about astrology?"

"Sure, I know a little bit, but tarot's my specialty, you know."

"Well, that might work. Do you have time to meet with me today? The sooner the better. I have a major personal catastrophe here, and I need to get some perspective on it quick!"

"Okay, Ann, I hear you. I can meet with you at noon. Would that be okay?"

"Yeah. That would be great. Can you run some astrology charts for me in the meantime?"

"Sure."

"I don't know times of birth."

"Well, that's okay. We'll set the time at noon. We can get something out of it, anyhow."

"Okay." I gave her the information, and two hours later ducked out of the office.

"I'm going for a long lunch," I told the women in reception, avoiding eye contact. "I'll be back about 1:30." I stepped out into the sunshine and crossed the street. It was a six-block walk to Linda's office. I set off at a quick pace.

The phone call on Saturday had been a disaster. Bess's father, Dr. Dawn, had answered the phone. He must have been waiting for me to call. After I explained who I was, he laid into me for tracking them down, for intruding on their lives, for reneging on my agreement never to contact Bess. He was angry and forceful.

There'd been a fire-storm raging under my skin, but I wasn't going to let myself get defensive.

"You sound upset," I'd interjected. "Would you like to talk about it? I'm paying for this call, and I'll be happy to listen to your concerns." *Oops. That may have been a bit patronizing*, I realized after it was too late.

Unfazed, he'd started up again. No, he didn't want to talk about it. I should have contacted them through the adoption agency, not directly. The agency would be sending me a letter from Bess. And I should stop bothering his sister-in-law, Mrs. Lockhart, too.

"Bess wrote me a letter?" I'd asked, amazed at this apparent *non sequitur.*

"Yes, you should have gotten it," he'd shot back.

I could sense the receiver quivering in his hand. He was ready to hang up on me, and I had exactly one more chance to say something to him.

"I want you to know how thankful I am that Bess went to intelligent people like you," I'd squeezed in, cringing at how ironic it might sound just now.

Dr. Dawn had hesitated slightly; then he charged ahead, as planned. "Well, goodbye," he grumbled.

The whole ordeal had lasted three minutes. My insides still felt like they'd been slashed up by a hari-kari knife.

"A letter is coming," he'd said. Well, I could only imagine what it would say: "You slut, you bitch—you threw me away once—crawl back in your hole."

I leapt up the three marble steps to Linda's yellow doorway. I twisted the door handle and slipped sideways through the narrow set of double doors. A roly-poly woman, about 40, with short, brown hair, sat at the desk in the front office. I forced a smile at Teri and she rose to her feet.

"I ran those charts for you. Let's go upstairs."

I followed her up the curved wooden staircase, then through the narrow upstairs hallway to the front room on the second floor. Linda's fat, white cat, Crystal, was curled in the pillow-lined window seat, facing the street. She looked up when we entered and started licking her paws as I settled myself in the soft, tan sofa near the window. Teri plopped down on a big white floor pillow across from me and waited for me to speak. The room was quiet except for the wet little pops of tongue on fur.

I studied the floor and spewed out my story. Teri knew about my search for Bess, so I just gave her the latest installment, ending with the disastrous phone call two days before.

"I feel terrible, Teri. All my guilt comes up in spades. It's true I broke my promise to never contact them. But I tried to be as gentle about it as I possibly could. I don't know. Maybe Dr. Dawn was just trying to protect Bess, but he has a Ph.D. in communication, for Pete's sake . . . he didn't have to yell at me like that," I whimpered. Finally I looked up.

Teri's hand groped for the astrology charts. "Well-educated doesn't mean he's dealt with the issue of his infertility on an emotional level yet," she reminded me, glancing down at the charts.

"Oh, boy." She straightened up and looked me straight in the face. "This man has his Sun, his Saturn, his Venus, his Mercury, *and* his north node in Aquarius. Do you think that could possibly make him a little wee bit temperamental and inflexible?" she asked, twisting up the corners of her mouth. "I wonder if these planets might happen to be clustered in his eighth house, where adoption falls."

My ears were ringing. I gazed at her and sighed. I hadn't even thought to check this out ahead of time. What an idiot I'd been.

"Ann, that really could explain his reaction. If his planets in Aquarius are in the eighth house, he would have a tendency to be temperamental and inflexible about other people's possessions—an adopted child—get it?

"And, oh, gosh, look at this!"

I leaned over to look at where she was pointing now.

"A Moon and Mars in Libra. Ann, this is a man who likes everything to be on an even keel. He does *not* like emotional upsets. He does not like them at all! And if his Aquarius is in the eighth house, his Moon and Mars are in the fourth—'the home.' That means he likes emotional upsets at home least of all. And, since Mars is there, he'll fight about it."

I crossed my right arm over my chest and used my left hand to prop up my face. The cat plopped down onto the couch and curled up beside me. I reached out to stroke her silky fur as Teri's explanation slowly sank in. Then, weighted down with sadness, I sighed deeply. "Well, that would make a lot of sense." I closed my eyes a moment and listened to my breathing. "So, what do I do now?"

"Would you like to do a tarot reading? Maybe there's a question you could ask that would help you know what to do."

I shifted forward on the couch. "Yeah, but what? I want to respond in some way. . . ." The cat sprang off the sofa and paraded towards the door.

"Try to come up with a question that can be answered yes or no."

My eyes darted around the room. Books, candles, *objets d'art* all blurred together. "Okay. How about, 'Shall I write a letter now or wait a while?'"

"Teri, Bess's twenty-fourth birthday is coming up this Friday." My eyes began to burn. "I promised myself I'd tell her how much she means to me before then. That's one of the reasons I made that stupid call when I did in the first place." My index finger dug into my chin. "Really messed up, didn't I? Should have been more patient."

Teri looked up, her eyes full and gentle. "But now you've got to deal with her father first, right? What would you write to him?"

I picked at my eyebrows and sighed. "Well, let's see. I could apologize for the intrusion. I do mean that sincerely—though, damn it, I sent a letter and *told* them I was going to call."

I bit my thumb and let out another sigh. "I could tell him I know he was just trying to protect Bess. I could explain to him that I'd tried many times to contact him through the adoption agency, but they would never cooperate." I leaned back, crossed my legs, and stared into space for a few seconds. "Oh, I know, Teri," I said, wedging my thumb nail up under my top teeth. "I could tell him that I don't want to intrude, but I just want to be available to give medical information."

Suddenly, my eyes lit up and I slid to the front of the couch. "There's an angle that might work. You know, my heart stopped in 1981," I explained. "There's a chance, God forbid, that Bess may have inherited my arrhythmia."

"Oh, that will get him," Teri rejoined. We laughed with glee.

"And it's *true*, too."

"How do you like this?" Teri stiffened her face and her voice took on a mock-serious tone. "Oh, Dr. Dawn, by the way, your daughter's life might be saved by medical information I have. But if

239

you want to ignore me, that's okay. . . ."

I rocked back and forth with laughter. "Might just do the trick."

Teri reached over to a low table beside us and picked up her deck of tarot cards. "Okay, let's do a reading." She carefully unfolded the red silk cloth in which they were wrapped, took out the tarot cards and shuffled them. She divided them into three piles and then spread the cloth on top of the table.

"Choose one," she said, rolling up her sleeves.

I opened my hand and passed it slowly back and forth over the three piles. Which pile was mine? I would know by the faint energy I would feel from that stack of cards. I chose the pile in the middle, and Teri laid out them out. . . .

I felt much steadier a half-hour later, when I passed through the double doors into the sunlight. Teri had done two readings. They both looked positive about the situation overall, but clearly advised waiting until after Bess's birthday to react to what had happened Saturday. As I turned north and then headed east for the office, the old brick townhouses with white marble steps seemed to say, "Be patient." But my mind was already spinning with another set of plans.

37 - The Door Opens

Our receptionist's voice jarred my eyes from the computer screen. "Ann, line one." I fumbled for the phone.

"I thought you'd want to know. A letter came for you today from the adoption agency," Ned said in a low voice.

My body began to quake. "Oh brother, that must be it."

He didn't reply.

"Man, I'm a bundle of nerves today. Can't get any work done. Only good thing I did was go see Teri. Boy, learned a lot from that. Tell you about it later. Meanwhile, I'm trying to write some letters, one for Bess and another for her dad. Maybe I can send them later, after this dies down a little. Anything to keep the door open. Can I bring them home?"

"Sure. Do you want me to read you the letter that came in just now?"

"No, I don't think I could bear to hear it on the phone. Might as well just come home now and get it over with. Stupid to stay here. Can't work anyway."

The unbearable tension was rising again; from the pit of my stomach, it surged up to my throat and stuck there, right around my Adam's apple. I hoisted myself out of the chair, collected my things, and left the building.

Around the back of the office, a row of cars flanked the chain-link fence dividing our property from that of the office next door. As I plodded towards my car, I noticed poison ivy twisted in the chain links in front of my car. *That's a terrific omen*, I thought to myself, while unlocking the car door. I flung my briefcase on the floor behind the driver's seat and got in. I just sat there for a moment.

Are you really ready to go home and face this? I asked myself.

Well, there isn't much choice, came the reply. *Delay won't help the agony any.* Like a robot, I turned the key, put the car in gear, and backed out of my parking space.

I buzzed up the alley, following a trail of last week's cherry blossoms. The tree at the corner had already faded from heavenly-splendor pink to dusty gray, and sloughed off petals were piling up in cracks and crevices like dust bunnies.

Then my inner voice spoke: "Perhaps there was no way you could have anticipated their response," it gently reminded me. "No matter how you try to buffer it, people have a right to their responses. You had no way of knowing about their private unresolved issues, hopes, and dreams. How can anyone know? Things can turn out badly in spite of noble intentions and carefully-laid plans."

There's truth in that, I told myself. *Why do I always think I can fix it so people won't be upset? I forget people are responsible for their own responses. There's only so much anyone can do. I'm not God.*

A face flashed in front of me—a thin, deeply-wrinkled face. It belonged to one of my genealogy clients, an adoptive father I'd had lunch with a few months ago. His faded blue eyes had grown moist, listening to the details of my search to date. When I finished, he gently told me his daughter's story.

"My first wife and I adopted two children in the early 50's." His wrinkles spread into a soft smile. "I've been a genealogist for many years. I knew how important it would be for my adopted children to know their roots, to have information about their birth families available, so they could understand themselves better. My wife and I always knew that our children had two families, not just the one we supplied.

"Last year, my daughter finally asked me to help her find her birthmother. I was surprised how quickly we managed to do it. It only took us three months."

"And has your daughter contacted?"

"Yes, she did. We had found out ahead of time that the birthparents were married and had four other children. We naturally thought they'd be thrilled to hear from their long-lost first-born."

"So, what happened?"

"Donna called, and her birthmother answered the phone. When Donna identified herself, the birthmother was absolutely furious. She got hysterical and told her she didn't want anything to do with her, ever."

My eyes spread open. "Whew! How did your daughter take it?"

He crossed his arms. "It certainly wasn't the reaction she was expecting."

"What a shame! I know a dozen birthmothers who would have collapsed in tears of joy if their child had contacted them. Your daughter's birthmother must have a lot of unresolved guilt about the surrender."

"I think it was Jung who said, 'A small evil becomes a big one through being disregarded and repressed.' I told that to Donna, anyway. She's trying to be philosophical about it. Meanwhile, I must say, her birth siblings have been wonderful. They threw a big party for her. They call her up all the time. One of them even flew all the way to California to visit her recently."

"I'm glad she got that out of it, anyway."

The wrinkled face faded, and, somehow, I found myself making the final turn up our street. *Unresolved issues can cause "nice" people to be rejecting*, I reminded myself, backing into a spot in front of our house. *I wonder what raw wounds I opened for the Dawns.*

Daffodils were blooming in my front yard, as they had been a year ago when the call from Mary Anne had come. But that seemed to have happened in another lifetime. I got out of my car and dragged myself up the brick walkway to the front porch. Like precious ointment, hope spilled out, drop by drop, with every step I took. I stood in front of the door and inserted the key. It clicked, I pushed, and the door scraped open. Ned was standing there. I dropped my briefcase on the floor.

"Give me a hug," I sighed. The pressure of his embrace slowly trickled calm down my spine. I sighed and stepped back.

"Okay, where's the letter?"

He pointed towards the dining room. There it lay, on the wooden side board, where the envelope containing Bess's birth certificate had first appeared. I glanced up at the dark, somber face in the Rembrandt print that hung on the wall above and tore the envelope open. My numb fingers extracted two sheets of paper.

The first was a cover letter from the agency:

I'm enclosing a letter from your birthdaughter, Bess Dawn. She has requested that any reply be sent back through the agency, and we will forward it for you.

Best wishes, Ms. Sweepaway

"Well, finally—a civil letter from the adoption agency," I quipped. My eyes met Ned's. "Here goes."

I removed the agency's letter to reveal a neatly typed four-paragraph letter. A loud buzzing sound filled my head. I took a deep breath and concentrated hard.

Dear Ann,

I have just recently become aware of your dedicated efforts to contact me. After checking with the agency through which I was adopted it was confirmed that you are, indeed, my birthmother. I also became aware that you have been trying to contact me for a number of years. I certainly admire your persistence. It has indeed paid off.

The room began to spin around. I could hardly get a fix on what she was trying to say. My eyes began to burn; I read on. "I have thought about you many times during the past 23 years. I have often wondered what you look like, what types of things you enjoy, and who you are as a person."

My face broke into a grin. "Ned, she says she's thought of me." The tears were flooding in.

His baritone voice lilted, "Well, of course she has."

I hushed him and glanced ahead, then began to read out loud. "Listen to this: 'I recognize the strength and courage you must have possessed to help you through the difficult circumstances of my birth. I realize that you didn't feel you were able to raise a child at that stage of your life. You did what you felt was best for both of us at the time. Thank you for caring enough about me to do this.'"

The paper rattled in my frigid hands as I passed it over to Ned. "Oh Ned, she's beautiful. She . . ."

My face was too contorted; I couldn't go on. I hunched over in quiet sobs while Ned scanned the letter and then read me the rest aloud. She talked about her studies, her interests and hobbies, and she asked about her sisters. She'd signed it, "All my love, your first daughter."

Ned and I looked at each other through our tears. I took the letter back from him and read it twice from beginning to end. My throat was swelled up, and when I tried to speak, I could not. All I could do was cry—so I cried and cried.

I cried that my search was over, and I cried that I'd been blessed with a kind and sympathetic daughter. I cried that she could understand and forgive my decision to surrender her. I cried that she was whole and complete. I cried that she had opened a door for me to be a part of her life.

Joy seeped into my body—gradually at first—then the floodgate broke, and I began jumping up and down. A long, high squeal escaped through my clenched teeth. I hopped into the living room towards a Morris Louis print that hung over a low bookcase. Its kaleidoscope of colors reached out to my joy. Tears streaming down my face, I jumped up and down, squealing to it, time after time after time. When I stopped jumping, a wide grin that I couldn't remove was plastered all over my face.

I grinned and cried the rest of that day and all the next. I went to choir practice that night and grinned and cried; I went to work the next day and grinned and cried. I simply could not speak about what had happened. Every time I tried, I would cry. I carried my letter with me everywhere, and I read it silently to myself over and over again.

Bess had written on March twelfth. It had taken 14 days for her letter to reach me. If only I had been a little more patient. Had the phone call ruined everything? Did Bess know about it? Did she still feel okay about me now? Only time would tell. Meanwhile, our two souls had touched, and nothing would ever be the same again.

38 - Penance

Saturday, June 30, 1990. The endless black pavement glared, and its heat shimmered up my legs. I was somewhere between Chester, Pennsylvania, and Wilmington, Delaware, my wide-brimmed hat cast the slightest of shadows. I balanced my sign and dabbed more sun tan lotion on my red, sore face. *Don't think, just keep walking*, I told myself. Sweat dribbled down my back, but I plodded ahead . . . left foot, right foot, left foot, right foot . . . mile after endless mile. The only thing that mattered was the sign I held high: "Root for Adoptees' Rights."

Chained together, we stretched along the roadside fifty yards or more, flashing our signs at passing cars. Sometimes, we chanted slogans or sang our theme song, "We Want Open Records." But now, with the heat grinding into our bodies and a long way to go, we merely trudged after one another in weary silence.

On either side of the highway spread endless commercial blight. Meanwhile, I was trying to imagine how cool water would feel sliding over my blistered body in the motel swimming pool later that afternoon. *Can't be too much longer. Only have to do sixteen miles today.* We'd be done by mid-afternoon. We'd swim and rest, have dinner around a big table later, and then "rap" about "it" deep into the evening. At 7 a.m. tomorrow, we'd pile back in the RV, ride to wherever we stopped today, and walk another leg. I glanced behind me at the RV, our rolling oasis/adoption rights billboard. It was creeping down the road, as always, just behind the last marcher.

We had just begun to climb a little hill with houses set back from the road when a black motorcycle roared by. I turned my sign its way, and the biker twisted around with a puzzled look. Two minutes later, he zoomed back and pulled up just ahead of us. We shuffled to a stop and stared. The popping motor fell silent; he dismounted. Finally, when he took off his helmet, we all gathered around him. He was a good-looking young man, about 30.

His gaze darted from one face to another. "What are you guys doing out here? What's this all about?"

Our leader Joe Soll stepped forward and made his pitch for adoptee rights. (Joe had started this March last year, vowing to repeat it *every* year, until adoption records were opened. A New York psychotherapist in his early fifties, Joe was an adoptee himself, who'd been battling the New York City courts for eight years, without success, to get access to his birth records.)

The young man listened intently and then looked down. "I'm an adoptee." He said it like a confession one makes in the dark.

We all beamed and Joe put his tan arm on the biker's shoulder. "Welcome. Wonderful to have you. What's your name, son?"

Our new friend was still looking down but his mouth curled up in secret excitement. "Bob," he mumbled.

Joe invited him to walk with us, and they speedily arranged to park the bike at a nearby shopping center. The van would follow and bring him back. Meanwhile, the rest of us would take a short breather by the roadside.

Soon, the gravel crunched and the RV's engine was panting behind us again. Bob popped out, and I reached back inside the RV and grabbed him a sign. When he took it, his jaw seemed to lock.

"Wow—I've never done anything like this before."

"That's okay," I replied. "Neither have I." I introduced myself and told him how I'd joined the group only yesterday at the Liberty Bell in Philadelphia.

His face brightened. "This is so *neat*. I can't believe I just kind of drove by you guys like this. My adoption's something I've been thinking about a lot lately." He glanced at me and then studied the ground. Sweat was already beading on his brow.

"And we just sort of showed up for you today, eh?" I hitched myself to the chain of marchers and began shuffling forward with the others. Bob fell in beside me. "So, are you thinking about searching—?" I asked. My muscles groaned as they fell back into our march stride.

"Well, yes. I've been in therapy for a long while now, and my therapist and I have been discussing it. My adoptive family's nice, but I've always been so different from all of them. It's made me feel like an ugly duckling."

His face scrunched up and his words began to tumble over one another. "I'd just like to fit in some place. Just once, I'd like to meet people who look like me, think like me, and enjoy the same sorts of

247

things I do. Know what I mean?"

I nodded, my chest heavy with guilt, my eyes stinging.

"I'd like to find out how I'm connected to the human race." Then he lowered his voice. "I used to act out when I was younger." He shot me a quick glance to see if I disapproved. "I got myself in some trouble. But then, about five years ago, I started going for therapy. That's helped a lot."

We were walking on black macadam now, and it blistered. I wiped the wet from my eyes. "Things have been rough, eh?"

"Yeah, but I've been kind of lucky, really. I've always had friends who support me." His foot pinged a can into the gutter and then he pierced me with a sharp look. "Something gnaws at me, though. If I could find my mother . . . do you think she'd want to know me?"

I reached out and touched his shoulder. "Most likely she would, Bob. You can ask any of the birthmothers here on the March. They'll all tell you the same thing: it's impossible to forget your own child."

He shifted his eyes without moving his head. "The adoption agency told me my birthmother was a college professor. Guess she was afraid I'd ruin her career."

I told him about the shame and guilt I'd suffered back in the '60s, while a passing car beeped. We both gave the car a wave.

"Hope times have changed," he said, winking at me. "Now that I have myself pretty much back together, I'd like to have a chance to meet my own mother."

I wiped the sweat off my upper lip again and smiled back. "Go for it, Bob. What a wonderful gift that would be for both of you. Your mother's probably a very sensitive person—just like you."

We crunched along as another string of cars whooshed past and two more cars beeped. Finally, Bob broke the silence, asking about *my* search. I told him I'd found my daughter last March.

"That's great. Have you met her yet?" he asked.

My face tightened. "No, but I'm going to next month."

The ground began to slant upward, and I concentrated on my breathing. There was a mountain of fear out there for every searcher. How did we get the courage to climb it? It helped to have a pressing need.

Finally, I spoke up. "It would be great for you to know your birth family, Bob. Think how much you'd learn about yourself! I never appreciated genealogy myself until my cousin wrote a book on my mother's family a few years back. Learned about our talents and our flaws—and even about where our social values came from.

"I have a theory on that now," I continued. "I think a family's values are forged each time a parent faces a severe personal crisis. Always thought they were some kind of holy rite before. But listen to this:

"After my grandmother died, my mother discovered some old letters that were once in Great-grandma's attic. I remember my great-grandmother; I have her bedroom set. She was a very proper old lady, but the letters showed that her husband was an alcoholic and that, in spite of aristocratic airs, they lived in dire financial straits. But it had all been kept a secret. My mother and her brothers and sisters had never known. The secret would have been buried forever if it hadn't been for those letters.

"Now, do you see what I learned from that?" I peered at him intently. "Our family deals with serious, shameful problems by hiding them. Appearance is all." I gestured to the air. "See? My mother never knew about the alcoholism, but she learned from her mother's knee that shameful problems should be hidden. You can bet that's one reason she dealt with my unwed pregnancy the way she did."

Bob shook his head. "Okay. I see what you're saying. So, the values *my* birthmother grew up with influenced *her* decision to surrender me." He bit his lip, and we trudged along in silence for a while. Ahead, tires screeched as someone stopped for a red light.

"So, Ann—" His voice jarred me. "What are you going to say to your daughter when you meet her next month?"

My heart started racing. I swallowed hard.

"I want her to know about her father, her medical history, and her genealogy, and I want to tell her what I just told you about family social values. I want her to understand what it was like for me back then, so she can know my decision to surrender her had nothing to do with her personally."

When I turned to look at him, his dark eyes were glistening.

I rattled on. "I'm going by myself this first time, so we can work through our issues about the past in private. Then, we'll have something to build on."

Bob cleared his throat and smiled. "That's very inspiring," he said. "I hope *my* birthmother will be open to knowing *me*."

"I hope she will too, Bob." I touched his shoulder again. "And if she's not up to it, don't take it personally. It just means she still has some work to do on herself. She may not have dealt with the past yet.

"Look how long you've been in therapy. . . . Me, too. . . . I've been doing human-potential work for 11 years now." Our eyes connected. "I think it's an ongoing process. You just have to take her hand, wherever she's at, and walk forward together."

I unbuckled myself from the chain and excused myself. "I'm going in for a little while. Need a drink of water. Just walk up to anybody and start talking."

"Thanks," he said, flashing me a bright smile.

I waited for the RV and motioned for it to stop. A blast of cool air greeted me when I climbed in. I propped my sign in a corner and opened the little refrigerator under the sink. The bottle of mineral water slid in my hot hand. I poured myself a large drink, gulped it down, and then refilled my cup. My water held high, I stumbled back to the U-shaped bench at the rear of the van. A young man with straggly black hair was slumped in the corner. His eyes blinked open then shut as I sat down beside him.

"Hi, Denny." I held a mouthful of water behind my teeth for a moment. Its coolness bathed the inside of my mouth.

"Hi, yourself. What did you say your name was?"

I took another sip and told him. "Did I hear you're walking all the way from New York City to Washington, D.C.?"

"Yep. All the way, baby."

"That's a big commitment." I drained my cup and tossed it in the trash. At that, he straightened up and gradually opened his eyes.

"There's a lot of pain out there. There's a lot of brothers and sisters out there singing the 'Lost Mother Blues.' We've got to get adoption records open so people can heal." He leaned forward and rooted in his pouch for a tan flier. "I'm working out a Twelve Step program for adoptees." He held one out to me. "Like AA."

Our heads pitched forward when the driver stepped on the brakes. "Yup. Being adopted gives people the same sort of pain as alcoholism or drug addiction. I know: I've been through all of that. Now I'm fighting back. Do you know that adoptees are twice as likely to end up in jail or in therapy as non-adopted persons?" His jaw was set. "Think about that."

"That's quite a statistic."

"Did you see today's paper?" He reached over and picked it up from the back window shelf. "Some poor American Indian woman had both her babies taken away and adopted 25 years ago. She just managed to locate them. One's dead; the other's in jail."

The van jerked again and stopped this time. A heavy-set woman with curly hair boarded. Denny stood up.

"Hold up," he shouted to the driver. "I'm getting out." He picked up his hat, twisted the handkerchief on his neck, and made his way towards the door of the RV. "Got to go sing some more of those 'Lost Mother Blues.'" He grabbed his sign. "See ya' all later," he said, stepping out of the van with a wink.

The newcomer grabbed a drink from the cooler and staggered back to the bench. "It must be a hundred degrees out there," she moaned, mopping her brow.

"That's why I'm taking a break. I haven't had a chance to talk to you yet. You're Melanie. Right? Did I hear you're walking the full distance, too?"

"That's right," she gasped.

"Can I ask why you're doing this?"

"I lost my son to adoption. He's 30 years old," she said, still huffing. "How about you?"

I reported finding my daughter recently and then asked about her search.

Melanie sighed and looked down. "I finally know where he is," she said carefully. "I found him about a month ago."

When I pressed her for details, she told me about how her father had arranged for a private adoption. The lawyer, a friend of his, had left the file sitting beside her before the surrender hearing. When he walked away, she had scribbled down the name and address found inside and had carried it around for thirty years without really

251

understanding what it was.

"When I finally got up the nerve to go to an adoption support group meeting a few months ago, I showed it to a man who offered to help me, and it turned out to be all we needed. It was the name and address of my son's adoptive parents, and they still lived in the same house."

I'd been holding my breath, and now I let it hiss out. "Boy, were you lucky. What did you do next?"

She continued in a measured tone. "I did a little research before contacting my son. He has a master's degree and works for a big insurance company in Rhode Island. He's tall and good-looking like his father." Her eyes twinkled with pride, but I could sense something was wrong. "It turns out he was raised by a Catholic, Italian couple," she went on. "I'm Jewish, but I really didn't care about the religion of the adoptive parents. Also, he's married but no children yet."

My chest was tightening. "Have you talked to him yet?"

Melanie grimaced and proceeded in a monotone. "Once, three weeks ago."

Something was wrong. I didn't know what, but I had to prod her on. "I just talked to my daughter for the first time about six weeks ago. How did it go with your son?"

When Melanie looked up again, there were tears in her eyes. Finally she spoke. "Well, there's a problem," she said softly. "He didn't know he was adopted until I told him."

"Oh, wow," I whispered. Heat jabbed my cheeks while we sat together listening to the rattle of the van's air conditioner. Finally, I reached over and touched her hand. "What in the world did you do?"

"Well, it was very awkward." She ran her fingers through her hair. "I had sent him a brief letter and my picture before I talked to him. I had told him I was his birthmother and asked him to call. He called up right away and was very kind and polite. He simply told me I must have the wrong party because he wasn't adopted." Her face reddened with frustration. "But I'm *positive* it's him; he looks just like his birthfather!"

She took a deep breath and looked away. "On the phone, I told him everything I had about time and place of birth, and he agreed it was all correct. But his parents have pictures of them leaving the hospital with him, so he prefers to just leave things the way they are. He won't meet or talk to me." Her eyes flared with anger. "He won't confront his adoptive parents, *who lied to him all these years.*" She dabbed them with a tissue then and looked down again. "So what do I do now?" She gave a little shrug.

I sighed and slowly shook my head. "I really can't imagine what I'd do."

"So, what about your daughter?" she asked, after a pause.

I told her about how I'd contacted, including the disastrous phone call and the letter I'd gotten from Bess two days later.

"Never did figure out what happened until much later. Bess and I wrote back and forth, and then she finally called me. On Mother's Day! She called at 10:00 p.m. and we talked until 1:30 in the morning. It was the most incredible gift."

Melanie's eyes glistened.

"Anyway, would you believe, they never got my letter until two weeks *after* I called. I never imagined the mail service was so bad. That was bad enough, but then her dad thought I'd gotten Bess's letter, too, which specifically said I should write to her through the agency. No wonder he was mad.

"Haven't gotten that misunderstanding straightened out with her parents yet, but Bess's been wonderful, anyway, and I can't wait to meet her in July. Can I show you her picture?"

Melanie nodded. I fumbled for my wallet and whipped out the picture Bess had sent me. The image was small, but you could see she was a very pretty girl with long dark hair and dark eyes.

"Oh, she's beautiful," Melanie cooed.

"She's a beautiful person, too," I said wistfully.

Melanie let out a long sigh. "You're one of the lucky ones." She wiped her eyes and then put on a big smile.

"So, you're going to meet your daughter in a few weeks. You must be thrilled."

My voice thickened. "I am," I agreed, "but I'm scared to death, too."

Melanie squinted at me. "Why?"

"I'm so afraid I'll screw this up. Here I have the best daughter in the whole world, but something inside says, 'You don't deserve it.' I just know my subconscious mind will find some way to sabotage this relationship."

She narrowed her eyes and leaned back. "What do you mean?"

"That's what I always do when I think I don't deserve something. It just happens before I realize what's going on. I might figure it out later, but by then it's too late." My eyes started to tear. "I still feel *really guilty* about giving her away, Melanie. That's why I'm here on the March." I took a deep breath; my voice grew stronger. "I'm here to do penance and rid myself of that guilt. I figure four days of pounding pavement in 90-degree-plus heat for adoptees' rights should sweat some of the guilt out of my system." I chuckled to myself. "Say, I think it's time for me to hit the trail again."

My knees were stiff, but I made myself stand. Melanie called to the driver to stop, and we both stumbled to the door of the van and picked up our signs. As I turned the latch and opened the door, a wall of heat hit me. It nauseated me, but there was a cause to fight for and a wrong to right. I clipped my chain to the long chain stretched between the other sweaty bodies, and proudly stepped off, my sign held high to passing cars.

39 - Meeting/Mending

"We will be shutting the power off for approximately ten minutes while we disconnect some cars here in New York," the conductor drawled over the loudspeaker. A few seconds later, motors ground to a halt, plunging the train into black silence. A strange ringing filled my ears.

Slowly, my eyes adjusted to the dark. The light from the underground station filtered through the train windows, casting an eerie glow over the motionless car. People around me tittered uneasily until the bustle outside on the platform gradually relieved our sense of isolation.

So . . . I'd made it to New York. Fourteen more hours, and I'd be in Quebec, meeting Bess for the first time. She'd said I could stay with her friend. Her parents wouldn't know. She'd meet me at the train station. *That's tomorrow at 11 a.m. Can I be ready by then?* It seemed impossible. I held onto one faint hope: that the long train ride would give me time to prepare.

An idea flashed: why not use this quiet darkness? I fingered a small pouch of mottled gray silk slung on my neck. Slipping it off, I pulled open the pink drawstrings and groped inside. I removed two small, tattered squares of paper and squinted over the first in the dim light.

> *I prayed to experience God's peace.* And God within me responded. Then you must release everything that is not peaceful. You must release the pain of the past and all fear of the future, for they will block your experience of peace. . . . If you would feel my love, you must let go of all that is not loving in your heart, mind, and body. . . . If you would bathe in joy . . . you must release all resentment and anger . . . . If you would hear my voice, yours must be still.

I inhaled deeply, breathed out, and squeezed my eyes tightly shut in the darkened car. "May the Life Force make it so," I affirmed. I carefully refolded the prayer and fished out of my bag two little stones. One was a rough blue ball of azurite about the size of a pea. I balanced it between my forefinger and thumb while I smoothed out the other tattered piece of paper.

"Azurite," I read. "Let go of old belief systems, expand awareness." Pressing the small rock against the middle of my forehead, in the third eye area, I concentrated and silently moved my lips.

"Yes, the old belief systems of guilt and punishment, let them go," I prayed. "Help me expand into a new awareness of grace and reconciliation."

I took another deep breath and lay the azurite in my lap. Next, I felt for the translucent, pink stone called kunzite. A chunky stone, it seemed like a cross between mica and crystal—glossy and solid, yet lightweight—and it radiated a strange power into my hand.

I clasped the kunzite over my heart and waited. Soon there was a strange sensation of heat and throbbing, as if the stone were pulling out poison.

I glanced down at my crib sheet. "Kunzite—transforms emotional blockage. Manifests the mature state of the heart: open, clear, secure, strong, vibrant, radiant, balanced and loving. Use it to let go of fears and sorrows that bind the heart."

Fears and sorrows that bind the heart. My heart has been bound with fears and sorrows for as long as I can remember. I held the stone to my chest and prayed, "Power of the Universe, clear sorrow and fear from my heart. Cleanse me of these poisons."

I stopped my breath and focused on that thought. Finally, I released it, and inhaled.

The kunzite tight in my fist, I dug out another stone—a small, deep purple pyramid of amethyst. "Amethyst symbolizes the ability to transform one reality to another." I pressed the cold pyramid of purple to my third eye. "From guilt, limitation, and the past; to love, freedom, and the future," I affirmed.

I placed the amethyst on my lap and drew out my little wand of pink tourmaline—"the giver of love to the material realm"—and a small clear quartz crystal—"the symbol of coming into alignment with cosmic harmony." I clustered the kunzite, the pink tourmaline, and the clear quartz crystal over my heart.

"Blast away that grief and sorrow. Blast away that old fear, those feelings of guilt and inadequacy. Make room for the flow of Love,"

I affirmed, clenching my fist and squeezing my eyes tightly shut.

The hum of lights and whirl of fans announced the return of power. I looked around self-consciously and stuffed the papers and most of the stones back in my little silk purse. The kunzite and the tourmaline, however, I kept in my fist, enjoying the warmth that pulsed up my arm when I held them. But I soon stowed them away, as well. *People will be coming.* I drew the pink strings shut, slipped the leather thong around my neck, and tucked it all under my blouse, where no one could see.

The metal door to the train car clattered open, and in swaggered the conductor. "Take all your belongings off the seats," he barked. "We will have a full train tonight. Every seat will be occupied. Clear off your belongings."

People shuffled their suitcases across the metal floor, lifting and scraping them into the overhead racks. I stowed my suitcase above, like the others, and then pondered what to do with the flowers I was bringing to Bess. If only I could get them to Quebec without crushing the pink-spotted lily petals.

I was shifting them from the seat beside me to the floor between my legs, when the train door flew open and the new passengers rushed in. *Who will choose me?* I wondered. Many people passed me by. Finally, a smart-looking young woman stopped and lifted her small suitcase onto the overhead rack. She settled herself beside me, looked over, and smiled.

"Are you going all the way to Quebec?" I asked.

"Yes. A friend of mine is getting married there tomorrow. I'm going up for the weekend. And you?"

Shall I tell her or keep my mouth shut? I wondered. *Oh well, she doesn't know me. It would be good practice to talk about it.*

"I'm going to Quebec to meet my daughter for the first time. You see, I gave her up for adoption 24 years ago, and I just found her this past March." I flushed with embarrassment and then winced, annoyed with myself

"Wow. That's really exciting," she replied.

A splash of relief trickled through me. "That's very kind of you. Can you tell how nervous I am about this? Part of me is still saying I had no right to search. I battle with that thought constantly."

"But I think it's great that you found her. I'm about your daughter's age, and if I'd been adopted, I would want to know my background. My family's from Czechoslovakia. I wish I knew more about them. So tell me, how did you find her?"

As the miles and hours rolled by, I told my new friend the story of how I'd found Bess . . . from Mary Anne's phone call to that story's sad denouement, from meeting Clara and her sister to negative blood tests, from the miracle of getting Bess's birth certificate to the serendipitous phone conversation with Mr. Cowgill. And then I told how I'd connected with her, combatting negative forces all the way.

As I retold my story, my hands slowly warmed and my voice relaxed. *I DO deserve this reunion after all*, I finally allowed myself to think. *I've certainly earned it.*

Everyone else in the car had bedded down for the evening, by the time my companion and I bid each other good night. Drained, I leaned back and listened to the sound of metal wheels rolling over endless track. The darkened car rocked steadily through the moonless night. Tired but still sleepless, I reached for the affirmation card I'd brought. By the train's dim aisle lights, I read: "Any time one switches from Fear to Love, the outcome will be assured."

Just fill yourself with love, I told my buzzing brain. *Nothing else matters.* I leaned back and closed my eyes, letting the card fall in my lap. As the train rattled confidently through the darkness, its clickety-clack, clickety-clack seemed to say: "When one switches to love, switches to love, switches to love . . . the outcome's assured, outcome's assured, outcome's assured," lulling me into a deep sleep.

At precisely 10:50 the next morning, under a New Moon in Cancer, the train rolled into a dark underground station in Quebec. My seatmate and I wished each other well and went our separate ways. I made my way up the steps to street level, my stomach growing more queasy with each step I took. I tottered on, luggage in one hand, the huge bunch of flowers in the other.

At the top, I stood and searched every face eagerly. *Is she here? Will I recognize her? What if she doesn't come?*

The bottom dropped out of my stomach.

Just then, I felt a gentle tap on my shoulder. My breathing stopped. I turned around. There stood a lovely, small, dark-haired young woman, smiling broadly.

"Are you B-Bess?" I stuttered, easing my suitcase and carry-on bag to the floor.

She smiled and nodded, giving me a little hug. The room was spinning. I concentrated on balancing the flowers and hugged her back with my free arm. "Here, these are for you," I managed after our short embrace. *Does she look like me? Is she really my daughter?* I was dizzy with confusion and excitement.

"They're beautiful. Here, let me take them," she said with kindness, relieving me of their awkwardness. "Do you want a cup of coffee here, or would you like to go off to my friend's house? Are you tired from your journey?"

Travelers and shoppers flowed around us, but time stood still for me. I stared at Bess in a daze. *Well, she doesn't look much like me. She's small and dark, like him. She does have my teeth, though.*

"What did you say?" I stooped to pick up my shoulder bag and suitcase. "Sorry, I can't believe it's actually you. The last time I saw you, you were a tiny baby. Suddenly, you're a young woman." I was groping through a Twilight Zone. "It's going to take me a little while to get used to this. Let's go sit down and get some coffee."

We started walking towards the McDonald's inside the station. "But I don't have any Canadian money," I suddenly realized.

"That's okay," Bess smiled. "I'll treat."

I grinned and followed her into the restaurant. I settled down at a back table, while Bess went for coffee. "Remember your promise. You said you'd tell her everything about you, her birth family and why you gave her up. This is your chance," a strangely familiar voice seemed to say. And so, over coffee, I began.

We talked as the early lunch crowd came in and were still only beginning as the late lunch crowd departed. We sat across from each other at a Formica table, with the flowers and lost time between us. I touched Bess's hand and told her everything I knew about my past, our family's past, the social milieu of the 1960s—and about the promise that had brought me here. She listened and listened, her sensitive face mirroring every up and down in the story I told.

Finally, the restaurant's noise and pace picked up again as the early dinner crowd began to filter in. My throat was hoarse; my body, tired and cramped. I limped out from behind the table, bone-

259

weary; yet it seemed a great weight had lifted from me. I looked and saw her as I first had—a radiant face, framed by a full head of dark hair. I remembered the wrenching force that once had told me the adoption would wrong her. I remembered how powerless I'd felt. I remembered my sole, anguished gift to her—a promise to find her again, someday. A deep sigh of satisfaction escaped my lips.

I kept my promise, I silently shouted to the Forces of the Universe. Tears brimmed up. It hadn't been easy . . . but what did that matter now?

That thought drifted off dreamily, like a cloud. In its place I saw a sun-swept shore. The flood of the stormy past had receded. The shore was bristling with those new buds of joy I'd felt at her birth. They were taking hold at last.

* * * * *

. . . Love, stitch and mend, stitch and mend the torn fabric of our lives. The straight, strong needle of intention: lift it up. Thrust it down into the torn edge of the past—the time of your birth—draw it up under the torn edge of today. Catch the edges, pull the thread tight. The slender thread of sharing can mend and blend our lives again. Push the needle up and down, up and down. Rejoin what was torn when babe lost mother's arms: restore heritage to the babe; heir to her family of birth.

Precious daughter, you are first child to me—first grandchild and first great-grandchild to our family. Pretending otherwise has not changed the truth. Even unacknowledged, you have always been part of us. Stitch and mend.

Always, you have carried us with you, dark-eyed beauty with light olive skin. Eyes set close together, like mine; dark and large, like your father's. Your teeth, mine exactly; your lips, my dad's. Your prominent nose, stubby eyelashes—again, your father's. Your short-waisted body—built like mine; your stature— small and thin, like his. A gene-sorting wonder: Arabic face on a German-style body; Mediterranean eyes, American teeth. We are you, you are we, exotic beauty.

Love, stitch and mend the torn fabric of our lives. The straight, strong needle of intention: thrust it down through the lost dark past. Point it up. Pierce the edge of today. Draw the thread tight across the gap of time. . . .

Today, today—she's on her way. Hot August sun, when will she come? Can she find me, sweat-drenching August sun, beating down on me perched on black car hood waiting? I look down at my magazine, feigning calm, while fretting thoughts swarm inside like pesky flies. Patience. It's not time yet, I tell myself. (Car door slams.) I hope they can figure out where I am. I should have told them . . .

"Hello, Ann," she says with a little kiss and a little hug, startling me. Magazine collapses. "We found you!"

In dumbfound wonder, I watch while my wildest fantasy takes form: she climbs in my car, eager, beaming—off to meet her new relations, to share my world/her world of might-have-been, is-too.

Straight, strong needle of intention: thrust down; point up. Draw the thread tight across the gap of time.

We begin with her two half-sisters, at the home of their father, Adrian. Plunging down a long, dirt drive, our car winds into his wooded world of gardens and ponds. Motor stops. Out we climb. The girls, inside, juggling stomach butterflies, call hello—while Adrian, radiating joy, rushes to us and seals Bess with his approval. The girls come—tenative, like first spring buds which warmth will soon open into full flower. The three slip away to explore country hillsides, fish ponds, frogs and new sisterhood.

Adrian prepares a gourmet meal, served on china with crystal. We sip wine and pumpkin soup, feast on London broil, asparagus, etc., while overlooking winding garden wonders. Our merriment bubbles like clear stream water over rounded rocks.

I float home in ecstasy—me and the three young women I conceived and nourished in my womb—the three whom I birthed and heard draw first breath. How I've longed for this moment: the three—knowing each other, together at last. I am complete.

Love, stitch and mend the torn fabric of our lives. Pierce the edge of today. Draw the thread tight across the gap of time.

She likes our house; fits nicely in the guest room. The sisters play. I stay out of their way and watch as likenesses are discovered and, one by one, tastes compared. They show and tell, share secrets, conspire together.

They play and take a hundred pictures, slowly discovering each other/themselves. They think the same, value the same, react the same—and they each look different, my bouquet of daughters. One is short and dark; one, medium and light brown; one, tall and red-headed. All different, all the same.

. . . **I listen to the hum of sisterhood being woven on the loom of love. They bond. I am full . . . .**

Away from home we venture to weave in others, strengthen the family tapestry. First, my father's sister—warm, accepting, glad for me. Flurry of welcome—so much to tell. Then dinner. We all hold hands around the table while Uncle says the prayer—then dive into chicken corn soup, jello salad, pickled eggs and beets, homemade rolls and jelly, cobbler dessert. Next, first-ever family portrait of me with all my girls. After-dinner yard tour: neat rows of vegetables, flower beds, golf-course-manicured lawn. We depart with the essence of love lingering on us like precious perfume.

Mother's house is next. I sigh, remembering who we've been to each other: two bleeding wrestlers, squared off, frozen in time.

Now think of this, the heavy weight pressing on my solar plexus groans. *True, you have never surrendered—but where is victory? and what price paid?*

Love, stitch and mend the torn fabric of our lives. Straight, strong needle of intention, thrust through the black hole of the past. Pierce the edge of today. Thread, draw tight across the gap of time.

Mother greets us with extreme cordiality and unresolved feelings. Watch and see. Meals, carefully planned, eaten on schedule; card games, sightseeing—programmed to fill the gaps of time. Watch and see.

Delighting me, the new granddaughter plays cards as sharply as her grandmother—clears dinner dishes (without coaching), scoring big points. Watch and see. A Sun-in-Aries/Capricorn-rising pair—more alike than they know. Watch and see. They'll figure it out eventually.

A box of old pictures, our common past, is up for grabs. We scramble through the photos. Mother narrates. "See your father, sick with pneumonia? Almost died when he was five. See our storybook romance?" (They were so slender, young, and happy.) "He was my first and only: the way love *should* be."

More pictures. Mother, her white satin wedding gown trailing in the snow; my grandfather, good-looking, middle-aged, proud father of the bride. My father's father, a young man with his first wife (who died and was never spoken of again), looking self-assured and wearing grey instead of the preacher-black I'd always seen. Later, my parents, my brother and I, polishing our light green 1952 DeSoto. Big family reunions in our two-car garage, with everyone grinning around the table (green ping-pong table, draped with tablecloths). Dad in uniform, shoulders back, marching proud as punch with his beloved band; and me—gangling—a cheesecake shot from adolescence. Me, in Europe, days before getting pregnant, and one year later, at my grandparents' fiftieth anniversary (my parents and I sharing a shameful secret: the first member of the new generation had just been born and banished).

But, even so, you have always been a part of us. If unspoken, not forgotten. Eldest great-grandchild, eldest grandchild, eldest child you have always been. Now we acknowledge and reclaim you, our daughter and someone else's, too. We rejoice at your homecoming.

Last, we go to see my brother Fred—he who helped me find you, who named a daughter after you. "Don't mind Mom," says he. "Of course she likes you, but she hasn't figured out how to show it yet. Give her time. Please know: you are profoundly welcome. You make momentous difference here. Your coming gives great joy— for now, we are complete."

His hot tub bubbles and hums around us. I and my daughters three—warm, submerged in a hot tub womb. Like playful puppies, the younger two come over to me. Each tucks her head under an arm. We laugh and snuggle. The warm bubbles flick at our backs. Fred's camera clicks and flashes over steamy gurgles.

A profound longing fills me then. It arises from deep inside; its primal cry consumes me. I want to hold my first-born—my arms ache for her. I beckon. She comes. The others give way. Bess's small, wet body slides weightlessly onto my lap. I wrap my arms around her. She lets her head lie back on my shoulder. As I feel her whole body pressed lightly against me, my being melts in bliss. And in that timeless space—like an old icicle—a useless illusion cracks off, shatters, tinkles into nothingness. Then the truth throbs through me hot and strong.

"You have always loved her," moan my tingling arms. "You *are* her mother—one of two."

. . . Live together, heal together; stitch and mend the torn fabric of our lives, O Love. Balance with me at the edge of lost time. Leap with me into the abyss of now. . . .